NOT JUST JANE

Rediscovering Seven Amazing Women Writers Who Transformed British Literature

Shelley DeWees

NEW YORK • LONDON • TORONTO • SYDNEY • NEW DELHI • AUCKLAND

FIRST EDITION

Designed by Jamie Lynn Kerner

Library of Congress Cataloging-in-Publication Data

Names: DeWees, Shelley, author.
Title: Not just Jane : rediscovering seven amazing women writers who transformed British literature / Shelley DeWees.
Other titles: Women writers who transformed British literature
Description: New York : Harper Perennial, 2016.
Identifiers: LCCN 2016001019 (print) | LCCN 2016012417 (ebook) | ISBN 9780062394620 (paperback) | ISBN 9780062394637 (Ebook)
Subjects: LCSH: Women authors, English—Biography. | English literature—Women authors—History and criticism. | Women and literature—Great Britain—History. | English fiction—History and criticism. | BISAC: BIOGRAPHY & AUTOBIOGRAPHY / Women. | BIOGRAPHY & AUTOBIOGRAPHY / Literary. | HISTORY / Europe / Great Britain.
Classification: LCC PR111 .D49 2016 (print) | LCC PR111 (ebook) | DDC 820.9/9287—dc23
LC record available at http://lccn.loc.gov/2016001019

ISBN 978-0-06-239462-0 (pbk.)

16 17 18 19 20 OV/RRD 10 9 8 7 6 5 4 3 2 1

For AJ and Saul

CONTENTS

NOT JUST JANE

INTRODUCTION

WILD AND EXTRAORDINARY STORIES OFTEN HAVE COMpletely ordinary beginnings, and this one, the story of how I became obsessed with seven British women, is no different. It happened one summer evening a few years ago, sometime after I had packed up and moved from Montana to South Korea with my husband to teach college-level English. I had found myself in Minneapolis, dreadfully jetlagged and dressed for a night at the theater. The city was in the midst of one of the worst heat waves in its already well-broiled history, and considering this formal occasion had called for my prettiest closed-toe pumps and a structured skirt, I was feeling rather wilted and impatient by the time I sank into my seat.

I waited in the hushed, darkened, delightfully air-conditioned space, and when the curtain finally rose to reveal the illuminated set, I was reminded of the reason for my coming despite the heat: this was an adaptation of one of the most important books of my then-thirty-year life, *Pride and Prejudice*, and there I sat, about to see it performed on the professional stage. That I had been able to come to Minneapolis at all, able to visit friends at exactly the right time—friends who I hope will forgive me for what I've written here—was a stroke of unreasonably good fortune, as this happened to be the final performance of the show.

At that time, there was no author more dominant or more valued in my life than Jane Austen. I'd read and reread her books; I'd seen every film adaptation; I'd wondered aloud to many patient friends about the miseducation of Marianne Dashwood, pointed out the notes of Gothic parody in *Northanger Abbey*; I'd even come to enjoy certain fan fiction based on Jane's* settings and characters; and I'd begun writing book reviews for the ravenous online Janeite community (which I loved). My early twenties had been a blur of academic books, conferences, seminars, and trips to remote subarctic archipelagos in pursuit of a graduate degree in ethnomusicology—which is, essentially, the anthropology of music. (It was this course of study, with its emphasis on the social and cultural context of art, that ignited my passion for literature even as I remained busily devoted to music research.) But, later on, in my stormy post-MA years, Jane's novels became places of refuge in a land of turmoil, buoys on a sea of uncertainty as I, like many other graduate students, wondered whether I'd indulged myself too long in the comforting bosom of education. I was hooked—*addicted*, you might say—to Jane. *Sense and Sensibility*, *Mansfield Park*, and all the rest were, for me, fast passage to a land of delicious fantasy, one of misty gardens and snug cottages in Devonshire; of hours

* After enjoying such a lengthy and personal relationship with Jane Austen and Charlotte and Emily Brontë, use of their last names seems not only unnecessary but even a little coldhearted. Thus, for our purposes, these brilliant women—and the seven lesser-known ones in this book, to whom I've become equally attached—will be referred to by their first names in most cases, for they are to me, and soon will be to you, dear friends.

spent reading and writing (without wondering whether it was worth it); and of marriage to a wealthy man who had no other care in the world except me, one who offered a stress-free love nest and an exquisite, comfortable life. It was a blissful picture, and I reveled in it.

Yet, attractive as it was, as I progressed out of my post-graduate haze, this land of sugary perfection became cloying. I yearned for stiffer stuff, stories with more menace, more dramatic density. So I walked down the well-trodden path from Jane to her successors, Charlotte and Emily Brontë (Anne Brontë too, but to a lesser extent, because—as I'll discuss in greater detail—in terms of style her writing stands strikingly apart from that of her more romantically inclined sisters and was, as a result, less appealing during a time of my life when escapism was more important than realism), and found a whole *other* fantasy to cling to, this one darker and more brooding, though. *Jane Eyre* and *Wuthering Heights* filled my head with images of wind-swept moors, cloud-curtained fields, dark, barren houses, and crumbling ancient stones, and my heart with a feeling of forlorn, untamed coarseness that offset the warmth and refined rosiness of Austen's universe. (This disparity—wildness in place of calm; unbridled passion in place of sweet, decorous admiration from afar—Charlotte Brontë herself acknowledged: she allowed her characters to explore the darker side of love, the heated, confusing, *consuming* side of it—but Jane? In Charlotte's opinion, Jane had hedged her ladies and gentlemen behind "a carefully-fenced, highly cultivated garden with neat borders and delicate flowers," where "no open country—no fresh air—no blue hill—no bonny beck" could encroach on a meticulously designed, balanced, harmonious plot.)

There I dwelt, with Jane and Charlotte and Emily, each experience with them bringing more and more structure to my dreamscape. For nearly a decade, no matter which corner of literary England I chose to occupy at a particular moment—whether I wished to prance among the flowers or hunker down in the moss—as a place it was as powerful in my mind as the stories unfolding within it. Each time I reread *Shirley* or *Persuasion,* it felt like returning to a safe haven of beauty and poetry; simply by reading, I could effortlessly inhabit a fictional England. It was all so personal, so romantic, so intimate. The bleak landscapes and exaggerated satire of Dickens's and Thackeray's Englands just couldn't hold a candle to those of my literary ladies.

I could easily have stayed sequestered in these Englands were it not for that sweltering summer's eve in that air-conditioned theater. As the curtain came up, my heart was in my throat. How beautiful this would be, my dreamy reverie come to life: cottages and lace, elegance incarnate! And to be there, 6,200 miles away from my job and my apartment, at this exact moment in time, to see it—how lucky was I?

As you might already have guessed, it wasn't like that at all; it was a disaster. As soon as the curtain retreated into the proscenium arch, the orchestra whipped into a springy jig and five girls burst from backstage in peals of shrill laughter. Elizabeth, Jane, Mary, Kitty, and Lydia Bennet twirled and tittered, giggled and gossiped, whispering behind their hands as a parade of eligible bachelors dutifully danced before them. Ten minutes in, I could see it: this was saccharine silliness, the opposite of what I'd expected. Where was the poise, where were the delicate depths of feeling balanced by the gentle drawing-room ripostes that give Jane's fiction its witty edge?

Irritation bubbled at the back of my throat as I watched my beloved *Pride and Prejudice* turn into a kind of British *Bye Bye Birdie*. At my elbow, my friends were nudging me, trying to get my attention, as if to say, *Isn't this great, Shelley? Isn't it just so perfectly Jane?* But my mind was turning over with too much fervor to respond, for at that moment I'd been struck by a sobering realization: The world I'd dreamed of while reading Jane's novels was made of *my* constructs, *my* images. They weren't part of *Pride and Prejudice*; they were attached to *my* experience of reading it. And, as was quickly becoming apparent, they were not universal. Where I'd seen erudition, subtle wit, and quiet country vistas, the director of this play had seen flirtation and farce.

That night in the theater, my Austenian "castle in the air" (a phrase one of our forgotten ladies of literature, Sara Coleridge, used herself) tumbled down under the weight of my awareness—and the neighboring Brontëan palace was not far behind it. All this because of something I really should have seen coming. If Jane and Charlotte and Emily weren't purveyors of a certain English "sentiment," a malleable construct that appealed to our nostalgic (and aspirational) desires and onto which we could project our needs and adapt to suit our temperaments, emotions, and fantasies—especially in troubled times—would I, would *we*, still have been paying attention? Worse yet, I realized, was the burning question of greater import: what had we made of those women writers *without* such sentiment, those whose works didn't lend themselves as easily to transference and co-optation?

BACK IN MY CRAMPED APARTMENT IN SEOUL TWO WEEKS later, after some deliberation, I gawked at my bookcases in dismay and discovered that the appalling truth of my ignorance had been manifest all along, right in front of me. My Janes were crammed up against Emily and Charlotte; my copy of *The Professor* was stacked on top of *Middlemarch* and *Mrs. Dalloway*. There, staring back at me, was the uncomfortable truth: I had virtually no idea what existed between *Pride and Prejudice* and *Jane Eyre*; or, for that matter, between *Jane Eyre* and *Middlemarch*; or *Middlemarch* and *Mrs. Dalloway* (the latter two being the only other female British writers I really knew about).

Jane, Charlotte and Emily (and Anne) Brontë, George Eliot (aka Mary Ann Evans), and Virginia Woolf are all wonderfully talented writers, and their often quite socially subversive work undoubtedly transformed the British literary tradition—that's not up for debate, and diminishing their gifts and achievements is not at all what this book is about. Yet after my experience at the theater and the questions that had needled me ever since, I knew that they, along with the few select others who pop up on syllabi or have their writing adapted for a *Masterpiece* miniseries, formed only the tip of the iceberg. There had to have been other British women writing and publishing alongside them, and I decided to find out who they were, what they wrote about, and why their work was missing from my bookcase and from our cultural curricula.

STARTING IN THE LAST FEW DECADES OF THE EIGHTEENTH century and continuing right up until the beginning of the twentieth, female authorship in England bloomed at an unprecedented rate. Quality of life improved during the 1700s—due in large part to the innovations of the Enlightenment and the slowly dawning Industrial Revolution: Jethro Tull's seed drill and Andrew Meikle's threshing machine; Thomas Newcomen's steam engine, famously refined by James Watt and adapted to create the steamship (which could be steered by John Campbell's sextant); Edward Jenner's smallpox vaccination; Samuel Johnson's dictionary and Georges Lesage's telegraph; Richard Arkwright's spinning frame and Edmund Cartwright's power loom. As a result, families could now spend additional time and money providing their daughters with an education beyond the traditional female "accomplishments" and household management. And since these advances also pushed the working class out of the fields and into a growing number of wealthy homes to take over domestic responsibilities, an entire tier of British women was freed from housework. So, in the eighteenth century, in addition to dancing, sewing, drawing, and music lessons, a typical genteel woman—left with very little to do, otherwise—was also afforded instruction in reading, writing, arithmetic, French, history, geography, and, if she was very privileged, Latin and Greek. No woman, however, was so learned as to imperil the intellectual superiority of her brothers and father (whose curricula included Socratic critical thinking, philosophy, rhetoric, and law)—certainly not, as it was widely accepted that her education was not for the purpose of employment, but for attracting a worthy (read: wealthy) spouse and setting a good example for her children.

Once this goal—the *only* goal a female was supposed to have—was attained, young ladies were expected to put aside their studies, no matter their aptitudes or talents, and focus on their husbands and their own march toward becoming soft, affectionate, and, most important, unquestioningly compliant. According to the period's conduct literature, instructional books that were hugely popular among families of all classes throughout the eighteenth and nineteenth centuries, this "gentle and kind obedience to the wishes of their Husbands" was the most effective way for women to attain the love of men and "to reign triumphant in their breasts," forevermore, in true marital harmony. Reading, writing, and other intellectual diversions were thus excluded from a newlywed's list of "proper" employments. She might scratch a pretty verse here and there, but it was understood that literary pursuits were not to detract from the real purpose of her existence, which Elizabeth Gaskell puts best in her *Life of Charlotte Brontë*: women were "appointed to fill that particular place" within the home and family. "The quiet regular duties of the daughter, the wife, or the mother" could not be abandoned in order to make time for books, not even for "the exercise of the most splendid talents that were ever bestowed." Also often discouraged were friendships (especially with unmarried people), traveling, and even unguarded speech, for any sort of witty or sarcastic one-liner might "be wrought up into a family disturbance." Unless a wife was eternally chipper, ever on guard against bad tempers and peevishness, "what but domestic misery can be expected?"

Baldly stated, married women were entirely relative beings—that is, extensions of their spouses, mere "children of a larger growth" through which property and money passed. Yet they weren't giving up everything for nothing. In exchange for embracing meekness, chastity, and modesty, "the greatest glory and ornament[s] of her sex," as they were known, a married woman would receive the most significant rewards available to her in society. She relinquished the pursuits of her youth, the closeness of her family, and nearly all outward expression of intellectual or physical appetite, but in exchange she enjoyed public approbation, protection, elevated social status, a small yet important power of influence over a husband, a certain comfort and elegance of surroundings, and the tranquil satisfaction that comes from improving the pleasures and calming the nerves of those in her domestic sphere.

Finding comfort in this arrangement was a certainty, according to the conduct books—these "rewards" were always more than enough to sustain happiness, they claimed. In reality, though, this kind of life was almost invariably dreadful. Removed from her home and cut off from her family, unable to speak her mind and without any leisure pursuits (or, for that matter, any money of her own to spend on them), the newly wed lady was often plagued by boredom, loneliness, and despair. Pregnancy and parenting could alleviate some of this torture, as could extramarital affairs and secret book writing—and as we'll see, many women turned to one or the other, or both—but in countless instances, the grief was simply overwhelming. Illustrious hostess and wife of a Whig politician, Elizabeth Vassall Fox, wrote in her diary on her seventh wedding anniversary in remembrance of "the fatal day" when she was handed over "in the bloom & innocence of fifteen to the power of a being who has made me execrate my life since it has belonged to him." In her agony, she even considered suicide:

> *My mind is worked up to a state of savage exultation & impels me to act with fury that proceeds more from passion and deep despair than I can in calmer moments justify. Often times in the gloom of midnight I feel a desire to curtail my grief & but for an unaccountable shudder that creeps over me, ere this[,] the deed of rashness[,] would be executed.*

A married woman was to be civil, reticent, and, as Goethe put it in his novel *Wilhelm Meister's Travels,* to live "a life without external events—a life whose story cannot be told[,] as there *is* no story." Yet despite the physical and intellectual suppression in wedded life, a situation compounded by strict cosmetic and dietary practices (fasting, purging, tight-lacing, and others meant to reinforce the image of female frailty), spinsterhood wasn't an alternative to be favored. Until she was married, a lady spent most of her day trying to keep clear of the fog of boredom that was her constant companion. She might go to assemblies or to the theater, play cards, pick flowers, feed birds, visit friends with a chaperone, or prepare for the upcoming London season—and that could be fun, for a while, but for anyone of intelligence, it was intolerable. What of her polished mind? What was there to stimulate her in a world where she'd gone through nine London seasons and had only a tenth to look forward to?

Fortunately, an educated woman did have one respite. The late seventeenth and early eighteenth century saw exciting changes not only in the printing and distribution of books, but also in the public's ability to consume them, alone, in the serenity of their rooms. Before then, reading had been a public venture: an entire family would gather while someone read aloud from a very small collection of volumes, perhaps just two or three that were shared throughout the neighborhood. With the Age of Enlightenment, though, had come breakthroughs that allowed books to be produced at higher quantities for a lower price. In 1683, master printer Joseph Moxon had published what was essentially the first comprehensive manual of printing, *Mechanick Exercises on the Whole Art of Printing*, making the movable, modular-type process refined by Johannes Gutenberg available to all who wished to implement it. Yet Gutenberg's method was still incredibly labor intensive and costly. Composing each page required a vast inventory of individual letterforms that needed to be arranged by hand, for each printing of each individual edition. Production on a large scale using this process was impossible, nor could the method create enough books to keep up with the many surging advances in science and literature. Then, in the early 1700s, a new method, called stereotyping, whereby an entire page of type was cast in a mold to create a reusable printing plate, began to allow multiple presses in different locations to print the same content, and to produce new editions, at minimal expense, without having to reset the type for each page. (The invention of stereotype printing is generally attributed to Scottish goldsmith William Ged, but the method's origins are also tied to France; certainly, toward the end of the eighteenth century, it seems to have been the French who honed the technique.)

With a cheaply printed book now in hand, and a cheaply

made spermaceti candle waiting by the bed (thanks to the surging whaling industry in the late eighteenth century*), a reader could move out of the common room and into her own private space to enjoy reading at her leisure, while in the next room, her siblings and parents did the same thing. And because families now needed and wanted far more books than before, there was accordingly an enormous boom in the publishing of everything from novels to works of science, philosophy, travel, and history, followed by an explosion in lending libraries, which were poised to make a profit off the new influx of cheaply printed, inexpensive material. (One such library, William Lane's Minerva Library, boasted more than twenty thousand titles.) The result was a skyrocketing literacy rate in the population as a whole, but most especially among young, bored, well-educated, unmarried women with time to spare.

It should come as no surprise, then, that the overwhelming majority of England's early authoresses were single women from well-born stock. Their days were an endless whirl of self-improvement, justifiable only as a way to further adorn and refine them for a future husband—but their minds were cultivated enough to perceive their restrictions as they experienced them, at least to some extent (a psychological feat whose gravity cannot be overstated). It was only a matter of time before a bright

* Spermaceti, a waxy white substance found in the head cavity of a sperm whale, had been in use for candle-making since the early eighteenth century, but remained one of the more expensive options for household lighting (tallow candles, though smelly and dim, were far cheaper). The growth of the whaling industry, however, partly fueled by the demand for cleaner, clearer light, drove down the price of spermaceti candles during the 1800s and made them more accessible.

but underemployed British lady supposed she might do better than the current, mostly male, writers of her day.

She wouldn't be alone. In fact, so many women responded to their compulsory idleness by picking up a pen that, in my selection of subjects for this book, I was driven to confront—and release—my assumption that doing so would be a simple task. There were the sixteenth- and seventeenth-century breakouts Jane Anger, Mary Tattlewell, and Joan Hit-Him-Home, who, under their pointed pseudonyms, published scathing pamphlets in defense of women and demanded the right to an open conversation on their unjust intellectual suppression. Then came poet Anne Finch, the Countess of Winchilsea with her passionate protest of the "faults" of femaledom—"They tell us, we mistake our sex and way; Good breeding, fassion, dancing, dressing and play / Are the accomplishments we shou'd desire; To write, or read, or think, or to enquire / Wou'd cloud our beauty, and exhaust our time, And interrupt the conquests of our prime"—and playwright and poet Aphra Behn, a trailblazing upstart with a penchant for travel. Behn's experiences with the slave trade in Surinam led her to write *Oroonoko*, a work famous not just for its adherence to the newfangled novel form but also for having a slave as its hero. Before *Oroonoko*, Behn took great advantage of the fall of Oliver Cromwell and the Puritans, whose opinions against perceived "lewdness" had led to the dissolution of all theater companies in England during their time in power. Once the theaters reopened under Charles II, Behn jumped at the chance to write for the stage. Her plays were some of the most successful of the seventeenth century, and they paved the way for a succession of young female dramatists, beginning with Eliza Haywood and Delarivier Manley.

Britain's cadre of female scribblers expanded as the nineteenth century approached, ushering in with them the Industrial Revolution. Fanny Burney burst onto the scene with *Evelina* in 1778, which was quickly followed by Hannah More's poetry and Ann Radcliffe's famous Gothic work *The Mysteries of Udolpho,* both printed just as the effects of the French Revolution were beginning to transform nearly every aspect of life in England. Mary Wollstonecraft and her daughter Mary Shelley; Maria Edgeworth; Elizabeth Gaskell, who has some fame in modern England due to recent BBC adaptations: *Cranford* (based on Gaskell's *Cranford, My Lady Ludlow,* and *Mr. Harrison's Confessions*) and her *North and South*; and Christina Rossetti fit in among Jane Austen, Charlotte, Emily, and Anne Brontë, George Eliot, and Virginia Woolf—all of whom lived during the Hanoverian era of the monarchy and, in some cases, witnessed one (or as was the case with Woolf, who died in 1941, more than one) world war.

Pioneers, innovators, foremothers—these women were all three. They were also brave, for in this male-dominated society, becoming a published female writer was like branding yourself with a permanent mark of mortification, one that would be used unceasingly against you, your work, and your character from the date of your first step into the limelight until the end of time. Publishing was a competitive market for men, but it was an utterly harrowing one for women, and there was no sign of change anywhere on Britain's horizon, because the ideologies that had led to the unfair treatment of women writers were deeply ingrained in British culture. It bears reiterating that a young woman in eighteenth- and nineteenth-century England was believed not to be a whole human on her own, but rather a wife in the making. Her entire purpose was to reflect her husband's power and influence (or, as it often happened, to *give* it to him via her family property and connections), and in so doing, to replicate the happy "natural" system of patriarchy to which Britain was so thoroughly attached. A woman who was successful in this venture, in suppression of the self in favor of obedience to her husband, was rewarded with praise and greater social standing.

Aberrant behavior, on the other hand, was met with ire and abhorrence. "Boldness" in a female—self-assertion and public displays of talent or passion; proclaiming herself a nonrelative individual, whole in her own right; insisting that she had the power to think, to originate—all this was indicative of her abandonment of chastity and her potential for further unladylike activity, which, brought to the fullest terrifying extent, could include gambling, riding astride rather than demurely side-saddle, drinking, and (most grievous of all) engaging in infidelity. Publishing one's work was therefore tantamount to sexual profligacy, psychological instability, and a full renunciation of English values. A bold woman was an unnatural one; she'd overstepped her bounds and taken what wasn't hers.

IF A WOMAN WAS STILL DRIVEN TO PUBLISH, HOWEVER, SHE had some strategies for escaping public dishonor, or at least diminishing her vulnerability—and you'll see the women in this book employ them with great acumen. She could most certainly publish anonymously, and join the bulging ranks of authoresses whose books were attributed only to "A Lady" or "A Young Lady."

If invisibility wasn't acceptable, though, she had the option of manipulating her authorial image surrounding the book's purpose.* She could insist that writing for her was financially necessary, a desperate measure taken to save a young, genteel family fallen on hard times from the poorhouse. She could classify her work as a useful didactic tool in England's changing landscape (which was how the otherwise conservative Hannah More played it, not to mention Ann Radcliffe and Fanny Burney). She could downplay the importance of a given piece, describing it as "a mere trifle" or "an impromptu amusement." Or, finally, she could claim invalidism and justify her efforts as a way to escape the prison of her body. For the very few who would not publish unless it was with full, unapologetic openness, who refused any concession that might require self-deprecation or passivity—Mary Wollstonecraft comes to mind—the backlash from the reading public was often so furious that they were put off from writing, sometimes permanently.

Even after cloaking herself in one shadow or another to practice her craft, a burgeoning authoress still had to find someone to print her work, and while publishing for women was an exciting new market, promising potential gain, publishers had to be prepared to field the inevitable public opposition if a work were deemed too radical or permissive. Despite that risk, many publishers in the eighteenth and nineteenth century were quite

---

* See Mary Poovey, *The Proper Lady and the Woman Writer: Ideology as Style in the Works of Mary Wollstonecraft, Mary Shelley, and Jane Austen* (Chicago: University of Chicago Press, 1984) and Elaine Showalter, *A Literature of Their Own: British Women Novelists from Brontë to Lessing* (Princeton, NJ: Princeton University Press, 1977), for more on the intriguing interaction between authorship and feminine social expectation.

keen on giving women their voice. John Murray, founder of the eponymous imprint still around today, took on four of Jane Austen's novels and Maria Eliza Rundell's immensely successful *A New System of Domestic Cookery*, all written, according to his printings, "By a Lady." (Profits from Rundell's book were so great that Murray was able to buy 50 Albemarle Street, Mayfair, where, during his lifetime, some of the most influential literary figures would commune for evening chats.) Joseph Johnson nabbed tempestuous Mary Wollstonecraft's *A Vindication of the Rights of Men*. Thomas Cadell, too, appears to have been most agreeable to the ladies: together with his son and successor, the Cadell family gathered what was likely the most extensive list of female clients in England, including Hannah More, Ann Radcliffe, Fanny Burney, poet Felicia Hemans, historian Catherine Macaulay, and two of the women in this book, Helen Maria Williams and Charlotte Turner Smith.

SO MANY HURDLES, SO MANY ROADBLOCKS—A WOMAN'S PATH to authorship was circuitous and treacherous enough to make even the most intrepid female shiver in her stockings. As such, it really is a wonder that so many chose to make the journey—and yet, they did. Beyond my bookshelf, I discovered hundreds of other British women writers who were worthy of my attention. They were all trailblazers in their own right, often risking the loss of familial love, their futures as wives and mothers, and their reputation among people whose opinions mattered to them, all to see their work in print.

These women all deserve recognition, and I hope that one day they'll get it. For my purposes, however, the field had to be narrowed if this book were going to be approachable—and that process, the thinning of the bountiful forest of authoresses I'd discovered, was a complicated and lengthy one. I started by establishing some criteria, first with the time frame: I decided that the one-hundred-fifty-year span between 1760 and 1910, when the modern world was forming and when women began to write and publish in earnest, would be my focus. It encompasses my touchstones, Jane and Charlotte and Emily, and much of the social change that made their work and its publication possible, but extends enough beyond them to illustrate the enormous impact they had on the British novel.

The next criterion for an authoress's consideration was the darkness of the shadow under which she was hiding, meaning that the less attention she had, the better for my purposes. There might not be a film adaptation of Fanny Burney's *Evelina* or fan fiction forums devoted to the work of Harriet Martineau, but these two women still enjoy a fairly broad readership and are the subjects of discussion in lecture halls across the country. Anne Brontë may be the least talked-about of the Brontë sisters, but she's still remembered, still read. Who were the women *no one* was talking about? Those were the ones *I* wanted to talk about, the ones whom even my most rabid Janeite friends didn't know, the ones left out of an English major's curriculum.

The third, and final, criterion emerged organically, after I'd hit the books with my first two constraints in place. Every potential candidate was courageous and plucky; she'd negotiated the dangerous road to publication and had reaped the benefits of the risk. (Here I was reading her work, after all.) Yet there were precious few women with a tale of woe so amazing, so affecting, that I was compelled to pay greater attention. These were the women whose adversity went beyond a difficult publishing market and rigid social constructs, whose tribulations were of a much greater sort. Their journeys toward authorship required not only a pioneering spirit and a broad disregard for convention, but also pure, stout-hearted perseverance, an unabashed sense of self-worth, and, in many cases, a knack for getting out of life-threatening situations without losing their heads (sometimes literally). It was her *coolness,* her aptitude for blowing my mind, that finally hooked me onto each of my seven British women writers.

So this was how my group took shape, one by one. Seven ambitious women with inky thumbs shook their way out of the sifter and into my heart and head. All I had to do was give them their chance to speak.

What follows, as such, is not a book of literary criticism. It is a story, a collective biography, a narrative of anthropology and history. Each chapter is spent with the author *as* she writes, rather than looking back after the fact to judge what she created. How does she weave into the weft of these one hundred fifty years? How does she reflect the changing values of her tempestuous times? What was her day-to-day process of creation, however bleak and uncomfortable and mercurial it might have been, as she determined to make her voice heard?

Because these women have been languishing in obscurity for more than a century, most of my research couldn't be done remotely. No, I had to (*got* to!) zoom up and down the length of Britain's green and pleasant land for months at a time, from rainy Perth and Edinburgh in the North to Dover and Canterbury in the South, where I crawled into innumerable dusty library carrels with my stack of books and a pencil, tingling at the possibilities. I visited a few famous houses—those of Samuel Taylor Coleridge, the Brontës, Jane Austen, Thomas and Jane Carlyle—and many more as-of-yet unfamous ones. I got lost in Bristol, stranded in Berwick-upon-Tweed, and soaked to the bone in Folkestone, yet it was all intoxicating: These women were hard to find, but when I finally did track them down, I discovered a stupendously rich literary legacy.

I began with Charlotte Turner Smith, a bookish teenager turned child bride whose fame among the literati (Robert Southey and William Wordsworth especially) was even more remarkable considering she was rearing what would ultimately be twelve children, by herself, while she wrote; she managed this *and* became instrumental in the rise of the Romantics. (Jane was a huge fan.)

Smith's contemporary Helen Maria Williams also attracted Wordsworth's attention (devotion, more like), not to mention the rare praise of England's then-leader of the learned world, Dr. Samuel Johnson, which was likely a great comfort to her when she was getting upbraided in the press for her radical opinions. Williams had little patience for those who claimed that women had no place in politics; she herself ran in and out of wartime France, cataloging her experiences, and eventually produced an extraordinary firsthand account of the French Revolution as it unfolded day by day.

Meanwhile, back across the Channel, young Mary Robinson was using her ample beauty and cunning to elevate herself to one of the highest positions of all: mistress to the heir to the throne. She was an icon of fashion and a celebrity of the greatest sort, but as a gifted best-selling writer, she was also a keen observer of a rickety social system.

A few years later, after the fevered urgency of the French Revolution had cooled, an enigmatic enchantress named Catherine Crowe fomented a revolution of her own with her novel *Adventures of Susan Hopley; or Circumstantial Evidence*, which employed a plot strategy that led to an entirely new genre of literature: the detective novel. (It has been argued that *Susan Hopley* was the antecedent to Edgar Allan Poe's "The Murders in the Rue Morgue," and that Wilkie Collins, England's first sensationalist author, found inspiration in its pages.) Later in life, Catherine Crowe found even greater success with her 1848 treatise on the Spiritualist movement that was sweeping across England and America, of which she was an early adopter. Then, almost inevitably, she became the center of Britain's not-so-kind attention (and grist for Charles Dickens's nasty rumor mill) when the full extent of her eccentricities became known.

Sara Coleridge, on the other hand, never got that kind of notice—she labored under the long shadow of her father, Samuel Taylor Coleridge, for most of her life. Victorian propriety confined her to this obscurity, and to the very narrow road of a wife and mother. Still, she managed to make herself known nonetheless as the creator of the very first fantasy novel in English, *Phantasmion* (which displays an unprecedented and singular attention to worldbuilding), and as the purveyor of her father's genius to the modern world via her repackaging of his writings.

Finally, just as England was fully embracing the Industrial Revolution, Dinah Mulock Craik made her stand for the rising number of independent single women in England. According to her, women were *not* relative beings, but whole people, all on their own. Using her impressive business skills to support the propagation of her ideas in what were essentially, by today's classification, self-help treatises as well as fiction, Dinah lived very comfortably as a single lady during a time when this was nearly unthinkable—she must really have enjoyed watching her works become "more widely read than the productions of any other writer after Dickens," as one reviewer put it, not to mention her novel's placement just behind *Uncle Tom's Cabin* in a list of popular titles in 1863.

Yet if we were to measure the success of an authoress by profits alone, our last subject, Mary Elizabeth Braddon, would be the undisputed queen. Earnings from the sale of her two back-to-back best sellers, *Lady Audley's Secret* and *Aurora Floyd*, and from her serialized short stories and poetry, enabled Braddon to purchase and appoint an enormous mansion in Surrey for herself and her family. Scandal followed at every turn—she had children out of wedlock with a man who was already married (to a madwoman!)—but her prolific pen was there to garner support when she needed it. As a result, Mary Elizabeth and her assortment of nearly one hundred novels became ingrained in late Victorian culture.

These are the women whose stories I read, researched, and fell in love with, but as I studied their lives, I found myself in a constant state of befuddlement: how could a best-selling millionaire, or the inventor of a genre, or a war journalist in a petticoat, ever have been forgotten? For all their contemporary fame and fortune, for all their bravery, wit, and cunning, why have these seven authoresses been all but completely lost to us? Considering that Jane Austen published everything anonymously, and that the Brontës had almost nothing in the way of a public persona—Charlotte had a small one, Emily and Anne had none—it seems unimaginable that these women, who lived boldly in the limelight, could have been consigned to oblivion.

However, oblivion is where they have been. Currently their works are tucked away in the darkest corners of the market, produced cheaply and without elegance—that is, if they're in print at all. The very few biographies that exist on them are often fifty or a hundred years out of date, and any critical engagement with their writing is sealed behind the walls of academia: cloaked in unwieldy language, expensive to access, totally unattractive to all but the most dedicated scholars. Catch-all Internet sources like the *Oxford Dictionary of National Biography* and JSTOR, and even Wikipedia, are also woefully brief in their dealings with these formerly celebrated ladies of literature. They are not remembered, they are not canonized. But why not? Why would seven women so deserving of recognition have so little of it, or none at all, while a sisterhood of reclusive, scribbling parsons' daughters still endures?

What I came to understand was that, first and foremost, the game of lasting fame is an inherently unfair one. Aesthetic standards and the accompanying judgments are important to us—we're always dying to know which books we should read, which ones we should skip, which ones we should lie about having read (those by Tolstoy, Faulkner, David Foster Wallace), and which we should "forget" having read (say, the works of Stephenie Meyer, Dan Brown, and E. L. James). We're continually on the hunt for the Great Ones, always ready to cast off the Not-So-Great Ones, but when it comes to making these determinations, raw talent carries very little weight.

Consider, for a moment, Jane Austen. Decidedly a gifted writer, with Great Ones aplenty, she's upheld as the paradigm of English female authorship, and is known to all. Yet while she lived, her career looked a lot different—in fact, it paled in comparison with those of the seven women in this book. Jane's lifetime profits from writing were minuscule (£140 for *Sense and Sensibility*, £110 for *Pride and Prejudice*, and a paltry £10 for *Northanger Abbey*, which in modern currency would be around £9,000, £7,000, and £640 respectively*), and due in great part to her maddening, yet understandable, use of the "By a Lady" stamp, she received no popular acclaim and only the smallest slice of critical attention. How, then, did this country-dwelling authoress become essential reading?

Jane's miraculous journey from "a critic's novelist—highly spoken of and little read"—to a household name didn't happen simply because her writing is exceptional. (Indeed, if talent were the only deciding factor in the race to fame and fortune, our library shelves would look a lot different.) Rather, it was due to the efforts of just a few people that Jane was lifted out of the depths of irrelevance and into our hearts as a "major" novelist. A quiet, albeit constant thread of praise after her death; her nephew's well-timed 1869 biography, *A Memoir of Jane Austen*; and a pivotal Harvard dissertation in 1883, *Jane Austen: The*

---

* The value of currency has changed so drastically over the last two centuries that conversion is a troublesome process. But since relative values are often interesting, I've used MeasuringWorth.com and the many resources at http://www.ex.ac.uk/~R-Davies/arian/current/howmuch.html to give an approximation of this and other amounts in the coming chapters. March forward then, with the understanding that a certain interpretation is needed to fully grasp the economic worth of currency, and that I have not, in this instance, applied it as rigorously as it could be. Please refer to these websites if a more precise value is needed.

Critical Heritage, all helped. Yet it was Robert William Chapman's five-volume collection of Jane's novels, resplendent with illustrations of only the most appealing aspects of the stories (embodiments of the genteel English "sentiment" we've come to love, such as carriages and parties rather than donkeys or poor folk) that really set her apart from other authors and paved the way for her enduring posthumous celebrity. Jane's intrinsic value was there, but it was because of other people that she got to where she is today.

As illustrated in Chapman's scrupulous refashioning of Jane, this English "sentiment" sells. Jane, and Charlotte and Emily Brontë (though from a slightly different angle), reflect in their writing the England many people long for, a place where heroines are good and generous, unfailingly perceptive, and able to admit their faults (if they have any at all, which, in the case of Charlotte Brontë's heroines, is rare indeed). Deserving women are thus rewarded for their kind, warm spirits in the form of a union with men who submit themselves for polish and reformation under the women's gentle care. Unscrupulous people, on the other hand, are given their just deserts. Wayward Mr. Willoughby is condemned to an unhappy marriage; ditto for the conniving Mr. Wickham and his thoughtless bride, Lydia Bennet; Jane Eyre's icy aunt Mrs. Reed dies anguished and ashamed; Maria Bertram, for her sins, retires to a life of penance, disappearing from all good society. Still, at the end of these novels, all is serenity and calm, even if, during the course of the book, some darker and more contentious theme (like hunger, or death, or women's restricted role in society) has been broached.

In side-stepping any blatant engagement with the controversial issues of their period, Jane and Charlotte and Emily ensure readers' comfort in the last chapters—and here, it's worth a brief detour into the work of Anne Brontë, arguably the *least* famous (and culturally dominant) of the Haworth women, as an illustration. Under her pseudonym, Acton Bell, Anne published two novels, *Agnes Grey* and *The Tenant of Wildfell Hall,* which are now recognized (the latter making its way to television in 1996) but still, in comparison to the novels of her sisters, remain far less widely read. Whereas Charlotte and Emily embraced "the brooding, abusive Byronic hero" who presented an ever-alluring possibility of redemption, if only he could meet the right woman—and of course, he inevitably did—Anne "refused to glamorize violent, oppressive men."* Consider Heathcliff, from Emily's *Wuthering Heights,* and Frederick Lawrence and Gilbert Markham, from Anne's *The Tenant of Wildfell Hall.* Heathcliff terrorizes his pregnant wife and forces her to flee, whereas Frederick actually aids the flight of Helen, the heroine, from her prison of domestic tyranny. And when Helen refuses Gilbert's offer of marriage, he takes the news like a gentleman; contrast this to how Heathcliff behaves when Catherine does the same. (He doesn't handle rejection nearly so well.) Or, as another example, think about Anne's and Charlotte's two very different tales of a governess's experience, *Agnes Grey* and *Jane Eyre.* Jane's survival of a harrowing childhood is rewarded by what is essentially a pleasant post, despite the madwoman in the attic: Mrs. Fairfax steps into the role of the mother Jane never had; her charge, Adèle, reforms impressively under her care; and the

---

* Kate Beaton of *Hark! A Vagrant* fame, captures this perfectly in her popular comic "Dude Watchin' with the Brontës," found here: http://www.harkavagrant.com/index.php?id=202.

novel's fiery climax, though traumatic, is what allows Jane and Mr. Rochester to cement their relationship.

In Anne's *Agnes Grey*, after enjoying a far less dramatic childhood than Jane Eyre, becoming a governess is the heroine's choice—her loving family has fallen on hard times—but her experiences are vastly different to those of her counterpart. Both Agnes's positions put her in charge of children who are insubordinate—sometimes to the point of cruelty—and who, unlike Adèle, deny her the satisfaction of reforming their behavior. In further contrast, Agnes ultimately settles down not with the wealthy master of the house (having successfully tamed his wild ways and soothed his tormented soul), but with a kind, modest parson. "Jane Eyre is, in comparison, very fortunate," notes scholar Sally Shuttleworth.

Thanks to the Irish critic George Moore, who in his 1924 book *Conversations on Ebury Street* "demanded justice for Anne," she has emerged somewhat from Charlotte and Emily's shadow. But she is still "the forgotten Brontë sister," in part because, as one astute observer puts it, she "refused to wear rose-tinted glasses." Anne is "more honest than Emily and more unflinching than Charlotte . . . about the nature and violence of addiction. . . . But that doesn't make for great romance or cosy TV adaptations." And there's the rub: the world of Anne's fiction lacks the kind of romantic sentiment, the innocence, that makes her sisters' work so suitable for our castle-building in the sky. We can co-opt Charlotte's and Emily's, and Jane's, settings as places of refuge for our tired souls, seek shelter among the ivy-shrouded walls, and set up shop in an idyllic England where the houses are beautiful and so are the heroines (even if they themselves don't think so, as with Jane Eyre—they are, of course, not vain in the least). Poverty in this England is only dignified poverty, usually in the form of unspecified "debts"; good people ultimately get good things. And hardship? It exists here, but as a test of moral character—it proves the worth of those who endure it stoically, without bitterness. This is also the England where George Eliot's sun-drenched pastoral landscapes can be found, and where the unshakable "moral taxonomy" of her characters "can serve as a guide for living." (The power of this fantasy only increased after the Great War of 1914–1918, during which life in the real England was irrevocably changed; Clarissa also succumbs to its siren call in Virginia Woolf's *Mrs. Dalloway* when she reminisces about the halcyon days of her childhood in the English country village of Bourton.) *This* is the England many readers want, the England whose Arcadian heart endures through turmoil, and it is the England that Jane, Charlotte and Emily, and a cadre of well-intentioned editors, illustrators, and filmmakers have readily constructed for us.

It's an enchanting place, yes, but the actual England of 1760–1910 was nothing like it. The real England was embroiled in some divisive issues (the abolition of slavery and the French and Industrial Revolutions being among the most controversial)—it wasn't perfect, but it certainly was *interesting*, and it provided a backdrop for some riveting and wholly unromantic books that most of us have yet to read. The novels, poetry, travelogues, and nonfiction works of the seven women featured in these pages are startlingly different from the works of Jane and Charlotte and Emily Brontë, for these seven writers do not attempt to portray a romanticized England that doesn't exist. Rather, with a realistic approach that echoes Anne Brontë's, they embrace the turbulence of their time and reflect for their readers the dramatic and visceral emotions of a real world. Mary Robinson's semiautobiographical *Vancenza,* for instance, depicts her heroine's seduction and eventual betrayal by the Prince of Wales so irresistibly that the first edition sold out in a single day, making it the most popular novel written by a woman yet; Dinah Craik's *John Halifax, Gentleman,* which captures the rise of the struggling middle class in the 1850s, turned its authoress into a cheerleader for social change (and also made her a wealthy woman).

These books are no refuge—not every ending is a happy one, and not all loose ends are tied up in a pretty satin bow. Their heroines can be slippery and cunning, displaying liberal morality and behaving antithetically to their society's definition of proper femininity. Whisky is consumed, horses are ridden, adulteresses go on to have happy second marriages, and even murderesses beg the reader's sympathy. Their England is tumultuous, war-torn, and mired in problems, but it's also slowly revealing itself as a place where progress can be made, where unjust practices like slavery can be eliminated, and where women have freedoms they don't enjoy elsewhere. It is a world so very much like our own: unsettled, unpredictable, constantly changing. Their England can function not as a means of escape, but instead, as a window into history, in all its big, boisterous grandeur.

This book, however, is not meant to diminish the fantasy that many of us take away from the fiction of Jane and Charlotte and Emily Brontë, or trivialize the pleasure we find in it. Their romanticized and sentimental Englands—not always ideal lands, but on the whole less agitating to live in than our own—are just as necessary as ever, for they still speak to us and tap into our emotional yearnings in a way few others can. However, this project has given me an entirely new appreciation for the women of British literature: my view is wider, my bookshelves are fuller, my awareness of history is keener. So, as we soldier into the unknown, dear reader, fear not that Jane and Charlotte and Emily and the rest of the gang will lose their magic. Their world, the whole lovely landscape of it, will be waiting for you when you get back.

one

CHARLOTTE TURNER SMITH

[1749–1806]

IN THE 1700S, ENGLISH NOVELS WERE DOMINATED BY THE male picaresque tradition: a young, strapping, often unscrupulous hero moves in a straight line from one shenanigan to another. Much like the eponymous protagonist of Henry Fielding's 1749 bestseller, *The History of Tom Jones, A Foundling*, such a hero travels over hill and dale, falling in love here and sowing a few wild oats there. He might enlist in the military or start his own business (usually a less-than-conventional enterprise), and he most certainly gets into a few scrapes with the law, or even has a brush with death. After trotting about England impregnating servant girls and drinking with the locals, he finally settles down to a life of quiet respectability, just like Tom Jones.

For an eighteenth-century woman to write such a tale, however, was completely out of the question, and not just for reasons of propriety. In every practical sense, a life of freedom (of travel, of danger, of enterprise, of naughtiness and moral ambiguity) was entirely unknown to women, for theirs was a world of infinitely tighter boundaries than that of their brothers, husbands, or fathers. A woman could not wander aimlessly throughout the countryside on adventures, sleeping wherever she wanted, or with whomever she wanted; she would likely never even have set foot outside the borders of her family's land without an escort. When a woman's days were spent fussing over frocks and frivolities, and when she could count on one hand the number of people with whom she regularly spoke, she had no role in or even knowledge of a life that might lend itself to the kind of story that was popular in the eighteenth century. She was trapped in an almost unbearably small existence, one described by one female writer of the day as "tame and insipid"—"We awake in the morning, dress ourselves, go out shopping or visiting, and return in perfect safety to the same employment or amusements this day that we returned to yesterday, and which will probably engage our time tomorrow." What could she possibly have written about?

The one thing women *were* fully aware of, all too fully, was the overarching, exhaustive search for a husband, a search that dogged their existence from the moment of their birth. This was a female's sole reason for living, for she could never realize full womanhood (quiet, patient servility, gentle motherhood, moral rectitude) without first attaching herself to a spouse. Much of a girl's youth, then, was spent in anguish over whether some beau would ask her to dance, whether he would propose, and whether she should accept him. And since, as Catherine Morland puts it in *Northanger Abbey*, "people that marry can never part, but must go and keep house together," an enormous effort had to be made to ascertain a potential mate's interior character. Would he become brutish or violent when angry? Was he reckless? An alcoholic? A spendthrift? Did he have enough money to sustain both himself and a future family? Or, perhaps most important, were his affections merely a reflection of his greed for her dowry?

Mothers and friends could help a young lady with this decision and with the intricate process of becoming a good wife once the vows were said, but for more exacting detail, conduct literature could be counted on to provide some of the best instruction. Published exclusively by men initially, conduct books were meant to instill in women the values and comportment necessary for them to get along in an increasingly conservative society, and to prepare her to fulfill her "calling" as a tender, virtuous, sympathetic wife and mother. She was expected to become an ideal woman, fit for her domestic sphere, and for this, it was imperative that every respectable home have at least a few conduct books on hand. James Fordyce's *Sermons to Young Women* and John Gregory's *A Father's Legacy to His Daughter* were both extremely popular choices for the education of gentry daughters (as evidenced by their many, many printings), along with Thomas Gisborne's *Enquiry into the Duties of the Female Sex,* which insists that those women who rival "the most eminent men in depth and comprehensiveness of intellect" are variations on the natural state of things, and "useless to enlarge." A good woman, according to conduct literature, should instead busy herself with domestic life and elegance of taste, and with nurturing the kind of "acute sensibility" and "active benevolence" that would attract (and, later, please) a worthy husband.

Considering, then, how utterly bombarded eighteenth- and nineteenth-century women were with rules and regulations concerning their acquisition of a spouse (in books, at home, during their schooling), the choice of subject matter for an authoress of that period was a simple one: women wrote about love, in all its forms, from unrequited and predatory attraction to true, enduring, comfortable attachment. And soon, their quiet scribbling at the margins of society would become a brand-new literary tradition.

THE FIRST CLEAR SIGN OF A BURGEONING FEMALE LITERARY scene was Fanny Burney's *Evelina*, in 1778, followed shortly thereafter by her *Cecilia* in 1782 and *Camilla* in 1796; then Maria Edgeworth's 1801 work, *Belinda*, and Jane Austen's beloved *Sense and Sensibility*, in 1811. Each of these novels uses the heroine's path to marriage as the central plot, one fraught with questions of compatibility and emotional travail, full of ups and downs. In the end, though, all is made right once the heroine decides to allow her feelings of admiration and esteem to overrule her quest for fortune. (As it happens, however, the husband-to-be is already wealthy. Notably few heroines in works from this period must choose between love and utter poverty.) She marries, willingly and happily, and then zooms off to enjoy the best situation a society like hers can imagine: wifehood.

It all happens so perfectly: A handsome, moneyed man appears out of nowhere and makes the heroine's dreams come true. Everyone is content; no deserving soul is left out in the cold. Good people get what they ask for; scoundrels do not. Yet as delicious (and unlikely) a fantasy as these were, they were still dreamt up by women who, significantly, were unmarried at the time they produced them. Jane Austen, Fanny Burney, and Maria Edgeworth may have fully grasped the back-and-forth of the romantic process—it was ingrained in their lives, after all, via conduct literature and courtship novels—but they had no *real* experience of life as a wife beyond secondhand accounts. (Jane and Maria never would.) Thus, these narratives end where the authoress's knowledge does: at the altar.

Of course, reality extended far beyond the confines of such a precious affair, and few female writers understood this better than the ill-fated, harrowed, desperately overtaxed Charlotte Turner Smith. Like all daughters of the gentry, she grew up knowing she'd eventually have to leave the comforts of childhood behind for a profitable marriage. Her family's house in London and their sprawling estate, Bignor Park, near what is now the South Downs National Park in West Sussex, would both have to be given up—and this was no small loss, for her family was wealthy and prosperous. But for Charlotte, though, her books and papers were what she treasured most. From an early age she'd shown a talent for writing, and her father, Nicholas Turner (a poet himself), had encouraged her: in fact, she was only six years old when she drafted her first submission, a group of poems for *Lady's Magazine*, and though they weren't accepted for publication, the action speaks to her precocity. (It should be remembered that most of today's six-year-olds have only just figured out how to count backward from twenty.)

Pleasant though her youth was, Charlotte was thrown into chaos when her mother's death, from complications during childbirth, prompted Nicholas Turner to depart England for an expensive, luxurious, months-long bender that swallowed up the entirety of his fortune. Charlotte was left at home under the care of an aunt, and was therefore spared the torment of watching her father's disintegration, but she felt the effects of his actions when he returned to England. Now that the money was gone, drastic measures were needed to refill her father's pockets. He sold several of his properties and began courting a wealthy new fiancée, a Miss Meriton of Chelsea, who had twenty thousand pounds to her name—but it wasn't enough to offset his debts.

There was only one solution yet unexplored. When Turner had arrived home, he'd found Charlotte much changed since he'd so callously abandoned her at Bignor Park. She was now a charismatic beauty with a voracious mind, a graceful form, and fluency in French—a veritable fountain of potential for a suitor of her father's choosing. Soon it was announced that Turner, in his fifteen-year-old daughter's stead, had accepted a proposal from Benjamin Smith, the oldest son of a wealthy codirector of the East India Company. Smith had a supposedly bright future, and Charlotte was expected to marry him immediately.

In a letter written many years later, Charlotte likened her father's actions to a form of legal prostitution, but at the time, arrangements like this were not uncommon. Teenage gentry were typically betrothed before they reached their thirteenth birthdays, usually to people they had nothing in common with or, as was far too often the case, had never even met. The resulting situation was torturous for the new wife, yet the expectation, as Lord Halifax instructed somewhat crustily in his 1688 conduct book, *Advice to a Daughter,* was to accept the "disadvantages belonging to your sex." Knowing this, women sometimes avoided marriage for as long as possible, even choosing spinsterhood over becoming a bargaining chip between wealthy families.* Yet, for most, the freedom to refuse one's destiny was an impossible hope. Without the ability to earn their own way, women were at the mercy of those who controlled the purse strings: their fathers, brothers, and, ultimately, their husbands. Mary Astell, an English feminist and one of the fortunate few who was able to sidestep wifehood completely, asked the public for an explanation: "If marriage be such a blessed state, how comes it, may you say, that there are so few happy marriages?"

Lacking an income of her own, Charlotte would need to marry if she were to have any semblance of a life away from her overbearing father and his new bride. So, as she prepared for her arranged wedding—doing her "daily preparations for my journey to Hell," as Mary Wortley Montagu described it—she smoothed relations with her future father-in-law and did her best to make the transition as comfortable as she could. All this she did without knowing the truth of her situation: that twenty-three-year-old Benjamin Smith had zero interest in taking over the family business, as he'd promised, and that he'd already begun to descend into alcoholism. She also was kept ignorant of the many illegitimate children he'd fathered, and of his mounting gambling debts.

During the first months of wedded life, though, she really was quite happy. She basked in the sunlight of oversexed adolescence and felt herself fairly well satisfied in her spacious apartment. Like many willful young married women, she was

* Beyond Jane and Maria, there are a number of notable women writers who remained single for life, such as Louisa May Alcott, of *Little Women* fame, Emily and Anne Brontë, Emily Dickinson, and the popular Victorian novelist Marie Corelli.

annoyed with her mother-in-law, but she vented to a friend in a sassy, spunky letter that is also the earliest-known example of her writing:

> *I pass almost every day with the poor sick old lady, with whom, however, I am no great favorite; somebody has told her I have not been notably brought up [trained in household tasks], (which I am afraid is true enough), and she asks me questions which, to say the truth, I am not very well able to answer. There are no women, she says, so well qualified for mistresses of families than the ladies [her servants] of Barbados, whose knowledge of housewifery she is perpetually contrasting with my ignorance, and, very unfortunately, those subjects on which I am informed give me little credit with her . . . I have not seen any of their paragons whom I am at all disposed to envy.*

That her mother-in-law preferred the slaves' domestic skills to Charlotte's nonexistent ones made Charlotte harrumph, but over time this complaint would become the least of her worries. After the wedding glow dissipated, she discovered in Benjamin a lack of ability to concentrate on anything for long and a sulky childishness that would surface whenever he grew restless or bored. He was also indolent, inept at all things work-related, and clueless about money.

It quickly became clear how much Charlotte had already surpassed him in maturity, despite being eight years his junior. Her sense of isolation deepened, and the gravity of her mistake sank in:

> *No disadvantage could equal those I sustained; the more my mind expanded, the more I became sensible of personal slavery; the more I improved and cultivated my understanding, the farther I was removed from those with whom I was condemned to pass my life; and the more clearly I saw by these newly-acquired lights the horror of the abyss into which I had unconsciously plunged.*

Then there was the problem of children. She'd become pregnant just a few months after her marriage and delivered a son—no unusual thing. Then, immediately after the birth, she conceived again, then again, and five more times after that—eight babies arrived before she was twenty-five years old. Her first died of sickness; then came Benjamin, William, Charlotte Mary, Braithwaite, Nicholas, Charles, and Anna Augusta. (On average, women in England during this time would bear six or seven live infants—at least one of which would likely die before reaching adulthood—but many would produce double or even triple that number.) Charlotte was so hassled and besieged with babies, so overcome with responsibility, that bitterness began to brew in her gut; later, it would empower her to act.

For the moment, though, the real-life woe of pregnancy and childbirth was her reality. Jane Austen herself knew one woman who'd been "in for it," as she described motherhood to her sister, thirteen times over, and another, Mrs. Deeds, who would eventually become mother to nineteen children. The advice Austen gives poor Mrs. Deeds involves "the simple regimen of separate rooms," which was prudent guidance in a world without birth control. However, since the success of a marriage, arranged or otherwise, was determined by the number of offspring produced, women could easily expect to spend half their lives pregnant. The unending cycle of gestation and recovery (nine months of pregnancy followed by the obligatory month-long lie-in following) occurred with almost annual regularity.

In Charlotte's case, by 1775 her quickly expanding family had outgrown the London flat, so, much to her delight, they relocated to a small country home in Hampshire called Lys Farm. She and the children could ramble fields and swim in ponds, and she now had a garden, too. But Benjamin launched into its upkeep "with more avidity than judgment," as Mary Hays recounted in *British Public Characters*. Land was purchased, useless alterations were made, rare plants were bought and installed, and up went the debt—just as Charlotte realized she was expecting another child.

A baby girl, Lucy, arrived a year after their move to Hampshire, followed by another boy, Lionel, but after this tenth delivery, she wouldn't become pregnant again for another five years. This gap between pregnancies might have been the result of her advancing age and the corresponding difficulties of conception, but it also likely indicates her growing distaste for her husband. Benjamin's misuse of money and his increasingly violent temper had become more and more prominent in their life together. He subjected her to physical abuse, punching and kicking her, and in an incident she described to the Earl of Egremont in 1804, he even threw a hard loaf of bread at her head "without provocation at all but the phrenzy."

Yet some level of commitment on her part must have remained, because when the police finally came to collect on

Benjamin's debts in December 1783, Charlotte accompanied him to the notorious King's Bench Prison in London's Southwark right after she'd given birth to their eleventh baby, Harriet. The reasons for her doing so are unclear; perhaps her husband ordered her to come along, or perhaps it was out of pride that she chose not to desert him at this most opportune moment, or maybe it was a mixture of pity and concern that kept her by his side. The inner workings of any marriage are difficult to discern from without, and here they're especially befuddling considering the couple's rocky history and Charlotte's valid reason for not accompanying him: the children she had staying with her brother at Bignor Park (he'd inherited the property after their father's death). Nevertheless, for some reason, Charlotte moved to King's Bench to live out the winter with Benjamin.

Like most prisons of the day, King's Bench was almost unimaginably foul inside, with the noise of riots and fighting echoing at all hours, and as Charlotte later wrote in her novel *Ethelinde*, the "fierce and stern faces of the keepers" haunted her dreams. It's heartbreaking to imagine her lying there in the gloom, feeling the dismal weight of it all on her heart. She was away from her children, including her newborn, and by the spring she'd become pregnant yet again (thankfully, for the last time). Her husband was useless; all the money was gone. Yet despite, or because of, the sadness of it, Charlotte's time in prison marked a turning point: it was just the impetus she needed to start writing in earnest.

For this intelligent aspiring authoress, the way to liberation from King's Bench was quite clear: she would write, she would write well enough to get the debts paid, and she would do it now. She went straight to work in the fetid darkness and made her poetry debut just six months after Benjamin's arrest, in June 1784.

It's difficult to overemphasize the extraordinary accomplishment that *Elegiac Sonnets, and Other Essays* represented. That an unknown woman should first attract a publisher while her address was King's Bench Prison was amazing, but that she did it all in such a short time? Even modern minds have to boggle at the incredible focus and drive that kind of production would have required. She also bravely chose to publish under her real name, but masked her circumstances by scrupulously connecting herself with her childhood home, rather than her current one; the authoress of this new book was denoted as "Charlotte Smith of Bignor Park, Sussex." At the time, financial disgrace was nearly synonymous with social ruin, so the secret of her situation was protected, for now, but her interior torment was exposed for all to see:

Queen of the silver bow!—by thy pale beam,
Alone and pensive, I delight to stray,
And watch thy shadow trembling in the stream,
Or mark the floating clouds that cross thy way.
And while I gaze, thy mild and placid light
Sheds a soft calm upon my troubled breast;
And oft I think—fair planet of the night,
That in thy orb, the wretched may have rest:
The sufferers of the earth perhaps may go,
Released by death—to thy benignant sphere;

And the sad children of Despair and Woe
Forget, in thee, their cup of sorrow here.
Oh! that I soon may reach thy world serene,
Poor wearied pilgrim—in this toiling scene!

With such palpably aching language and Romantic sensibility—exactly the sort of style that was popular at the time—the success of the volume was all but ensured. Indeed, *Elegiac Sonnets* enjoyed instant acclaim and was into its second printing within the year, which enabled Charlotte to pay for Benjamin's release just seven short months into his sentence. Relief washed over her as her carriage blissfully bounced down the road toward her waiting children at Bignor Park, noting "the soft, pure air of summer's morning, breathing over the dewy grass" in comparison to the last seven months' "scenes of misery, of vice and even terror." It was almost too much for her to take in:

> *My native hills at length burst upon my view. I beheld once more the fields where I had passed my happiest days, and amidst the perfumed turf with which one of these fields was strewn, perceived with delight the beloved group from which I had been so long divided, and for whose fate my affections were ever anxious . . . After all my sufferings, I began to hope I might taste content, or experience at least a respite from calamity.*

Sadly, a brief respite was all she received. The profits from her book covered enough of Benjamin's debt to get him out of prison, but not to pay everyone off, and due to his continued and rampant overspending after his release, it was only a few months before the lawyers were again clamoring for his arrest. This time though, having exhausted all his resources and called in every available favor, Benjamin found no hope for legal settlement in England, and was forced to find shelter in France. Bitter, resentful, still pregnant (for the twelfth time), her fingers sore from writing, and with a list of ravenous collectors in her pocket, Charlotte gathered their children and moved to France to live out the winter. There, things quickly went from bad to worse.

Benjamin had gone ahead to France to find a house for the family, but the one he'd chosen turned out to be a crumbling château, rancid from the inside out, on a barren stretch of road between Rouen and Dieppe, a wreck he'd found through gambling buddies he'd only just met. Thoughtlessly, he'd also neglected to prepare the place for his wife and children's coming. This, after a grueling journey and a near-crippling bout of seasickness, Charlotte arrived in a state of exhaustion only to discover that she and several of the kids didn't have beds or bedding, and that many of the windows didn't have glass. In this, one of the coldest winters the region had ever seen, wood and food were in very short supply, and the nearest market was twelve miles away.

Unsurprisingly (although, from our perspective, perhaps belatedly), Charlotte finally went over the edge. She'd done everything she could, been as loving a partner as any cheating, pilfering husband could wish for, and had brought children into difficult circumstances. Yet none of it seemed to matter to Benjamin Smith, not even after she'd been to prison with him. He'd kept spending, kept gambling, kept getting in trouble (by now embezzlement had been added to his list of imprisonable offenses). Their marriage was a farce, and Charlotte was a woman whose pride wouldn't stand any more humiliation, even if it meant renouncing all that society expected of her. Though it would be two more years before everything was settled, she knew then and there, in 1787: the marriage was over.

Despite Benjamin's infidelities, his abusive temper, and his inadequacy as a father, the ways Charlotte could end their marriage were frustratingly limited. Her sole *legal* option for divorce involved the ecclesiastical courts and a private act of Parliament, but this route was so expensive that between 1700 and 1857 only three hundred people attempted it (nearly all of them men). The only alternative, then, was to abandon him, murder him, or wait what would seem like an eternity for his natural death. Charlotte chose desertion. She returned to England in the spring of 1785 with her children in tow, leaving Benjamin in France, while the *Times* was busily reporting every detail of another divorce, one that would captivate Charlotte (and, indeed, the entire English public) during this, the most transformative decision of her life.

In 1777, as the story goes, Mary Eleanor Bowes married a fabulously handsome man, Andrew Robinson Stoney, but soon realized he wasn't the dashing military captain he'd made himself out to be. In actuality, he was a poor lieutenant who'd secretly written libelous newspaper articles against Mary so he could win her heart by staging a duel with the editor who printed his words. Once Mary discovered what he'd done, Stoney imprisoned her in her own home and subjected her to physical and mental torture. He kicked, whipped, and hit her; burned her hair and face; raped her and the household servants; dallied with prostitutes in front of her; and on numerous occasions threatened her life. Yet, in spite of this laundry list of tyrannical cruelties, Mary had to make a monstrous effort to free herself from the marriage. Just to get the case heard in court, she had to find eyewitnesses (her own servants and hired help, who were themselves just as trapped as she) to prove what was happening. In the end, she was able to go to court only after a lawyer agreed to represent her for free.

Mary's husband appealed after the court found in her favor, then further responded by snatching Mary off a London street in the middle of the day and holding her at gunpoint, starving and terrified, until she was rescued more than a week later. Still, she managed to emerge victorious from each of the following two appeals made by her husband—three in total, which the courts unbelievably agreed to hear even after his obvious brutality—and was finally granted her divorce. Mary's fortune and children were returned to her, and Bowes was sent to prison, where he sired five more children with another unfortunate mistress.

KNOWLEDGE OF MARY ELEANOR BOWES'S FATE ADDED FUEL TO the fire already burning in Charlotte's heart, but with no money for a lawyer, she knew desertion was her only choice. It meant she would also have to give up profits from writing, her dowry, and any rights she had to property. Even so, this was a price she was willing to pay to avoid continuing with the life she had. So, social and fiscal consequences notwithstanding, she abandoned Benjamin after more than two decades of marriage. It was a decidedly anti-Jane thing to do—no "happily ever after" here, no fantasy—and it would lead to some decidedly un-Jane-like books.

WHILE SHE MOLDERED AWAY IN FRANCE, CHARLOTTE HAD busied herself with a pair of translations to keep herself occupied: a novel called *Manon Lescaut,* and *Les causes célèbres et intéressantes,* a collection of court cases. She was thankful for the distraction—"Amid the interruptions unavoidable in so large a family; when I could not possibly disengage my mind enough for original composition; it amuses, without fatiguing me; and is at least doing something"—but once she arrived back in England, the income insufficiencies of translation work made themselves known: it simply didn't create enough capital for a newly single woman and her children to live off. If the success of Fanny Burney and her peers Elizabeth Blower and Eliza Bromley were any indication, Charlotte would have to produce a novel if she hoped to make a living by her pen.*

In characteristic fashion, then, she sat down and immediately produced one, and since it was written in the months directly following her separation from Benjamin, it has the courageous bite of a woman on a mission. In the pages of *Emmeline, the Orphan of the Castle,* published in 1788 under her own name, she lambastes her wayward ex-husband and she does it very, very well. All fifteen hundred first-edition copies sold in just six months. Her publisher, Thomas Cadell (the man whose son and successor, Thomas Cadell the younger, would nine years later reject a request from Jane Austen's father to publish an early version of *Pride and Prejudice*), found *Emmeline* very promising and paid Charlotte two hundred guineas for the manuscript, more than he had originally pledged. Sir Walter Scott liked the book, too, calling it "a happy mixture of humour, and of bitter satire

---

* *Manon Lescaut* had to be withdrawn from the publishers after Charlotte was accused, falsely, of plagiarism. *Les causes célèbres et intéressantes* fared better. She repackaged and retitled it as *The Romance of Real Life,* and enjoyed a modest profit for her troubles. See Fletcher, *Charlotte Smith,* 82–86.

mingled with pathos." He confessed himself quite satisfied with the characters, and described them as "belonging to the highest branch of fictitious narrative."

Deserving as it is of high praise, *Emmeline* is different from the other female society novels on the market at the time, for Charlotte herself was different from other females. She held radical views on politics and feminism, and was not afraid to rewrite familiar scenes in her work to showcase just how unconventional her beliefs were. For instance, the abduction of her heroine in *Emmeline* mirrors a scene in Samuel Richardson's *Clarissa* (which he packaged as a conduct novel). Yet, in Charlotte's version, the heroine does not become a tragic victim of circumstance as in *Clarissa*. Instead, in an action that appears to reflect Charlotte's dissenting opinion of traditional values, Emmeline simply convinces her captor to return her to safety. Additionally, very unlike the characters in *Pride and Prejudice,* Charlotte's characters are not eternally unaffected, or beautiful; nor are they uncommonly fortunate or *un*fortunate. Also, because they were created by a woman nearly smothered in children, they're not removed from the often dreary reality of motherhood. Despite their different approaches, Jane Austen was a big admirer of Charlotte's work: *Emmeline* is mentioned twice in Jane's juvenilia (the only female contemporary of Jane's who is), first in *The History of England,* and later in her unfinished piece, *Catharine, or the Bower.*

The eponymous heroine of *Emmeline* is an orphan whose questionable birth leads to an isolated youth spent in a castle in the middle of nowhere, with only a housekeeper for company. Her past is shadowy, and her life is solitary, but she still attracts the affections of her cousin Delamere, who, "accustomed from his infancy to the most boundless indulgences, never formed a wish the gratification of which he expected to be denied: and if such a disappointment happened, he gave way to an impetuosity of disposition that he had never been taught to restrain."

Emmeline is not at all prepared to wed this spoiled dandy, or any other man. "I have a mind," she says, "which tho' it will not recoil from any situation where I can earn my bread by honest labour, it is infinitely superior to any advantages such a man . . . can offer me!" So when her cousin's attentions become too insistent, Emmeline flees for friendlier territory under the protection of her friend Mrs. Stafford, who is so obviously a copy of her creator that only the dimmest critic could have missed it. Mrs. Stafford lives a replica of Charlotte's life, and although it was a bold move to present private details in so unguarded a manner (and Charlotte later paid a dear price for her candor), posterity rejoices, because for one clear moment her innermost workings are revealed.

In Mrs. Stafford we see a busy mother who also happens to be educated, refined, and in possession of beautiful elegance. But her husband? He is a sham; irritable, abusive, ham-handed; and "ever in pursuit of some wild scheme." And just like Benjamin Smith, he spends far too much money on frivolous nonsense:

> *Mr. Stafford was one of those unfortunate characters, who having neither perseverance and regularity to fit them for business, or taste and genius for more refined pursuits, seek, in every casual occurrence or childish amusement, relief against the tedium of life. Though married very early, and though father of a numerous family, he had thrown away time and money, which should have provided for them, in collecting baubles.*

Mrs. Stafford has quietly suffered these long years, since her husband's shortcomings have led him to embrace some rather unsavory diversions, "vices yet more fatal to the repose of his wife, and schemes yet more destructive to the fortune of his family." And, as evidenced by her tendency to lapse into melancholy and to "gaze mournfully on [her children] 'till the tears streamed down her cheeks," it becomes apparent that the charge of motherhood has taken its toll on Mrs. Stafford. She's shrunken and lost, always trying to expect good things, but failing at acquiring them. Through her gloom, she explains the situation to Emmeline:

> *I, when not older than you now are, had a perpetual tendency to fancy future calamities, and embittered by that means many of those hours which would otherwise have been really happy. Yet has not my pre-sentiments, tho' most of them have been unhappily verified, enabled me to avoid one of those thorns with which my path has been thickly strewn.*

On the outskirts of the narrative is Adelina, an adulteress whose dalliances with a young lover leave her pregnant. At this point—where Jane Austen would have hot-footed it out of this unseemly territory, perhaps changing the subject to the news, as she does in *Sense and Sensibility* after Mrs. Jennings mentions her daughter's imminent confinement—Charlotte Turner Smith gets brave.* She spins an entire subplot around

*"'You may believe how glad we all were to see them,' added Mrs. Jennings, leaning forward towards Elinor . . . 'but, however, I can't help wishing they had not travelled quite so fast, nor made such a long journey of it, for they came all round by London upon account of some business, for you know (nodding significantly and pointing to

this soiled, unprincipled character and even goes so far as to allow the fallen woman to become friend and confidante to Emmeline, who later discovers her own happy circumstances: after learning that her deceased family was perfectly legitimate, she attains her inheritance and marries her true love. Adelina herself has the further unlikely good fortune of marrying the father of her lovechild (which can be interpreted as a barb directed at the sad truth of female legitimacy: that it can be attained only via marriage).

Readers were shocked; this kind of ending, where "bad" people enjoy good lives, was nearly unheard of in eighteenth-century England. Yet, though amazed that a character like Adelina could be allowed to live on happily, and stunned at Charlotte Turner Smith's courage, they read *Emmeline* voraciously and drove its popularity up, up, and up. Then the money rolled in, and Charlotte knew she'd found her path. She released *Ethelinde, or the Recluse of the Lake* the following year, and then *Celestina,* which immediately went into a second edition and dropped more than £250 in her pocket (well over £24,000 by today's standards). *Elegiac Sonnets* had also been expanded and printed four times since its initial publication, and went out in its fifth edition in 1789, just after *Emmeline,* earning Charlotte a further one hundred eighty pounds that

---

her daughter) it was wrong in her situation. I wanted her to stay at home and rest this morning, but she would come with us; she longed so much to see you all!'

Mrs. Palmer laughed, and said it would not do her any harm.

'She expects to be confined in February,' continued Mrs. Jennings.

Lady Middleton could no longer endure such a conversation, and therefore exerted herself to ask Mr. Palmer if there was any news in the paper.

'No, none at all,' he replied, and read on."

year alone. These were some of the most significant wages she'd ever see for her poetry.

IN 1791, CHARLOTTE AND HER BROOD MOVED DOWN TO BRIGHTON in search of, as far as has been surmised, cheaper living and "lively company." The southern seaside town had recently been furnished with an opulent monarchical mansion, the Royal Pavilion, which attracted many stylish partygoers and their accompanying hangers-on. The Prince of Wales himself frequently visited the area for romps with a lady who would eventually become his common-law wife, Maria Fitzherbert. (Four years later he would be subjected to an arranged marriage that was, of course, a complete failure.) Forty-two-year-old celebrity Charlotte Turner Smith plunged herself into Brighton's liberal society; politics, philosophy, and some great café culture intellectualism were all hers to enjoy.

The temptation for Charlotte to join in the fun must have been irresistible. She was surrounded by like-minded people (radicals, even) and finally free to expound on her very developed, very antiestablishment ideas. After all her suffering and servitude, she'd grown to heartily despise the British government, for it had abandoned her in favor of the patriarchal status quo. The system wouldn't grant her a divorce, which enabled Benjamin to pillage her earnings whenever he felt inclined; nor could it settle her father-in-law's estate—even now, fifteen years after his death, the money he'd left her and her children was still caught up in red tape, and it would be thirty-six years before an agreement could be reached. (*Jarndyce and Jarndyce*, the lawsuit that "[dragged] its dreary length before the Court, perennially hopeless," in Dickens's *Bleak House*, is eerily similar, so much so that some scholars have pointed to Charlotte 's case as the direct inspiration for the story.)

She was fed up with the English system of law, and the timing was auspicious—there'd been an insurrection at the Bastille, the nobility were fleeing France, enthusiasm for liberty was bubbling over into revolution, and it was all spreading across the Continent like wildfire. Intrigued, and likely more than a little curious, Charlotte quickly "caught the contagion." As her sister, Catherine Ann Dorset (a writer of children's books), later commented, communion with "some of the most violent advocates of the French Revolution" in Brighton filled Charlotte's head with ideas. So, in 1791, she went down to France to see for herself. Helen Maria Williams (see chapter 2), Thomas Paine, and William Wordsworth were among the many writers already there, and while little information about her trip survives, we can easily assume it was productive: once she came home to England, she produced a new novel with extraordinary speed and passion, activity symptomatic of a woman keyed up on the energy of revolutionary Paris.

Desmond, published in 1792, tells the story of Geraldine Verney, who, like Mrs. Stafford, is chained to an unworthy mate. In this case, the husband is a glorified Tory misogynist who thinks women are "good for nothing but to make a show." The main storyline is superimposed over the French Revolution, and Geraldine struggles against her husband just as the French people struggled against their monarch: as prisoners of war. Slavery, women's rights, inequality, and political representation are all major discussion topics, and as a result, this is Charlotte's most feminist, and therefore most incendiary, work. Yet the real intensity of her proud Girondist views is most easily seen in her venomous preface, one so crusading that, beginning in 1800, her publishers dropped it from later editions:

> *As to the political passages dispersed through the work, they are for the most part, drawn from conversations to which I have been a witness, in England, and France, during the last twelve months: in carrying on my story in those countries and at a period when their political situation (but particularly that of the latter) is the general topic of discourse in both; I have given to my imaginary characters the arguments I have heard on both sides; and if those in favour of one party have evidently the advantage, it is not owing to my partial representation, but to the predominant power of truth and reason, which can neither be altered or concealed.*

Desmond isn't partial; it's accurate—or so Smith claims. By opening an already polarizing book with such confidence, however, she was bound to lose friends. Thomas Lowe, the husband of one of her Brighton chums, refused ever to be in the same room with her after learning of her opinions, and though her sister, Catherine, chalked up the resulting ripple of condescension to envy—she wrote that the "host of literary ladies in array against her," in their discomfiture about such boldness, were "armed with all the malignity which envy could inspire!"—much of Charlotte's devoted fan base was alienated by the new political fervor in *Desmond*. Even still, where one person put it down, another picked it up, for *Desmond* spoke to a new breed of reader, one who looked to appreciate novels not only for their entertainment value, but for their social commentary as well.

Fresh and innovative, *Desmond* also drew the attention of other female fire-breathers, like Mary Wollstonecraft and Helen Maria Williams, both of whom were writing politically charged works of their own. Happily for Charlotte, the success of *Desmond* brought her deeper into this circle of reformers. She even had the honor of being remembered at a toast in November 1792 to cheer on the good fortune of the French military—"[to] the Women of Great Britain, particularly those who have distinguished themselves by their writings in favor of the French Revolution, Mrs. Smith and Miss H. M. Williams!" (These two authors had met and befriended each other in France, likely through their mutual connection William Hayley.)

This kind of grand attention heralded a big change. Novels were becoming a means of intellectual discourse and could no longer be written off as mere empty-headed lovelorn diversions. And though it would be decades before women stopped apologizing for writing novels—before Jane Austen stopped having to defend her family as "great novel-readers and not ashamed of being so"—*Desmond* was pioneering in enabling women to set a high standard for their own brand of sharp, judicious literature on topics other than husband acquisition. Later, George Eliot and Harriet Martineau would push much harder against the bounds of lowbrow "women's" novels, but Charlotte was ahead of the curve. *Desmond*, and her following work, *The Old Manor*

House, were more than just cute stories; they spoke to the high-minded, and to those who wished to be so.

Politics brought diversity to Charlotte's career, but her passionate liberalism wouldn't last. In August 1792, a raging horde descended on the Tuileries Palace to take the royal family into custody, and among the hundreds of casualties was the Princesse de Lamballe, who was torn to bits by the crowd. A few weeks after this assault, some fourteen hundred people were slaughtered in a wave of killings later called the September Massacres, and as news of this butchery started to filter through the freedom songs coming from France, Charlotte backpedaled on her radicalism in revulsion and disgust. The bloody Reign of Terror left her reeling, and unfortunately it would also leave her next novel in shambles.

She began this new work at an opportune moment. She'd been invited to stay at the home of longtime friend and patron, William Hayley, along with a handful of other artsy types, includes the poet William Cowper and the painter George Romney. In this enlightened company, she had several rare weeks of uninterrupted time to devote to writing and to present raw chapters to an astute audience. Here, she flourished, and through Romney's letter to his son we can see that her presence among them was just as appreciated:

> *I was near a month at Mr. Hayley's, where I met Mr. Cowper and Mrs. Smith . . . Mr. Cowper is a most excellent man; he has translated Milton's Latin Poems, and I suppose very well. Hayley is writing the life of Milton, so you may imagine we were deep in that poet; every thing*

belonging to him was collected together and some part of his works read every day. Mrs. Smith is writing another novel, which, as far as it is advanced, is, I think, very good. She began it while I was there, and finished one volume. She wrote a chapter every day, which was read at night, without requiring any correcting. I think her a woman of astonishing powers.

This new, "very good" novel, *The Old Manor House*, revolves around an estate, Rayland Hall, which bulges with characters whose lives act as a grand metaphor for the condition of Britain and her people. We see the inept politics of the higher-ups; the lower, baser, looser attitudes of the household staff; and the grungy contraband smugglers scurrying around the basement. Even the rickety house itself is analogous to England, but this symbolism isn't obvious; it creeps in only after constant, careful observation of Rayland Hall, and never really coalesces until this speech—which, oddly, comes from an occupant of the servant's hall, where such perspicacity isn't generally found:

But she said to me, says she—"When you have done that job, Jacob, I wish you would just look at the wainscot under the windows . . . it's as rotten as touchwood [tinder], and the rats are forever coming in," says she; and says she, "I never saw the like of this old house—it will tumble about our ears, I reckon, one day or 'nother, and yet my lady is always repairing it . . . the wainscoting of this here end of the wing has been up above a hundred years; and we may patch it, and patch it, and yet be never the nearer; but, for my part, I suppose it will last my time," says she.

The establishment is falling apart, warping under the weight of its haphazard construction and compromised from the inside by the menace and trickery of its inhabitants. Mrs. Rayland and her team of overlords are the aristocracy, members of an old society that won't easily budge from its castles or decamp from its manicured gardens without a fight. Yet while the artistocrats favor inequality, and embrace formality and tradition, the servants below them live well—*better,* actually, because they have the kinds of expectations that are far more easily met. (One servant, Betsy, who has no need for marriage and is content as a mistress, is also able to shrug off several nasty insults delivered by her superiors, names like "silly baggage" and "nonsensical ninnyhammer," because, being so worldly and broken in, she's aware of their irrelevance to her real worth.) Even lower in the household are the cellars, where the real scum resides. Here dwells a population of men who, "knowing they are to expect no mercy, disclaim all hope, and resolutely prey upon the society that has shaken them off," crawl through the bowels of the house with bits of stolen treasure in their pockets, unwanted above, unwanted below.

In the middle of all this mess, our young hero, Orlando, and his lover, Monimia, are trying to escape abroad to a life of adventure. They're fed up with the constraints of society and constantly rebelling against life at Rayland Hall, "where the elderly police the young and talented." In the beginning of the novel, their aversion is apparent; they practice little discretion in their midnight escapades in Monimia's room (at the top of a hilariously priapic tower), and they leave far too much evidence around than is considered advisable. It's the same defiance that pounded within the hearts of many Englishmen and -women at the beginning of France's conflict; it's brash and brave, even a little foolish.

BUT AS CHARLOTTE SCRATCHED ORLANDO AND MONIMIA'S story into her parchment, the revolutionary tune across the Channel had started to change keys. When they heard what had happened, Charlotte and her Girondist friends were forced to append their views of the conflict: they were still in support of reform, but the appalling actions used to attain those reforms had to be stopped.

This model was easy enough to embrace while she stood among her radical brethren, but at her writing desk, the situation was trickier. Now that France's war had turned ugly, she began to have doubts about her spirited nose-thumbing of aristocracy in *The Old Manor House*. Orlando and Monimia now appeared reckless and cocksure, just like the radical Jacobin progressives inciting violence in France. Also, whatever her personal opinions, Charlotte was not in a position to run roughshod over people's antiwar sensibilities—that meant losing readers, an unacceptable consequence for a woman whose children were still in need of financial support. She'd paid for her two oldest boys, William and Nicholas, to travel to India to take up careers in the civil service; Charles had joined the army, a less costly (but more dangerous) career choice. Lionel, her most difficult child, was constantly causing expensive trouble at school. He was finally expelled after leading a revolt so dramatic that "the troops had to be called out," as Lionel's great-grandson recounted, but Lionel returned home to Charlotte that day and told her "not to worry . . . the only difference it made was he would have to become a general instead of a bishop." Charlotte was shocked, and also relieved—she'd never again have to pay his school bill. (And Lionel *did* become a lieutenant general.)

To play it safe in a sense, Charlotte chose to place her novel in the past and to speak not on the French Revolution but on the American War of Independence, where her hero does a tour in the British army. At the time she was writing, this was a less risky campaign and provided indirection, to shield her from scrutiny. By choosing not to write of the present day, as she had in *Desmond,* she was able to comment on conflict, tyranny, and political representation without the danger of being accused of overzealous optimism—she would lose fewer friends, and maintain a stronger readership, if her *Desmond* troubles didn't repeat themselves. To further cushion herself, she adjusted her main characters' sentiments to reflect more subtlety, and in so doing, she shows a deftness that dazzles.

As the novel progresses, Orlando and Monimia begin to wonder if their scheme for a brazen life abroad is too far-fetched. Wouldn't they be happier if they just followed the rules? A customary courtship, perhaps, followed by marriage and inheritances, or, as evidenced by Orlando's need to join the army, a profession? Accordingly, their sexy evening encounters fizzle into banal, unchallenging conversations, the tone progressively more fitting for good English ladies and gentlemen. Yet, ingeniously, Charlotte places their meetings directly next to Rayland Hall, where the foundation stones are "half shaded with brushwood . . . so mantled with ivy, they could hardly be distinguished." We never know if the infrastructure is holding fast or crumbling alongside the young couple—all is hidden.

Orlando's compliance with the norm is threatened when, later in the novel, he questions whether his deference to tradition is costing him too much. He decides in the affirmative and attempts to leave, but Nature slows him down, and he reassess, one last time:

> *While he pursued these contemplations, the way became almost impassable; for a small current of water filtering through the rocky bank, had spread itself over the road, and formed a sheet of ice, on which his horse was every moment in danger of falling.*

He is forced to dismount and walk, effectively ending his revolt and setting himself on a more suitable path, one that is ultimately worth his while: In the end, he marries Monimia and inherits Rayland Hall. He repairs and refurnishes the manor, and "being rather solicitous to give to those he loved future tranquility," he forgets about any revenge that would only "make him more sensible of his present felicity." He is no longer a revolutionary, and as a result, his ending is happy.

Charlotte's oblique portrayal of Britain aside—as a rickety, isolated, and bizarre house resplendent with phallic symbolism and held upright by moldy, decaying walls—this proper ending was criticized by her more radical peers for leaving the reader with a sense of defeat; such absurdly good luck as a result of adhering to the status quo was exactly the sort of thing radicals did *not* want to see. Yet, for the many readers who longed for France's war to end peacefully, and for those who had balked at Charlotte's zealous politics in *Desmond*, her strategy in *The Old Manor House* was perfectly executed. The novel is considered by modern critics to be her masterpiece.

Still, for many of her supporting patrons, the damage from her earlier political position was irreversible, and in 1797, even as her novels and *Elegiac Sonnets* continued to garner a modest income, change was on the wind. As the new century approached, her popularity decreased dramatically. Her work was inundated with bad reviews, and she saw dwindling sales. She was harangued in the press for her treatment of the French Revolution, both from the conservative and liberal point of view. This, in combination with a number of other factors—a saturated market that had seen a new work of hers every year for more than two decades, her unremitting social denunciation, the arguable though not wholly inaccurate claim that her writing quality had gone down—this led to a broad decline in readership. Unfortunately, Charlotte's increasing bluntness in her prefaces about her strained circumstances made her even less approachable. This one, from the sixth edition of *Elegiac Sonnets*, is particularly desperate, and led to an even greater reduction in her popularity:

> *I wrote mournfully because I was unhappy . . . you know the circumstances under which I have been labouring; and you have done me the honor to say, that few Women could so long have contended with them. With these, however, as they are some of them of a domestic and painful nature, I will not trouble the Public now; but while they exist in all their force, that indulgent Public must accept all I am able to achieve—"Toujours des Chansons tristes [always sad songs]!"*

Charlotte was aware of the mercurial nature of the market, and she was no stranger to bad reviews. In response to her first novels, one critic wrote to *The Morning Post*, "Charlotte, my dear! I'm really hurt / To see you throw about your dirt / And give yourself such dreadful labour / To soil and vilify your neighbor." Another praised the abilities of "Mrs. Charlotte Smith, Mrs. Inchbald, Mrs. Mary Robinson, Mrs. &c. &c.," but went on to claim that, despite her qualities, Charlotte was "too frequently whining or frisking [cavorting] in novels, till our girls' heads turn wild with impossible adventures." Fellow poet Anna Seward bit back, too. In response to a review lauding Charlotte's poetry—which Seward considered plagiaristic—as better than Shakespeare or Milton, she wrote with scorching sarcasm:

> *You say Mrs. Smith's sonnets are pretty;—so say I—"pretty" is the proper word; pretty tuneful centos [sic] from our various poets, without anything original. All the lines that are not the lines of others are weak and unimpressive; and these hedge-flowers to be preferred, by a critical dictator, to the roses and amaranths of the two first poets the world has produced!!!—It makes one sick.*

However inured Charlotte was to a little criticism, her slackening momentum in the late 1790s was palpable enough to prompt her to attempt less divisive work. She tried her hand at playwriting with *What Is She?*, and enjoyed moderate success in children's literature with *Rural Walks;* its sequel, *Rambles Further*, a young reader's history of England; and *The Natural History of Birds, Intended Chiefly for Young Persons*. She also produced a set of tales with a decidedly Romantic-era flair, *The Letters of a Solitary Wanderer*, which emphasized simplicity and the importance of the natural world, and finally returned to her poetic roots with *Beachy Head*, published posthumously.

⁂

In many ways, Charlotte Turner Smith's awful marriage and the ensuing demands of motherhood can be considered the largest influence on her work; she was a gifted authoress, but a professional one. She wrote for survival rather than self-fulfillment, and was therefore forced into a position of ostensible compromise of her ideals (via either coded language or overt flip-flopping) in order to maintain public favor. She was "deserving of admiration," her sister wrote, in that she "exerted herself with as much zeal and energy as if [Benjamin's] conduct had been unexceptionable," but in so doing, she'd destroyed her own life: "To a mind so ingenuous as hers, there could not have been a more painful sacrifice of talents at the shrine of duty." In the end, she was destitute and bitter; most of her belongings had to be sold in order for her to avoid debtor's prison.

Despite all she'd been through, however, Charlotte still had many reasons to be proud. On the power of her wits alone, she'd managed independently to raise her children up and out into prosperous adulthoods. Only some of them were still alive when she died in 1806, of what was probably uterine cancer, but they had exciting years ahead. William and Nicholas were both successful in India; Harriet enjoyed a comfortable, happy marriage with a Mr. William Geary; Charlotte Mary stayed contentedly single; and Lionel, the rebel-rousing expellee, became governor of Jamaica and was awarded a baronetcy as a result. Sir Lionel Smith, First Baronet, in perfect concordance with his abhorrence of slavery, had the thrilling personal honor of ending the practice in Jamaica after the Slavery Abolition Act of 1833. A vehement abolitionist herself, Charlotte, we can imagine, would've been very proud.

While not all her children were as lucky or as prosperous as Lionel—Charles lost a leg in battle, Lucy left her husband and returned home with three young children, and Anna Augusta and George both died young—Charlotte enjoyed strong connections with all of them as she aged. However, her estranged husband, Benjamin, did not. Having stowed himself away in Scotland under an alias, he saw the gulf between himself and his family grow wider with every passing year. Charlotte refused to see him, and with good reason: he'd attempted to take advantage of the draconian divorce laws and filch her earnings on more than one occasion (sometimes with success). As a result, any semblance of latent devotion—be it laced with pity for his miserable existence, or not—had long evaporated. He died eight months before she did, while imprisoned (again) for debt, and when his obituary ran in *Gentlemen's Magazine*, he was identified only as "the husband of the justly celebrated Mrs Charlotte Smith."

Charlotte's crucial position among the most important writers of the 1700s has not been properly restored, and perhaps that's a result of poor access to her novels and poetry. Nevertheless, her merit was widely acknowledged by England's learned community; she even received the rare approval of Robert Southey, poet extraordinaire:

> *Though she has done more and done better than other women writers, it has not been her whole employment—she is not looking out for admiration and talking to show off. I see in her none of the nasty little envies and jealousies common enough among the cattle. What she likes, she likes with judgement and feeling, and praises warmly.*

Such an ovation, and from the man who would later try to deter Charlotte Brontë from authorship—"Literature cannot be the business of a woman's life, and it ought not to be"—is notable, but our literary debt to Charlotte goes further. She had a colossal breadth of influence across the genres, from poetry to novels to children's literature, and her style within each arena rippled down through a generation of Romantic-era successors: Wordsworth and Coleridge benefitted greatly from her experiments in poetry, provided as they were with a chance to transcend known forms and the classical aesthetic. They also found great inspiration in her style (big emotion wrapped in intricately structured packages) and ran with the Smithian ideal that poetry was best initiated out of solitary and sporadic musings, surrounded by nature's overarching majesty.

Indeed, to Charlotte Turner Smith, the natural world was everything to art, and her eminent peers took note of this. Sir Walter Scott said that Charlotte "preserves in her landscapes the truth and precision of a painter." (He went on to borrow some of her more pioneering strategies for his *Waverly* series.) William Wordsworth applauded her faculty to compose "with true feeling for rural nature, at a time when nature was not much regarded by English poets."

Jane Austen also felt, and was grateful for, Charlotte's contributions. In *Catharine, or the Bower,* embedded smartly in a dialogue about books, is Jane's thinly veiled letter of love: The heroine, Kitty, describes *Emmeline* as "so much better than any of the others" and declares herself to be "delighted" with Charlotte Turner Smith's novels. "They are the sweetest things in the world," she says.

two

HELEN MARIA WILLIAMS

[1759–1827]

In 1787, when Charlotte Turner Smith was packing her bags to leave her husband, a little poem appeared in *European Magazine* under a pseudonym "Axiologus." The author had just finished reading Helen Maria Williams's *Poems in Two Volumes,* and was so moved by its contents that his long-standing adoration of Williams deepened into unbridled celebrity worship:

> *She wept.—Life's purple tide began to flow*
> *In languid streams through every thrilling vein;*
> *Dim were my swimming eyes—my pulse beat slow,*
> *And my full heart was swell'd to dear delicious pain.*

Life left my loaded heart, and closing eye;
A sigh recall'd the wandered to my breast;
Dear was the pause of life, and dear the sigh
That call'd the wandered home, and home to rest.
That tear proclaims—in thee virtue dwells,
And bright will shine in misery's midnight hour;
As the soft star of dewy evening tells
What radiant fires were drown'd by day's malignant
pow'r,
That only wait the darkness of the night
To chear the wandering wretch with hospitable light.

The poem is titled "Sonnet on Seeing Miss Helen Maria Williams Weep at a Tale of Distress," and its swooning author was seventeen-year-old William Wordsworth. He would go on to become poet laureate and to write one of the most important works of the nineteenth century (*The Prelude*), but at this moment he was just a sentimental teenager with a crush. This wasn't a fleeting one, however: still hooked, and eager to meet her, he decided four years later to take matters into his own hands and orchestrate a run-in with his beloved authoress. She'd never heard of him, despite being the center of his first-ever published work, but surely she'd be amenable to meeting an ardent fan? Also, Williams was now in France, and Wordsworth had long been searching for an excuse to visit the Continent—this was his chance. Yet in order to appear legitimate, and to avoid looking like a deranged groupie, he would need a letter of introduction from someone who already knew Helen Maria, someone who could act as a bridge between this fledgling poet and his muse.

When he presented himself to Charlotte Turner Smith in Brighton one cold November day in 1791, this is exactly what Wordsworth had in mind. Though the exact date of Charlotte and Helen Maria's first meeting isn't known, it likely occurred in France just a few months prior (while Charlotte was gathering inspiration for *Desmond*), and because her time with Helen Maria was probably still fresh in Charlotte's mind, she was the best person for Wordsworth to approach with his request—and in order to get *this* meeting, he had to pull some strings with his uncle, Captain John Wordsworth, who worked for Charlotte's father-in-law at the East India Company. After spending a lovely afternoon with her, chatting in "the politest manner" and being shown "every possible civility," as he described to his brother, Wordsworth was indeed furnished with a letter of introduction. A few days later, he departed for France, ready to burst with excitement.

For two weeks, Wordsworth followed Helen Maria's path, from the Normandy coast through Dieppe and Rouen, but when he finally arrived in Orléans, he discovered he'd missed her by just a few days. To be denied his objective after weeks of traveling and months of planning was a letdown, "a considerable disappointment," as he later wrote, but the missed opportunity was also fortuitous. He lingered in Orléans, and later that winter met and fell in love with Annette Vallon, who bore his child the following December. It would be another twenty-nine years before he finally came face-to-face with Helen Maria Williams, but he remained consistently impressed and inspired by her work; he would even lift the title of her book verbatim (plus a comma) for one of his later publications, *Poems, in Two Volumes*, a work that, according to historian Richard Gravil, is "notable for many things, but most of all for its loyalty to the values entailed in Miss Williams' brand of sensibility."

Born in London in 1759 to Charles Williams, a Welsh army officer, and Helen Hay, Helen Maria Williams (her sister, Cecilia, came a year later) was the second youngest in a blended family.* Charles had another child from a previous marriage, a daughter called Persis, and together the family was abundantly happy until his sudden death in December 1762, when the girls were still infants. Helen Maria hardly ever mentioned this event during her life, but in her 1823 *Poems,* she writes of "early sorrows" and of a tendency to be melancholy as a child. Her upbringing was one of strict reverence for Protestant values, and in her early youth she was a devoted service attendee at Princes Street Presbyterian in Westminster. It was the leader of this congregation, a learned and amiable man called Dr. Andrew Kippis, a close friend of the family, who would later become one of the most important people in Helen Maria's life.

At some point after her husband's death (though it's not known precisely when), Mrs. Williams decided to move herself

* There are conflicting reports around the year of Helen Maria's birth. Her death certificate corresponds with her birth in the summer of 1761; other resources, like Encylopedia Britannica, place it in the first weeks of 1762. I was finally able to track down her baptismal record from St. James's Anglican Church in London, which is dated July 5th, 1759, and in this record—which, notably, includes the correct names of her parents, unlike others—her birthdate is shown as June 17th, 1759. The Oxford Dictionary of National Biography corroborates this.

and the three girls to Berwick-upon-Tweed, England's northernmost town, where she could be in closer contact with her Scottish relatives. Little is known about these early years, but it is apparent that, even within Helen Maria's provincial circumstances, there was enough intellectual stimulation to bring forth her literary talents. Though she was the first to admit that her education was fairly narrow—"confined," she later called it—she made the best of her situation in chilly Berwick and managed to become well read despite the distance from London. (Her early writings reflect an obvious knowledge of the current styles and trends of the day.) She was Berwick's clever young upstart, and clergyman Percival Stockdale would later recall that "the graces of her mind, were *then,* as attractive, and charming, as those of her person. She had a tenderness, and a delicacy of soul; and was a sincere friend of all order, moral, civil, and religious." It can be discerned from Stockdale's conspicuous italics that he wouldn't always be counted among her friends—indeed, he would eventually come to despise her—but at this point he was like everyone else: taken with this clever country girl and her elegant intellect.

Her literary pursuits included poetry, and buoyed as she was by the constant support of family and friends, she confidently put pen to paper at an early age and began to hone her style. Thus, when Mrs. Williams moved the family back down to London in the summer of 1781, twenty-year-old Helen Maria hit the ground running, and with Dr. Kippis's encouragement and connections she was able to publish her first work, *Edwin and Eltruda: A Legendary Tale,* just six months after arriving. Dr. Kippis himself provided the introduction, a somewhat apologetic piece that asks the public's indulgence for this innocent, slightly uninformed piece of poetry:

> *The young Lady who is the writer of the following Poem is a native of London, but was removed, with her Family, in very early life, to a remote part of the kingdom, where her sole instruction was derived from a virtuous, amiable, and sensible mother. In so distant a situation, she had such little access to books . . . Should there be found in [Edwin and Eltruda] many marks of an elegant and pathetic genius, to these not only the candid, but even the judicious critic will direct his principle attention; and will be disposed to forgive the simplicity of the story, and that diffusion of sentiment which is so natural to a youthful mind, in its first essays in composition.*

Charitable gestures, but not really necessary; *Edwin and Eltruda,* written anonymously "By a Lady," per the custom preserving female modesty—one that Helen Maria, like Charlotte Turner Smith, would eventually cast aside—and published by the illustrious Thomas Cadell, was a bright beginning for the burgeoning authoress. The story opens in England's northwestern Lake District, where a war hero lives in a lonely castle perched on the shore of Derwentwater (the same area where Sara Coleridge would spend her youth). He's conquered all his foes, but has somehow remained a gentle soul, which is almost too bad, because within the first pages we realize he's a recent widower and has come to this castle "To feel the fulness of despair / The woes of hopeless love," and to remember the "partner of his breast," Emma, with whom he'd shared so many happy memories. His baby girl, Eltruda, is a ray of sunshine in this gloomy place, and the man's suffering diminishes as he watches her bloom into the perfect, benevolent romantic heroine. Eltruda spends her days doing charity for widows and sick children, and the evenings praying that her heart will open wider still to the needs of others. She has a great love for nature and cannot bear suffering in any living thing—dying flowers are nursed back to life, fallen insects are mourned, baby birds found on the ground are returned to their nests—and when her lover, Edwin, appears (as he does seemingly from out of nowhere), she falls in love not with his bank account or his dashing stature, but with his "liberal mind" and his "gen'rous, ample heart":

> *EDWIN, of every grace possest,*
> *First taught her heart to prove*
> *That gentlest passion of the breast,*
> *To seel the power of love.*
> *Tho' few the pastures he possest,*
> *Tho' scanty was his store,*
> *Tho' wealth ne'er swell'd his hoarded chest,*
> *EDWIN could boast of more!*

Unlike many women's tales, though (and very much unlike the love stories from Austen and the Brontës) this one isn't meant to end "happily ever after." War comes to the countryside, and one "death-fraught day," Eltruda's father is killed in battle at the hands of her own dear, gentle Edwin, who is among the soldiers on the opposing side. Eltruda dies of a broken heart, and Edwin follows:

> *He feels within his shivering veins*
> *A mortal chillness rise;*

Her pallid corse he feebly strains—
And on her bosom dies!

Drawing as it does on well-worn tragedy traditions, the work at first glance seems pretty commonplace. Characters are predictably benign: a lonely father; his "lovely, peerless maid" of a daughter, who is beset by uncontrollable outside forces, and with whom a soldier finds comfort before inadvertently bringing the evils of the world into their haven. Their deaths are also entirely certain. It is a familiar premise—think Shakespeare—but where *Edwin and Eltruda* departs from the norm is in its treatment of conflict. Here, war isn't glorious—it's bloody and reckless, filling the world not with heroes but with "lone widows" and "weeping mothers." Families and lovers are torn asunder, homes are lost, and private lives destroyed amid conflict; there are no waving banners and no proud, victorious fighters, because under that veneer of bravery lies the suffering of the masses. It is an uncomfortable truth to examine, and an unusual focus for a twenty-year-old country girl. Yet despite its troubling nature, Helen Maria would return to this theme again and again.

This unorthodox approach brought her a fair amount of success, and thanks to Dr. Kippis and his high-minded circle, she was instantly transported into London's intellectual elite and surrounded by new admirers, many of whom had their own top-notch friends. One such connection happened to be Fanny Burney's younger sister, who made note of Helen Maria's popularity at a party in 1782. Charlotte Burney had been enjoying the company of a Mr. Mathias, "the very drollest of the droll . . . he was so excessive[ly] comical that before I had recovered from one laugh, I was shaking with another." Mr. Mathias was all hers for a time, but was soon whisked away to meet the lady of the hour, "author of Edwin and Eltrada [*sic*], a legendary tale, a pretty girl rather . . . Mr. Blunt senior came and took [Mr. Mathias] off to introduce him to Miss Williams, and then I had scarce any more fun with him."

Writer and patron of the arts William Hayley—the same Hayley who, ten years later, would host Charlotte Turner Smith, George Romney, and William Cowper at his home, where Charlotte would begin *The Old Manor House*—was another of Helen Maria's new fans. He was so enraptured, in fact, that he dispensed with her name altogether and instead chose to call her "the young muse" in his writings. She's mentioned frequently as one of Hayley's worthier pursuits: "I am engaged to drink tea with Mrs. Bates [a singer], on Thursday next, at the house of the young muse, who is also musical."

In Hayley's letters we can also glimpse Helen Maria's relationship with Elizabeth Montagu, cofounder of the influential Bluestockings, and whose efforts to bring scholarly discourse to women led to her ascension as Queen of the Ladies Who Lunch. By the 1770s, Mrs. Montagu's Mayfair salon had become a hive of literary culture, where big-name writers like Samuel Johnson and Edmund Burke would gather with avid male and female listeners. For an emerging authoress, to be invited to an event there was surely an undeniable thrill. Helen Maria must've been over the moon when, as Hayley reports, Mrs. Montagu "behaved with the most friendly politeness to her" after they'd dined together. Helen Maria then explained to Hayley that she intended to show her appreciation by dedicating her new epic poem, *Peru,* to Mrs. Montagu, of 23 Hill Street, where Hayley was headed later that same morning, and he showed "the highest approbation of her design" before leaving for lunch:

> *I proceeded to the great Mrs. Montagu, and was honored with a tête-à-tête in her magnificent [Hill Street] mansion. Our whole discourse turned on the poem of the young Muse, which she criticised with infinite spirit and judgment, and with the most friendly severity.*

Even after finding places in the poem requiring "friendly severity," Mrs. Montagu clearly approved of the dedication in her name, because when *Peru* went to print the following year, 1784, it was accompanied by an effusive introduction, "To Mrs. Montagu," a sentimental recounting of the generosity and "moral beauty" of the authoress's patroness:

> *Far other homage claims than flatt'ry brings*
> *The little triumphs of the proud to grace:*
> *For deeds like these a purer incense springs,*
> *Warm from the swelling heart its source we trace!*
> *Yet not to foster the rich gifts of mind*
> *Alone can all thy lib'ral cares employ;*
> *Not to the few those gifts adorn, confin'd,*
> *They spread an ampler sphere of genuine joy.*

Another noteworthy tidbit in the first pages of *Peru* rested on the title page, where Helen Maria this time insisted that her real name be stamped, rather than "By a Lady." It was an audacious move, but she had no reason to be timid—her new connections among the Bluestockings had elevated her work into the highest circles, the positive responses she received spurring her forward with strength.

Like *Edwin and Eltruda* and her 1783 poem "Ode on the Peace," celebrating the end of the American Revolution, *Peru* deals with the sentiment behind a conflict, in this case the fall of the Incan Empire at the hands of Spanish conquistadors led by Francisco Pizarro. As with "Ode on the Peace," her choice of topic is further indicative of a growing boldness: she *would* speak on politics, a conceptual sphere where women weren't typically allowed. Helen Maria makes no promises about her scholarship, however. She explains in the introduction that she "has not had the presumption even to attempt a full, historical narration," and instead tells the tale through a succession of love stories: Alzira witnesses the murder of her fiancé, the ruling monarch of Peru, on their wedding day, and kills herself in anguish; Almagro is forced to part with his beloved wife, Cora, in order to stage a brave resistance against the invading conquistadors; Zilia watches her father die in peace after a long, horrific torture at the hands of Pizarro's men.

Helen Maria's approach is in some ways, as Jane Austen asserted of herself, "partial, prejudiced, and ignorant." Written seemingly without regard for any underpinning political view, and showing little acknowledgment of the potential "good" that could, arguably, arise out of conflict, *Peru* could be dismissed as a small-picture way of looking at history. Yet, in venturing into this territory, Helen Maria was a stranger in a strange land. Ladies of this era had very little experience with anything outside their limited domestic sphere, and she was no different, as her disclaimer in the introduction affirms. She'd never traveled to the places she was writing about, and she didn't have access to any of the philosophical debates men were enjoying in the library after dinner. Many politicians and writers were expressing concern about the exploitation of South America, but while they were busily touting the accuracy of their accounts, explaining exactly who had done what to whom, Helen Maria's more personal approach implored the British public not to be apathetic to the pain of "an innocent and amiable people."

Her attempt at humanizing the conflict is in sync with her blossoming style, one that would evolve into her own brand of protest poetry: she used this same approach (seeing conflict through the lens of human relations) in "An American Tale" and "Ode on the Peace," and later to tackle the slavery debate with *A Poem on the Bill Lately Passed for Regulating the Slave Trade.* In each of these works, she argues, with perfect sensibility, that the subjugation and suffering of the innocent should not be tolerated; how could it, once their personal pain is revealed?

Helen Maria's overtly emotional portrayals of war serve as another example of the mechanisms women writers were forced to use to survive prevailing social norms. As moral compasses, protectors of goodness, they were only tolerated in the realm of politics and current events if they hid behind their cloak of womanly sensibility, appealing to the heart rather than the head. Even if she did have the proper knowledge, a woman could not cast aside her sentiment and enter political discourse like a man: that was grounds for castigation and social exile (as Helen Maria would eventually find out, at great personal cost). It wasn't as a scholar, then, that she, and other women like her, would be cherished, but rather as an "arbiter of moral standards." Yet an authoress's being so patently female, presenting herself as a conglomeration of potentially unstable and illogical emotion, enabled critics to subject her to a kind of scrutiny that a male author would never have had to endure. A reviewer could not, in this system, separate a work of literature from the gender of its creator, and this resulted in reviews not only of the work, but also of the authoress's personal standing. Was she a "good" lady? Did she uphold the values of femininity?

However, if she were to balance her approach, choose her words with great care, a skilled female writer could create a work with a subversive political message and actually be praised, rather than chastised, for it. Indeed, Helen Maria Williams eventually became so practiced at this technique that reviewers denied or ignored her politics altogether (even when it was most conspicuous, as in her famous *Letters from France*) and commended her for a "tender, pathetic, and pleasing" style. She'd found the sweet spot: emotional and tenderhearted, with just a dash of forward-thinking boldness—and the critics adored it. They applauded her loveliness of temper, her animated spirit and polished decorum, her "sweetly harmonious" versification, and her ability to write with "no small degree of sublimity." Female reviewers, especially, roundly praised her efforts. Anna Seward noted in *London Magazine* how this "poetic sister" had, "with daring hand . . . seized the epic lyre—with art devine." (This same issue featured two sonnets from thirty-six-year-old Charlotte Turner Smith.) Biographer, novelist, and poet Elizabeth Ogilvy Benger was also rather taken with the "tuneful Williams," who unveiled the woes of Peru "with such pathos . . . We feel their sorrows, weep their fate anew."

Not all her readers found her so arresting. Horace Walpole described Helen Maria and the other (to him) unoriginal women authors as "harmonious virgins" with "thoughts and phrases

[that] are like their gowns, old remnants cut and turned." Still, most of London was head over heels for this poetess. Her explosive combination of upstanding womanhood, authorial talent, and subtle yet attractive "sense" (beautiful words from a beautiful mind) produced "a literary star of the first magnitude." Helen Maria's methodology also seemingly allowed her books to be disseminated widely among a female audience that, under other circumstances, would have received nothing of the kind.

AS TO BE EXPECTED, THE NUMBER OF PEOPLE WHO WISHED TO make Helen Maria's acquaintance skyrocketed during the 1780s. She even happened to meet Dr. Samuel Johnson, an unquestionable leader of British literary culture, who by now was extremely ill and nearing the end of his life. His accomplishments were many, his writing known to everyone—the *Oxford Dictionary of National Biography* still describes him as "arguably the most distinguished man of letters in English History"—but on a balmy evening in May 1784, he was just another of Helen Maria's worshippers. In his *Life of Samuel Johnson,* James Boswell recounts the enormity of Johnson's regard for her:

> *He had dined that day at Mr. Hoole's, and Miss Helen Maria Williams being expected in the evening, Mr. Hoole put into his hands her beautiful "Ode on the Peace;" Johnson read it over, and when this amiable, elegant, and accomplished young lady was presented to him, he took her by the hand in the most courteous manner, and repeated the finest stanza of her poem; this was the most delicate and pleasing compliment he could pay . . . Miss Williams told me, that the other time she was fortunate*

enough to be in Dr. Johnson's company, he asked her to sit down by him, which she did, and upon her inquiring how he was, he answered, "I am very ill indeed, Madam. I am very ill even when you are near me; what should I be were you at a distance."

IN 1786, HELEN MARIA WILLIAMS COMPILED WHAT WOULD BE her last book of poetry for almost forty years, *Poems in Two Volumes* (the title William Wordsworth would later commandeer). Within its pages appeared a ten-canto poem that heralded an upswing in her radical sensibilities, "Part of an Irregular Fragment, Found in a Dark Passage of the Tower," which depicts an abandoned, haunted apartment in the Tower of London. Featuring angry wraiths who, in one way or another, have been slain by the monarchy, the poem edges uncomfortably toward implying that the leaders of England are well acquainted with murder—they're maniacal killers, in fact, "smear'd with blood," and that makes the volume's dedication to the queen all the more insolent and cheeky. In a poem that, even to a modern (jaded) reader, is menacing and lurid, Helen Maria blatantly thumbs her nose at the establishment, but it appears that her message was, again, so well encrypted that its politics was overlooked: reviewers noticed in *Poems* not her overstepping of any boundary, but rather, the "simplicity, tenderness, and harmony" that had "justly obtained her no inconsiderable share of reputation." To today's readers, however, the magic of "Irregular Fragment" likely has nothing to do with "tenderness" and "harmony," but rather, with its explosively abrupt, heart-pounding ending as the protagonist attempts to flee—and fails:

As, starting at each step, I fly,
Why backward turns my frantic eye,
That closing portal past?
Two sullen shades, half-seen, advance!
On me, a blasting look they cast,
And fix my view with dang'rous spells,
Where burning frenzy dwells!—
Again! Their vengeful look—and now a speechless—

Helen Maria was as dexterous as ever at disguising her opinions with the guises of feminitiy—it was a good thing, too, because the roiling political landscape in France was about to bubble over into revolt and test her skills as never before. Yet, despite her deft encryption of them on the page, Helen Maria's leftist views were already known far and wide: as one of London's biggest celebrities, she'd spent nearly ten years surrounded by the city's most liberal minds, first as a guest and later as a host in her own right, so they weren't terribly shocking. She had forged friendships with some of the most influential voices in the debate over France's gathering storm, and was even close with a few members of Parliament, most notably Benjamin Vaughan, a key player in ending the American Revolution, and abolitionist William Smith (Florence Nightingale's grandfather, incidentally).

The "revolution debates" took a personal turn for Helen Maria when, in 1785, she became acquainted with Monique Coquerel du Fossé, a French expatriate with a tale of woe so affecting that Williams would use it as the central plot in her next work, *Letters Written in France in the Summer 1790*, the first volume of her *Letters from France* series. "What, indeed, but friendship, could have led my attention from the annals of imagination to the records of politics; from the poetry to the prose of human life?" it asks the reader. What indeed? For a poet to turn away from poetry and toward the "records of politics" required a profound change in focus, and that's exactly what occurred when Helen Maria met the du Fossés. Her connection to them was, in addition, very advantageous: their sad story would act as an allegory for the French Revolution as a whole, serving Williams's narrative purposes in *Letters* to much success and ultimately speeding her to greater notoriety.

Monique du Fossé's husband, Antoine, was the eldest son of the severe and unjust Baron du Fossé of the Parliament of Normandy who, according to Helen Maria, lived the maxim "Rather to be dreaded than beloved." As a father, he was cold and stern; as a feudal lord, he was utterly ruthless: "[He] considered the lower order of people as a set of beings whose existence was tolerated merely for the use of the nobility . . . if it were the great purpose of human life to be hated, perhaps no person ever attained that end more completely than the Baron du Fossé." Here is our demon of the *ancien régime* of France, a crooked upper-cruster, an evil tyrant. Just like Louis XVI, the Baron du Fossé forced his dependents into submission without regard for their wellbeing and, again like Louis, eventually found himself in the throes of a full-blown uprising as a result.

Antoine du Fossé, who grew up in complete opposition to his father, with "the most amiable dispositions . . . the most feeling heart," rebelled by settling "in the bosom of conjugal felicity" with Monique and marrying her in secret, against his father's wishes. The Baron responded to this defiance (as any bully would) by using his status in a system of oppression: he obtained an official document, a *lettre de cachet,* that enabled him to imprison his son indefinitely. Since the thirteenth century, these *lettres* had been used to remove inconvenient people from society, without trial. Radicals and troublemakers in particular, some of whom would become famous, were targeted: Voltaire was twice the victim of a *lettre de cachet,* first for writing a libelous poem (a false accusation, for which he spent nearly a year in prison) and later for drawing arms against an aristocrat who'd mocked his pen name. The Marquis de Sade also spent time in jail—thirteen miserable years—because of a *lettre* signed by his mother-in-law. And because the power to release these poor souls rested solely with the king, the *lettres de cachet* came to represent everything wrong with the French monarchy: cruel overlords acting independently of the justice system to impose control over an unwilling people. Like Dr. Manette in Dickens's *A Tale of Two Cities,* who was brought to the edge of sanity because of a *lettre,* these prisoners were obliged to spend their lives in jail at a nobleman's whim.

For young Monsieur and Madam du Fossé, the *lettre de cachet* meant evasion, destitution, and ultimately separation for three long years. So affronting was this injustice to Helen Maria Williams that she wept while recounting it in *Letters*: "Oh, my dear, my ever beloved friends! When I recollect not only that these were real sufferings, but that they were sustained by *you*! My mind is overwhelmed with its own sensations.—The paper is blotted by my tears—and I can hold my pen no longer." By the time Monique du Fossé met Helen Maria, the former had been reunited with her husband, but the couple wouldn't return to France until four years later, in 1789. In the interim, Monique stayed in England to teach French and ended up with Williams, first as a pupil and then as a companion.

These events, and the other very exciting ones occurring in France at the time, presented an opportunity for Helen Maria to witness real political change; for her, they would also help right the wrongs done to her own cherished loved ones. "A friend's having been persecuted, imprisoned, maimed, and almost murdered under the ancient government of France, [this] is a good excuse for loving the revolution," she wrote in *Letters from France*. So, in 1790, when Madame du Fossé asked her to visit the family at their home, twenty-nine-year-old Helen Maria put down her poetry and embarked across the Channel, on what would be the most important, and revolutionary, journey of her life.

When Helen Maria Williams arrived in Paris, the city was united in celebration of the first anniversary of the fall of the Bastille, the Fête de la Fédération. It was likely one of the largest parties yet to occur in Europe, attracting almost fifteen thousand men, women—soldiers and policy makers, social leaders, musicians, flag bearers—and schoolchildren to the ruins of the Bastille at five in the morning to form a colossal procession. People waved and cheered out their windows and from rooftops as the parade moved through Paris, to the Champ de Mars (where the Eiffel Tower stands today), taking refreshment along the way from generous families at their doors, kneeling in the streets to give thanks, and promising to infants in the crowd that they would "imbibe, from their earliest age, an inviolable attachment to the principles of the new constitution," as Helen Maria describes. This constitution was not yet written, even as one politician after another took an oath to it before the masses following this procession, but despite that unfinished business, France was "transported with joy." Even through torrential rains, the spirit of the crowd was positively jubilant—people shouted, "Nous sommes mouillés à la nation" (We are drenched for the nation) and "La révolution Française est cimentée avec de l'eau, au lieu de sang" (The French Revolution is cemented with water, instead of blood) over the din of drums and dancing.

Helen Maria was completely overtaken on that day in July. The first Fête de la Fédération represented the beauty of democracy in action, a shining display of the power of a people who wanted change, rose as one, and took it as their own. These events commemorated France's uprising against a despotic regime that, as the du Fossés' experience exemplified, had long abandoned any semblance of justice. Bloody conflicts between Catholics and Protestants the century before had led to tight governmental control at the hands of Louis XIV, who despite the penury of his people spent an outlandish amount of money building the palace at Versailles. The lower classes were overburdened with taxes, food shortages were rampant, and rebellions were frequent. Yet all these problems were essentially ignored. The next king, Louis XV, made life *worse* by gambling away France's remaining assets in the Seven Years' War against England—those financial losses were staggering. So, by the time Louis XVI came up, the country was nearly bankrupt. At Versailles, though, life continued on unencumbered for Louis and his young wife, Marie Antoinette, who were both imprudent and licentious. Their various silly sundries and crackpot schemes (including, famously, numerous residences for the queen and a working model farm, Hameau de la Reine, where she would dress up as a peasant and play house) further enraged the starving public. To make matters worse, Louis was helping finance the American Revolution, almost entirely with high-interest loans. Further scarcity, and the rising cost of bread, had the lower classes choked with desperation. The situation was dire, and the Parisians couldn't, *wouldn't,* take it anymore.

So, on July 14, 1789, a throbbing mass of underfed, overtaxed people, thoroughly enraged by their repressive government and anxious about the increasing military presence in the city, attacked the Bastille. As the go-to prison for the unfortunate victims of *lettres de cachet,* the Bastille embodied all the malevolence of France's corrupt monarchy, and the success of its capture showed unmistakably that a full-on revolution was at hand. The government was finally forced to act, and the following year, it made many unprecedented changes to its crumbling structure. The newly convened National Assembly dissolved noble privileges, which essentially put an end to French feudalism; local bodies of government were put in place to prevent abuses by the monarchy; peasants were released from their tithe obligations to the Church. Yet the most affecting change came about when the National Assembly's basic tenets were collected and published in its Declaration of the Rights of Man and Citizen, bestowing as-yet-unheard-of freedoms upon France's people and setting the bar for constitutions around the world. (The United Nations' 1948 Universal Declaration of Human Rights, for instance, is based on this French prototype.) Freedom of speech, religion, and press; fair taxation; free access to public office regardless of rank; and administrative transparency laws were all established.

As Helen Maria and the rest of England were strongly aware, there were troubles in enacting the new laws: Jews and free blacks were not given full citizenship until two years later, and women were still excluded from all political processes. Nevertheless, France was progressing faster than any other country, including the United States, to extend equal rights to all. The insurrection at the Bastille had been a success, and there was worldwide celebration for the changes it cultivated. Especially in England, where the *ancien régime* of France had long been a topic of schismatic discourse, the early days of the Revolution were heralded as a victory, "a triumph in the warm hope, that one of the finest countries in the world would soon be one of the most free," as Hannah More described it. Even as a known conservative, More joined in exultation at the fall of the Bastille, and she wasn't alone. This comment from Samuel Romilly has been recognized as the quintessential English response to the French Revolution:

> *I think myself happy that it has happened when I am of an age at which I may reasonably hope to live to see some of the consequences produced . . . it is certainly true, that the Revolution has produced very sincere and very general joy here [in England]. It is the subject of all conversations; and even all the newspapers, without one exception, though they are not conducted by the most liberal or most philosophical of men, join in sounding forth the praises of the Parisians, and in rejoicing at an event so important for mankind.*

Thus the happy feelings at the Fête de la Fédération—where Helen Maria Williams sat in the grandstands above the Champ de Mars, witnessing "the triumph of human kind . . . the noblest privilege of human nature"—where Helen Maria found the inspiration for the rest of her life's work, were not wrongly placed. "It required but the commonest feelings of humanity to become in that moment a citizen of the world . . . I shall never forget the sensations of that day." The country stood poised at a new dawn. Horses galloped, flags waved, cannons blasted, and as King Louis and Marie Antoinette took to the stage to vow their support for New France, "every sword was drawn, and every arm lifted up . . . [the king's] solemn words were re-echoed by six hundred thousand voices." In the silence that followed, after "the cries, the shouts, the acclamations of the multitude," the sun blazed out from behind the rain clouds and compelled the people to "call upon the Deity to look down and witness the sacred engagement they entered . . . you will not suspect that I was an indifferent witness to such a scene, Oh no!"

Helen Maria Williams, at this point, displayed the antithesis of indifference, much like Charlotte Turner Smith upon returning from her own trip to France. After touring Paris and Normandy for a few weeks—making sure to visit the ruins of the Bastille, "which so many wretches have entered never to repass . . . human creatures dragged at the caprice of despotic power"—Helen Maria went back to England and penned her own *Desmond*: the first volume of her *Letters from France*. The work was purchased and printed, again, by Thomas Cadell, who had published her earlier poetry *Edwin and Eltruda* (not to mention Smith's *Elegiac Sonnets*) along with Williams's only novel, *Julia*.

The fame of Thomas Cadell's imprint notwithstanding, the latter of these works has been somewhat ignored, for at first glance it doesn't fit into the politics-in-a-petticoat persona with which Helen Maria Williams has been associated. Upon closer inspection, however, *Julia* shows us that, even when removed from the genre in which she was most comfortable, Williams was still plugging away at politics in her covert style. Where this is most obvious is in the poems interspersed throughout the novel (which portrays a love triangle among the protagonist, Julia, her best friend, and her best friend's husband), most specifically the longest poem of the work, "The Bastille: A Vision." Again, it appears as though reviewers failed to notice this abrupt and fairly tangential slice of unladylike rhetoric, and here it's particularly mystifying as to why: was Helen Maria's message *so* well concealed that, even with a conspicuous title such as "The Bastille," it still failed to incite objection? Indeed, Helen Maria is most adroit here in covering her tracks; she even uses a male intermediary to narrate the poem, thereby distancing herself and her heroine from the politics of it. Still, it seems odd that her opinions should have been overlooked, and thus dismissed.

Perhaps it was with this in mind that Helen Maria penned *Letters Written in France*, her most overtly political contribution. This nonfiction narrative follows the same pattern as her earlier historical poetry: rather than simply recounting events, she speaks with the voice of sentiment. To this end, nearly a third of the book is taken up by the du Fossé family, whose story of suffering urges the reader to be empathetic, to feel what the du Fossés felt; and most critics found the effect quite stirring. *Monthly Review* thought the du Fossés' adventure was perfect for the occasion, that "if any thing were wanting to increase our detestation of tyrannical government, that purpose would have been effectually answered by this little history of the private distress, and unnatural cruelty, which these virtuous and innocent victims endured." Helen Maria filled the rest of *Letters* with a retelling of those events of her trip she deemed important, including the Fête and visiting the Bastille, and along the way peppered her observations with meditations on nationalism, humanity, and the trouble with "Englishness"; the work was "part history, part journalism, part melodrama, part documentary."

LETTERS WRITTEN IN FRANCE RECEIVED VERY FAVORABLE reviews. Most of the major newspapers gave it high praise, including *The Analytical Review,* which noted Helen Maria's "talent of chatting on paper in that easy immethodical manner"; they extolled the book as having "confirmed the very favourable opinion we have entertained of the goodness of the writer's heart." Another reviewer, again speaking of hearts, said it had "so much the air of romance . . . the sum of the whole is, that, after various sufferings, enough to melt even a heart of stone."All heart and no head—this was the only way a work like this, created as it was by a female commentator, could ever be interpreted in a market swarming with men. And though *Letters* is little known today, at the time of its debut, it was lauded as one of the first published responses to the Revolution, and consequently, its creator and her ardent views were known throughout the land despite critics' refusal to acknowledge them in her work. Case in point: In an anonymous satirical cartoon, *Don Dismallo Running the Literary Gauntlet,* appearing in 1790, Helen Maria Williams, drawn in a pink and light green frock, is first in line to whip essayist and philosopher Edmund Burke, depicted as a fool, as he runs past. (Also depicted, variously as Justice, Liberty, et al., were many prominent, pro-Revolution members of society, including Richard Price, Richard Sheridan, John Horne Tooke, Whig historian Catharine Macaulay, and Anna Barbauld.)

The cartoon's imagery is telling, especially considering the butt of its joke. Burke had recently given voice to a growing faction of people who weren't so sure about the state of things in France. Appearing just two weeks before Helen Maria's own work on the matter, Burke's *Reflections on the Revolution in France* took the opposite stance: it warned the people of England to control their emotions, to be wary of letting their fervor overwhelm their senses, not to allow the heart to vanquish the head, as it were. *Reflections* calls for "conformity to nature" in the quest for liberty, and draws attention to the benefits derived "from considering our liberties in the light of an inheritance"—as in: the place you occupy at birth should be the one you're comfortable with. Burke claimed that the traditional model had always worked for England, and that France might, "if you pleased, have profited of[f] our example, and have given to your recovered freedom a correspondent dignity . . . [you had] in some parts the walls, and in all the foundations of a noble and venerable castle . . . you might have repaired those walls; you might have built on those foundations." His was an opinion that was steadily gaining momentum over the course of the fall and spring of 1790–91. The English people, watching from the safe haven of a society that, notably, had been built on the same kind of classification system the French were attempting to jettison, began to wonder if this outrageous uprising could end well. Burke didn't think so:

> *Laws overturned; tribunals subverted; industry without vigour; commerce expiring; the revenue unpaid, yet the people impoverished; a church pillaged, and a state not relieved; civil and military anarchy . . . Were all these dreadful things necessary? Were they the inevitable results of the desperate struggle of determined patriots, compelled to wade through blood and tumult, to the quiet shore of a*

> *tranquil and prosperous liberty? No! nothing like it. The fresh ruins of France, which shock our feelings wherever we can turn our eyes, are not the devastation of civil war; they are the sad but instructive monuments of rash and ignorant counsel.*

As one of England's leading political minds, Burke had a lot of sway, so it wasn't long before he amassed a following and helped initiate one of the longest-running debates in English history. Like many politicians, though, he functioned in the realm of hyperbole in order to achieve a preconceived set of results. He employed florid language to paint the French royal family more sympathetically, as if they were gentle victims of circumstance—"[The Queen] bears the imprisonment of her husband . . . with a serene patience, in a manner suited to her rank and race, and becoming the offspring of a sovereign"—while at the same time making the mob look like frenzied, bloodthirsty demons, inflating the presence of violence and sparing the reader none of the gory details, even if they were fictitious. Presented in this way, his conservative views seemed not only valid, but also understandable.

However, in his haste to reinforce his political position and remove the emotion from what was obviously an emotional situation, Burke entirely misconstrued the mood in France. When Helen Maria Williams returned there in September 1791, after making her intentions to stay widely known in a new poem, "A Farewell, for Two Years to England," she found not a pile of broken rubble—the "fresh ruins" Burke mentioned—but a glorious "region of romance," as she styled it in the second volume of her *Letters from France*. She continues in rapture:

> *Events the most astonishing and marvelous are here the occurrences of the day, and every newspaper is filled with articles of intelligence that will form a new era in the history of mankind. The sentiments of the people also are elevated far above the pitch of common life. All the motives which most powerfully stimulate the mind in its ordinary state, seem repressed in consideration of the public good . . . I sometimes think that the age of chivalry, instead of being past forever, is just returned.*

Her characteristically heartrending style paid off, despite whatever loss of legitimacy she perceived suffering from having to cloak her opinions in sentimentality. When she arrived at the du Fossé chateau in Rouen for the second time, her mother and sisters, Persis and Cecilia, were already there. For eight weeks they'd been cultivating the two families' affinity for one another—this would lead to a marriage between Helen's sister Cecilia and Monique du Fossé's nephew Athanase Coquerel—but they'd also managed to jump-start Helen Maria's celebrity career when, at a July 1791 meeting of the Rouen Society of the Friends of the Constitution, they presented to the congregation a newly available French translation of her *Letters from France*.

After reading her book aloud, the society's members wrote Helen Maria a wonderfully complimentary letter affirming her "pure and sensitive heart" (in accordance with her reviews) and her knack for portraying the French Revolution "in a way that mere glory-seekers have not come close to achieving . . . every citizen present applauded." She responded in kind, expertly reinforcing the heart-driven femininity that had allowed her to come so far: "Revolution is an event capable of providing the human spirit with the most sublime ideas, but the results it has already produced make it a topic not only for the mind but still more for the heart . . . how could I watch without compassion? I could not be more cognizant of the honor you bestow upon my work." Humble yet self-aware, Helen Maria captured the society's heart, and they conferred upon her a most generous gift in appreciation: three thousand copies of both their letter and her reply, printed at the society's expense, for circulation. This was an extraordinary gesture, which in combination with the new French version of *Letters,* meant big, big stardom on the Continent. By the time she left Rouen for Paris in December—missing twenty-one-year-old William Wordsworth in Orléans by just a few days—she was "the most famous English woman residing in France."

As she settled into her life in Paris, rapidly making new friends and reconnecting with old ones, and establishing a permanent residence that by 1792 would become, like Mrs. Montagu's Hill Street house, a hive of radical thinkers—all the while working on the second volume of *Letters from France*—Helen Maria Williams was forced to concede that Edmund Burke hadn't been wrong about everything. The abominable death of the Princess de Lamballe and the September Massacres had pushed the tumultuous situation in France to a breaking point. By the end of 1792, there were thousands of necks on the guillotine—Louis XVI's turn would come in January 1793—and dire circumstances all around. Square in the middle of it was our lady of sense and sensibility, Helen Maria Williams.

Family and friends implored her to return to the safety of England—how could she stay, scribbling away, while members of her circle were being dragged off to their deaths? Celebrity figure or not, in her stubbornness, she must have seemed insane. Yet even as she read letters from loved ones urging her to come home, and even as she herself was arrested and detained with her mother and sisters in Luxembourg Prison for six weeks, waking each day in constant fear of the guillotine, she would not withdraw her support for the Revolution. Like all the Girondists, she severely condemned the Jacobin Maximilien Robespierre and the brutality of the Reign of Terror, but she flat-out refused to renounce her principles; increasingly overt, she would always be looking to "join the universal voice, and repeat with all my heart and soul, 'Vive la nation!'" as she'd written in 1790. Many other writers and politicians, including Charlotte Turner Smith and William Wordsworth, scaled down their pro-Revolution remarks after the appalling the appalling execution of Louis and Marie-Antoinette in 1793, but Helen Maria would not, perhaps *could* not—thus further refusing to do what was expected of her as a woman.

To return to the small world of poetry and to her role as a decorous lady writer of the day, one among many moderately successful but undervalued, underpaid authoresses whose political opinions could not be openly shared? To live the traditional life of a "good lady" in Britain, staying under the radar and taking little credit for her own work? This had about as much draw for Helen Maria as a trip to volatile France had for most other Englishwomen. Her name was synonymous with the Revolution: her celebrity stemmed from it, her world was built upon it, her entire authorial self and voice were intimately connected to France. Leave now? Unthinkable. The French Revolution had enabled her to combine a flair for politics with her bewitching, Romantic style (intertwining, in her own way, the head and the heart) and to leave a lasting impression on a group of important people. She counted among her fans not just giggling novel aficionados, but also the literati and influential contemporary thinkers, the ones who were making history even as she related it. "All the stupendous events that usually fill the lapse of ages," she wrote, "[had] interwoven with every thing around me, linked with all my hopes or fears, connected with my very existence, and fixing irreparably my destiny." And that destiny seemed more and more to lie in France.

At some point, Helen Maria Williams had also become involved with a man, John Hurford Stone, who aside from being an early subscriber to her 1786 *Poems in Two Volumes* was also a well-connected member of the London Revolution Society. It is not known precisely how the two met, but based on the letters swirling among her friends, Stone's scandalous divorce in 1794, and a subsequent trip to Switzerland together, followed by a swift combining of their households, it can easily be surmised that he and Helen Maria were committed to each other. As to what level of commitment, whether in marriage or not, the details were never revealed, for on this matter Helen Maria felt no need to explain her actions, despite criticism; the press in particular was adamant that she divulge the intricacies of the couple's living arrangement for moral judgment, but she remained steadfast in her silence.

Perhaps it was because this was far from her first hostile interaction with the press that she handled it with such finesse.

Increasingly abandoning literary subtlety for blatant politicization, Helen Maria had come under attack in the papers for having succumbed to the "French disease" before she'd even met Mr. Stone (and had enjoyed what was likely an adulterous affair). A woman in support of revolution, especially in the face of violence, suggested a fundamental upheaval in traditional gender roles. Ladies who refused to shrink calmly into the woodwork of the parlor to contemplate their bellybuttons, who spoke even when they were told not to, who claimed their right to an opinion and to have a life outside the home, as a man would—such women were tearing at the moral fabric of society!

This opinion would become more pervasive as the nineteenth century approached, but as early as 1711, long before the beginning of the revolutions in America and France, women were instructed to be leaders of "faith, liberty, and country," not by taking to the streets, but by adhering to matronly normalcy:

> *As our English women excel those of all Nations in Beauty, they should endeavor to outshine them in all other Accomplishments proper to the Sex, and to distinguish themselves as tender Mothers and faithful Wives, rather than as furious Partizans. Female Virtues are of a Domestic turn. The Family is the proper Province for Private Women to shine in.*

Helen Maria Williams was doing nothing of the sort, what with her busy life among the intelligentsia and her rabble-rousing followers. Soon, public anxiety over wanton women such as she—those who'd yielded to their "monstrous political and sexual desires"—reached a fever pitch; they were "fallen," betraying both their sex and their homeland with their anti-feminine ways. In 1795, *The Gentleman's Magazine* published a ferocious piece accusing Williams of having "debased her sex, her heart, her feelings, [and] her talents" by subjecting "a regular government and a happy people [the English]" to the gritty nastiness of the French conflict. She and all the other corrupted ladies needed to be punished. Shockingly, a suggestion for how this should be carried out was borrowed from the French Revolution itself, more specifically, from the terrible case of Madame Roland: "[She] received a severe lesson [via the guillotine] of the dangers in which ambitious women involve themselves, by undutifully aspiring to notoriety in troublesome times, and by interfering with what does not regard their sex."

In a marked departure from the accolades heaped on Helen Maria by female critics early in her career, one of the most overarching and thorough lambastings came from another woman, Laetitia Matilda Hawkins, in her *Letters on the Female Mind*. Addressed specifically to Helen Maria as a response to the first two volumes of her *Letters from France*, Hawkins's work is a conservative rebuke against Helen Maria's liberal lifestyle and politics. She condemns the "vociferous clamour" of the French as "reasoning backwards" and, reinforcing conventional views, explains that neither she nor Helen Maria has much authority on the matter after a lifetime in the female sphere: "We are not formed for those deep investigations . . . male genius fetches its treasures from the depths of science, and the accumulated wisdom of the ages: the female finds hers in the lighter regions of fancy and the passing knowledge of the day." Revolutionary politics broke through this accepted mode of gendered thinking and created, according to Hawkins, some kind of half-woman, half-man amalgamation for which the world had no place; Helen Maria had essentially desexed herself, robbing her personage of all its womanly qualities. The consequences of such actions were grave:

> *Those whom nature, not withstanding all modern levelling, has made our lord and masters, may recollect that women ignorant were less a nuisance than they find women informed . . . It is not to be presumed that our rights, if we have any, are unalienable: it is as yet far from decided, that we are morally and collectively better for being wiser. Let us then[,] if we do not love darkness, be very careful to do nothing to provoke our superiors to take away the lamp they had allowed us.*

Our modern minds reel at that blatantly misogynistic threat (especially coming from another woman!), but it shows that women's lives were supposed to be apolitical—and in Helen Maria, we see a woman who shirks this most important tenet. As a result, she was considered a defective lady, a "strumpet," disloyal to her country and poisonous to her brethren. Even some of her old friends found her behavior deplorable. Percival Stockdale, who used to think so well of Helen Maria back when she lived in Berwick-upon-Tweed, explained that because of "the incense of flattery, and the intoxication of vanity," Williams was but a shade of what she once was: "The fallen fair one, whose deep descent I sincerely deplore . . . has adopted the meanest, the most degrading, and profane sentiments." Anna Seward, who had once praised Williams so lavishly, wrote of hoping for Helen

Maria's quick return to England so that she could cease looking upon her "in a state of cold alienation."

Beset by bad press, Helen Maria, it is not surprising, never again set foot on English soil and instead chose to live and work in France. She wrote two four-volume sets of *Letters from France,* cataloging the Reign of Terror and its aftermath up to the year 1796; a travel manual-cum-manifesto, *A Tour in Switzerland,* in which she both anticipates "the electrical fire" of revolution taking hold across the Swiss border and waxes philosophical while sitting on a glacier; and several more political books: *Sketches of the State of Manners and Opinions in the French Republic; A Narrative of the Events Which Have Taken Place in France from the Landing of Napoleon Bonaparte to the Restoration of Louis XVIII;* and *Letters of the Events Which Have Passed in France Since the Restoration in 1815.* She also used her formidable French language skills to translate several works, most notably Alexander von Humboldt's seven-volume *Personal Narrative of Travels to Equinoctial Regions of the New Continent*—the one Charles Darwin found so influential—and to write her final book, *Souvenirs de la révolution française,* published in the year of her death at age sixty-six.

DESPITE OSTRACISM IN HER NATIVE LAND, IN HER LATER YEARS Helen Maria Williams enjoyed a brilliant life as *the* English lady of Paris, entertaining many of the day's most famous politicians, philosophers, and literary gurus: American poet Joel Barlow, future Lord Chancellor of the United Kingdom Thomas Erskine, and all the others "particularly corresponding to her style of society," as Catherine Wilmot, a writer from Ireland and another of Helen Maria's illustrious houseguests, noted. "Senators, Members of the National Institute (in their blue embroider'd coats) and every one in the literary line" spent day after day, evening after evening, in her library, "in the midst of a delightful garden." Even as the Revolution came to a close, Helen Maria's work was still valued among a wide set of devoted readers, her passion for liberty holding strong against the chastising press.

Wilmot also noticed that Helen Maria consistently appeared dressed in full mourning clothes for her sister Cecilia, who had died suddenly in 1798. Williams was charged with the care of Cecilia's two young children, Athanase and Charles, from her marriage with Monique du Fossé's nephew, and together with Stone, she raised them into adulthood. She and Stone never married—at least, not publicly—but their relationship stayed constant until his death in 1818, and when Helen Maria followed him to the grave nine years later, it was next to him that her body was interred.

Helen Maria Williams wrote bravely—even as the threat from Robespierre (and later, from Napoléon Bonaparte) led her to seek shelter on more than one occasion, and often to fear the guillotine for herself and her family—as a war correspondent and a voice for those who had none. When dissenters accused her of a lack of sympathy for nobles who'd lost property during the war, she responded with perfect acuity in the hope for a better world: "Must I be told that my mind is perverted, that I am become dead to all sensations of sympathy, because I do not weep with those who have lost a part of their superfluities, rather than rejoice that the oppressed are protected, that the wronged are redressed, that the captive is set at liberty, and that the poor have bread?" She paid a dear price for her candor, however. Due in large part to persistently negative chatter in the press and her too-close-for-comfort association with Jacobin agitators, Helen Maria's name faded from popular culture once France's conflict settled and nineteenth-century ideals took hold. The writing was on the wall even while she lived: in 1818, William Beloe wrote harshly that she "forgot the lessons of her youth" and "forsook the land of her forefathers" only to become a "paramour . . . with a presumptuousness and impertinence, a determination to palliate and excuse." He asks, "What is she now? If she lives (and whether she does or not, few know, and nobody cares), she is a wanderer—an exile, unnoticed and unknown."

three

MARY ROBINSON

[1758–1800]

BY THE LATE 1790S, THE DEBATE OVER WOMEN—THEIR nature, and the "proper" capacities in which they could exert themselves—was heating up, as Helen Maria Williams discovered to her detriment, but it was certainly not a new point of contention. One hundred fifty years earlier, in 1640's *The Women's Sharp Revenge*, Mary Tattlewell and Joanne Hit-Him-Home accused men of being "lime twigs of Lust and Schoolmasters of Folly" who, by their habitual censure of smart females, kept half of humankind firmly tamped down, "reviled and railed at, taunted and even terrified, undervalued and even vilified." Both sexes responded to this decidedly radical treatise with an avalanche of conduct pamphlets outlining, with varying levels of patronizing rudeness, how a virtuous woman was to go about her life.

She was not to busy herself with finery and fashion, for

"sober shows without" led to "chaste thoughts within" (and, as one discourteous writer reminds us, plain women can still satisfy a sexual urge, "for foul water will quench fire as well as fair"); she was not to direct her attentions at anything beyond the scope of her home and family, so that she may love and serve, hear and obey, "like rich Jewels hang[ing] at your ears to take our Instructions"; and of course, she was most *certainly* not to take up her pen and, in the words of one Dorothy Osborne, "be so ridiculous else as to venture at writing books . . . If I should not sleep this fortnight, I should not come to that."

Precursors to the tsunami of conduct novels that would soon overtake the literary landscape, these "pamphlet battles" ebbed and flowed throughout the seventeenth and eighteenth centuries with steady regularity, never causing too much strife, yet never totally ceasing, either. The French Revolution and its accompanying deluge of radical ideas, however, raised the stakes. Buoyed up on a rising tide of increasingly vocal female authors was the issue of women's civil, marital, and legal rights. Many social commentators decided that the best way to proceed around this thorny topic was to separate the bad from the good—to delineate which members of the female sex were acting in a manner worthy of emulation, and which were not.

One of the most well-known examples of this type of rhetoric is clergyman Richard Polwhele's disputatious poem *The Unsex'd Females,* where the reader is invited to consider, with exacting and systematic tedium, "what ne'er our fathers saw / A female band despising NATURE's law / As 'proud defiance' flashes from their arms / And vengeance smothers all their softer charms." The remainder of the poem is a veritable *Who's Who* of radical women, with Polwhele's determination "is she a good lady, or a bad one?" hastily tacked on to reflect the trend of the day that, it will be remembered, required female literary contributions were to be assessed based on their authors' adherence to English gender norms, not the works' inherent value.

At the apogee of the debate, the "goodness" of a female authoress was determined, first and foremost, by how she wrote about the condition of women. Because they did so either not at all or in a manner that was chaste and not entirely out of line, Hester Lynch Piozzi, Elizabeth Montagu (an odd choice, considering she was the unquestioned leader of the progressive Bluestockings), and Hester Chapone all received Polwhele's approval as "proper" ladies. Female novelists could also be forgiven if, like Hannah More and Fanny Burney, their books functioned as conduct novels and propagated what Polwhele deemed virtuous ideals: "[A] mix with sparkling humour chaste / Delicious feelings and the purest taste." Or, if she wrote philosophy—Polwhele's exemplar was poet Elizabeth Carter, another Bluestocking, whose masterful language skills brought several important translations to the bookstores during the middle of the century; that, too, was acceptable.

In the opposing camp of "unsex'd females" were those authors who claimed to know things they shouldn't have; who, after a lifetime shut up in the female sphere, "sp[u]n webs of feeble reasoning on such subjects as original sin, free-will, fore-knowledge, the origin of evil, etc.," as *The British Critic* put it. Any woman, then, who commented on religious or political subjects was given an automatic black mark. According to Polwhele, Mary Wollstonecraft had awakened all the political mutineers of her time and thus deserved more castigation and blame than any of the others—Anna Laetitia Barbauld, Mary Hays, Ann Yearsley, and naturally Charlotte Turner Smith and Helen Maria Williams (chapters 1 and 2). Together with the subject of this chapter, Mary Robinson, they had all followed Mary Wollstonecraft into a place where darkness "quench[es] the pure daystar in oblivion deep":

> *[Wollstonecraft] spoke: and veteran BARBAULD caught the strain,*
> *And deem'd her songs of Love, her Lyrics vain;*
> *And ROBINSON to Gaul her Fancy gave,*
> *And trac'd the picture of a Deist's grave!*
> *And charming SMITH resign'd her power to please,*
> *Poetic feeling and poetic ease;*
> *And HELEN, fir'd by Freedom, bade adieu*
> *To all the broken visions of Peru[.]*

The boundaries of genre and comportment expressed in *Unsex'd Females*—that philosophy, as a subject, was acceptable for women, but political machinations were not; that "good" morality in female novels was imperative; that to work as a writer specifically to earn money was decidedly unladylike, unless, of course, it was the only thing that stood between a well-born lady and the poorhouse; that some women should be lauded and others condemned, regardless of their talent—were echoed in the conservative press. Charlotte Turner Smith was a sort of female antitype—"she may still produce entertainment, and even advantage to society, if she will abstain from politics . . . [for] the best of our female novelists interferes not with church or state"—as was Helen Maria Williams, who had a "decisive way of speaking, on matters far too perplexed for her sagacity, and far too abstruse for her acquirements." Here is our line of demarcation between "good" and "bad" women, and thus "good" and "bad" books—in much the same way that, in the previous century, when chaste royalist women writers like Katherine Philips were held above more daring ones such as Aphra Behn, critics were unrelenting in their inability (or refusal) to separate an author's literary merit from her sex.

The heftiest rebukes, however, were reserved for Mary Robinson. She was "vigorous and impatient," said one critic; "trash," said another. Her work, when it attempted to address moral and political causes, "went far *beyond her depth,*" and would have been redeemable only if she were to have "confine[d] herself to the fashions and manners of the times, without any vain attempt to investigate their causes." Yet this kind of censure would never have swayed a woman such as Mary. As an unapologetic Wollstonecraft disciple, she was vehemently, palpably, powerfully progressive—indeed, in her opinion, it would require "a *legion of Wollstonecrafts* to undermine the poisons of prejudice and malevolence" in this world of strict gender roles, where women were supposed to be modest and retiring (a dictate she would thwart most thoroughly) and where female intellectual pursuits were carefully controlled. Was the male intellectual the only one capable of writing, judging, and discussing? Of leading England? Mary, like so many of Polwhele's "unsex'd females," begged to differ:

> *Is not a woman a human being, gifted with all the feelings that inhabit the bosom of man? Has not woman affections, susceptibility, fortitude, and an acute sense of injuries received? Does she not shrink at the touch of persecution?*

Does not her bosom melt with sympathy, throb with pity, glow with resentment, ache with sensibility, and burn with indignation? Why then is she denied the exercise of the nobler feelings, an high consciousness of honour, a lively sense of what is due to dignity of character?

MARY ROBINSON HAD A LONG ROAD TO HOE BEFORE SHE WOULD become one of the most famous, most fashionable, most successful literary ladies in all of England. Born Mary Darby in 1758, she spent her childhood in Bristol, wandering the neighborhood surrounding her family home, which was next to the city's cathedral. It was a somber but beautiful place, and it inspired in young redheaded Mary a passion for the melodramatic: She memorized moving poetry, such as Pope's "Lines to the Memory of an Unfortunate Lady"; and "Elegy on the Death of the Countess of Coventry," by William Mason; and when she learned to play the harpsichord, she favored dark, passionate melodies over livelier ones. Roaming around the churchyard, brooding, listening to the great organ echo off the minster walls—one can imagine all sorts of odd ways this girl spent her time, but Mary never found fault with her upbringing or the independence it afforded her. If there was only one thing her mother did wrong, Mary felt, it was in giving her children "too unlimited indulgence, a too tender care, which but little served to arm their breast against the perpetual arrows of moral vicissitude."

Unprepared though they were for sorrow, Mary and her brothers would be thrown headlong into it when she was nine years old. That year, her father, Nicholas Darby, developed a scheme for a whaling business on the Labrador coast and duly departed England with a hundred fifty men, leaving his wife and children behind. His grand idea failed, however, and within two years he was forced to return to Bristol and sell the family home. Then there was further bad news: a mistress, Elenor, who'd traveled with him across the ocean to brave the freezing wilderness, would now be his full-time love.

Formally separated from Nicholas, the family would have to get down to business if they hoped to survive. For the elder brother, John, that meant work at a mercantile house in Leghorn, and for Mary and her younger brother, George, it meant school in London. Mary had already attended for some years Hannah More's popular academy in Bristol, just behind the town's cathedral and mere steps from her home. After her family's relocation to London, she was sent to a seminary in Chelsea run by Meribah Lorrington, an adroit, albeit unconventional teacher who instilled in Mary fierce self-sufficiency and an insatiable love of learning. "She was the most extensively accomplished female that I ever remember to have met with," Mary later wrote. "She was mistress of the Latin, French, and Italian languages; she was said to be a perfect arithmetician and astronomer, and possessed the art of painting on silk to a degree of exquisite perfection . . . All that I ever learned I acquired from this extraordinary woman." Mrs. Lorrington wasn't an exemplar of femininity (quite the contrary—she was a confirmed alcoholic), but her influence on Mary was truly substantial: the two grew to be close friends, even sharing a bedroom, and with Mrs. Lorrington's help, Mary applied herself to study and acquired an overarching fascination for books and poems; she even compiled a volume of juvenile poetry before she left school, one that would become her first publication. Though Mary was talented with a pen, it would be many years, however, before she wielded it in earnest. Long hours of study and silent mornings simply would not suit this blue-eyed, dimple-cheeked, auburn-haired teen beauty with the curving hips and legs. No, she would head for the stage.

In London—then one of the fastest-growing urban spaces on earth, where almost anything could be bought and sold—the theater was where fashionable society convened. If London was the center of the world, then the theater was the center of London, and this was where Mary wanted to be. She auditioned for David Garrick, the manager of the Drury Lane Theatre and an actor with stupefying star power (and, by the by, the first actor to be buried in Westminster Abbey). She was beyond excited to be chosen for the part of Cordelia in Garrick's adaptation of *King Lear,* which, coincidentally, she had seen a few years earlier when Hannah More took the entire school to a performance. Rehearsals were scheduled, and her training began.

Mary was well suited temperamentally to life on the stage, but her mother was adamant that such a life not be pursued—and with good reason. There was likely no worse place to send a fifteen-year-old girl in late-eighteenth-century England. A center of unchaperoned gender mingling generally fueled by rivers of alcohol, the theater was where the most libertine of ideas were on display, both onstage and off. During performances, the audience indulged in a no-holds-barred cacophony of bad manners: people would shout, brawl, and toss rotten food, all the while gawking at half-dressed actors and actresses onstage. As their temperatures rose, men could easily find relief with one of the many hundreds of wantonly waiting prostitutes (for, like any good business-people, they always knew where their clientele could be found).

Covent Garden and Drury Lane were to be avoided by anyone of moral integrity, and on this one point Mary's parents agreed, though admittedly her father was a bit more forceful about it: He wrote to his estranged wife, "Take care that no dishonor falls upon my daughter . . . [or] I will annihilate you."

All attentions were now directed toward finding Mary a more respectable path, and as it happened, there was a boy across the street who (it was supposed) could give her exactly that. A young protégé of an esteemed lawyer, Thomas Robinson had long shared a flirtation with Mary from his upstairs window without any obvious intention of pursuing a romance—that is, until he coordinated an encounter with her mother at a dinner party and spoke of his large fortune and brilliant prospects. This was the first in a string of deceptions, and after the seed was planted, it was only a matter of time—a few gifts here and there (books, mostly) and another dinner party—before Mary's mother could speak of nothing but marriage: "He was 'the kindest, the best of mortals!' the least addicted to worldly follies, and the man, of all others, whom she would adore as *son-in-law*." Yet Mary was still filled with dreams of the stage, "contemplating a thousand triumphs, in which [her] vanity would be publicly gratified," and was hesitant to enter into this arrangement; persuasion would be required to get her out of the clouds and down the aisle, and unfortunately for Mary, Thomas was particularly good at this kind of persuasion. He'd made quite an impression—a false one that Mary later described as "the source of all my succeeding sorrows—and soon the bullying and emotional blackmail, both from her mother and her would-be suitor, compelled Mary to give in. She bowed out of her emergent acting career and, on April 12, 1773, settled down to life as a wife, with no feelings for Thomas Robinson beyond a vague obligation:

> *My heart, even when I knelt at the altar, was as free from any tender impression as it had been at the moment of my birth . . . love was still a stranger to my bosom . . . I well remember that even while I was pronouncing the marriage vow, my fancy involuntarily wandered to the scene where I had hoped to support myself with éclat and reputation.*

Knowing that the creative life she'd hoped for was lost, Mary was already beginning to feel twinges of regret when Thomas's duplicity was revealed just a few weeks later. It's not known exactly how she discovered his untruths, but in any case, they were many. He'd claimed he'd inherit his rich uncle's money when he came of age, but he was already twenty-one and, in fact, only an illegitimate relative of the man whose fortune he'd boasted of for so long. He also had much more time remaining in his apprenticeship than he'd said. Thus, with no inheritance and almost no chance of success in his career—not to mention a penchant for those "worldly follies" Mrs. Darby was certain he'd have no part in—Thomas was perpetually penniless. Upon discovering the terrible truth of her situation, Mary was "the most wretched of mortals . . . the union which I had permitted to be solemnized was indissoluble." And to cap off her misery, Thomas insisted on keeping the marriage a secret, even as they departed for their honeymoon, to avoid trouble with another lady who hankered for his heart.

Downtrodden but not vanquished, Mary dealt with this inauspicious beginning by throwing herself into what she called "the broad hemisphere of fashionable folly." On credit, she and Thomas leased a big house, at 13 Hatton Gardens, outfitted it with furnishings and fabrics, and filled its wardrobes with the latest in expensive fashions; shawls, shoes, and custom-made hats and jewelry were purchased to go along with Mary's new gowns. She mentions two in particular as "sure to attract attention at places of public entertainment": a light brown lustring (glossy silk) with cuffs, and a pink satin number with sable trim she wore with her hair unpowdered, following the very freshest of trends. Looking so well done up, Mary burst onto the capital's social scene in her jaunty new phaeton (a carriage with an open top, much like a convertible) and immediately made a name for herself. She and her new posse strolled among the carefully tended trees and flowers in the pleasure gardens of Vauxhall and Ranelagh, attended concerts and balls in the evenings, chatted and giggled, and watched fireworks. She may not have been onstage, but she was certainly drawing attention.

Less than a year later she was "known by name, at every public place in and near the metropolis," but the Robinson coffers were empty. Thomas's drinking, not to mention his spending every last penny to live like royalty, had led to an almost complete disintegration of his professional life; his proclivity for gambling and visiting prostitutes only exacerbated the situation. Mary, in fairness, was equally responsible for the depletion of their finances—she had her own frills and diversions, servants and wardrobes—but in her *Memoirs,* she blames Thomas for having accrued debt prior to their marriage, and Thomas's biological father, Mr. Harris of Glamorganshire, for having withheld love: "Had Mr. Harris generously assisted his son, I am fully and confidently persuaded that he would have pursued a discreet and regular line of conduct." As it was, both Thomas and Mary were miserably unhappy, but their busy social calendars and pursuit of material splendor were a kind of consolation, along with the (more than a few) amorous affairs each had outside the gloomy marriage. Again, Mary felt guiltless on this account, having been denied the kind of "fidelity and affection which I deserved" in her loveless union with her husband. Still, if she were to continue on as a woman about town, she would have to find some extra income. So, at age seventeen, after having just given birth to her daughter, Maria Elizabeth, Mary Robinson dusted off her literary mind and set to it: "My little collection of poems [the juvenilia], which I had arranged for publication, and which had been ready ever since my marriage, I now determined to print immediately."

THE SLIM QUARTO VOLUME *POEMS BY MRS. ROBINSON* WAS A game-changer for Mary, but not because of its high sales or even its good reviews; on the contrary, critics gave only the very quietest of applause to its young authoress. As John Langhorne at *The Monthly Review* saw it, "Mrs. Robinson is by no means an Aiken or a More, [but] she sometimes expresses herself decently enough on her subject." (Anna Aiken later became Anna Barbauld, another of Polwhele's "unsex'd females" who can also be seen standing among the group depicted in *Don Dismallo Running the Literary Gauntlet*.) Another, at *The Critical Review*, was a bit friendlier, yet still fairly unimpressed. He described *Poems* as "distinguished by an elegant simplicity, unaffected ease, and harmonious versification," but added that "in two or three instances, the ingenious lady has been inattentive to the rhyme."

However guarded this praise seems, it's difficult not to agree with it—Mary's early poems are rather conventional compared with those from Charlotte Turner Smith and Helen Maria Williams. Yet among the thirty-two entries in *Poems* are a few snippets alluding to her potential. In warm and engaging verse, she shows how complicated themes like unrequited love and the growing divide between city and country life can be tackled with sweet sentimentality, such as in "A Pastoral Elegy":

Ye nymphs, ah! give ear to my lay,
Your pastime I prithe' give o'er,
For Damon the youthful and gay,
Is gone,—and our joys are no more.
That Shepherd so blithsome and fair,
Whose truth was the pride of the plains,
Has left us alas! in despair,
For no such a Shepherd remains.

In "Letter to a Friend on Leaving Town," most certainly the best poem of the bunch, she again approaches the opposing worlds of city and country and displays, with remarkable clarity, just how much experience she's already attained at age seventeen—and how her self-assessment has helped her understand the drawbacks of a life of "transient pleasures . . . [of] scandal and coffee":

Gladly I leave the town, and all its care,
For sweet retirement, and fresh wholsome air,
Leave op'ra, park, the masquerade, and play,
In solitary groves to pass the day.

Adieu, gay throng, luxurious vain parade,
Sweet peace invites me to rural shade,
No more the Mall, can captivate my heart,
No more can Ranelagh, one joy impart.
Without regret I leave the splendid ball,
And the inchanting shades of gay Vauxhall,
Far from the giddy circle now I fly,
Such joys no more, can please my sicken'd eye.
The town's alluring scenes no more can charm,
Nor dissipation my fond breast alarm;
Where vice and folly has each bosom fir'd,
And what is more absurd,—is most admir'd.

Mediocre public response notwithstanding, the real worth of *Poems* was quick to show itself. Just prior to publication, while Mary was correcting the proofs, Thomas's creditors came to the house and arrested him on a £1,200 debt (approximately £130,000 today). Unbelievably, just as Charlotte Turner Smith would soon do, Mary Robinson packed up her things and went to prison with her husband—and like Charlotte, she was now a destitute, but not defeated, young mother with a plan. In an action indicative of staggering confidence, she wrapped up a copy of *Poems* and sent it to Georgiana Cavendish, the Duchess of Devonshire, who immediately summoned Mary to Devonshire House and bestowed a healthy sum of money on her with "mildness and sensibility" and "a tear of gentle sympathy." And just like that, Mary and Thomas Robinson were out of prison.

With such extraordinary results, we can't help but wonder: what kind of eloquence and talent must Mary have shown in that letter to Georgiana, a woman she'd never met, to have elicited an invitation to Devonshire House and an offer of financial support? The duchess was roughly the same age as Mary, a writer herself, liberal-minded, and bound up in a terrible marriage; perhaps she saw a spark of ability (and maybe recognized a little of herself) in that wilted seventeen-year-old girl at her door with her little book of under-read poetry.*

Mary leveraged *Poems* into a lifelong friendship and patronage, and from then on, she never faltered in her attachment to Georgiana. Her next work, *Captivity*, was the first of many to be dedicated to the duchess, "Patroness of the Unhappy," for "the occasion of repeating my Thanks to You, for the unmerited Favors your Grace has bestowed upon me." With honeyed words, she celebrates liberation and looks to the future:

Bear me, sweet Freedom, on thy downy wing,
Teach me of thy superior Joys to sing,
Teach my fond Muse to wing its infant flight,
To that sweet scene where purest charms invite;
Where guiltless pleasures reign without control,
And godlike virtues harmonize the soul.
Sweet Liberty, to thee a Female pays
The slender tribute of these votive lays.

LIVING OFF THE DUCHESS'S GENEROSITY, THOMAS AND MARY Robinson headed back into the thick of London's social scene, but this time their mood was different. Financially they were in

* Being an avid gambler herself—and heavily indebted as a result—we can surmise that Georgina likely sympathized with the nature of Mary's plight.

a tenuous situation—Georgiana's money wouldn't sustain them for long, and Mary's poetry was bringing in only a pittance. Another source of income would have to be found, since Thomas had failed at becoming anything resembling a lawyer and was still up to his cravat in debts. What's more, compounding Mary's financial anxiety was the unavoidable truth that their marriage was defunct. Thomas's indiscretions "were both frequent and disgraceful," she wrote, with obvious bitterness: "Even though I was the partner of his captivity, the devoted slave to his necessities, [he] indulged in the lowest and most degrading intrigues . . . [with] women whose low licentious lives were such as to render them the shame and outcasts of society." Thomas was apathetic; he'd even been known to dally with prostitutes while his wife sat in the very next room.

Fortunately, Mary knew that both problems could be solved if she went back on the stage. In one swift stroke, it would support her lifestyle and assert her independence apart from her skirt-chasing husband. As an actress, Mary would be her own lady, with her own money.

In the three years since she'd been away from the theater, Mary's old coach, David Garrick, had retired, but the new manager of Drury Lane, Richard Sheridan, had seen her in past rehearsals as Cordelia and was elated to have her return. She worked tirelessly to prepare herself for her first role, as Juliet, "with zeal bordering on delight," and when opening night came, she strutted out from the wings in satin and lace and a floor-length veil, her heart "throbbing convulsively," and smashed it out of the park. Even the jaded critics knew they'd found a gem: "There has not been a lady on this, or the other stage [Covent

Garden], for some seasons, who promises to make so capital an actress," said the *New Morning Post*. The *Morning Chronicle* noted how "she appeared to feel the character . . . she gave the audience a better impression of [Juliet] than we can remember them to have received from any new actress for sometime past." "The young lady who performed the part of Juliet last night," as the *Gazetteer* remembered it, "was received with uncommon and universal applause." Though some commentators found small faults—one thought she wanted for polish of manner, another took issue with her walk, and others described a lack of maturity in her performance—Mrs. Mary Robinson was received with overwhelming positivity, and immediately landed her next role, as Statira in *Alexander the Great*, scheduled to open the following month; then as Amanda in *A Trip to Scarborough*. And as with everything else she'd done up until then, Mary excelled, even if things got rough: When the audience recognized *A Trip to Scarborough* as a rehash of Sir John Vanbrugh's *The Relapse*, for example, they began to boo and hiss, and the young star, instead of fleeing backstage like her fellow actors, turned and curtsied with her typical gutsy grandeur. "That curtsy seemed to electrify the whole house, for a thundering peal of applause followed."

Over the next three years, Mary's performances at Drury Lane steadily grew in popularity. She was particularly good with Shakespearean roles, and as a result spent much of the season engrossed in Ophelia, Lady Anne, and Lady Macbeth, along with characters such as Fidelia from *The Plain Dealer* (a scandalous cross-dressing "breeches" role); Araminta from a roaring comedy, *The Old Bachelor*; and Lady Plume in *The Camp*. She even put pen to paper for her own play, a farce called *The Lucky Escape*—the first of anything she'd written since *Captivity*—which reviewers described favorably: "The piece was well got up, and all the players acquitted themselves with credit . . . prettiness and sentiment in the language [is] strongly characteristic of the author."

Mary's salary was commensurate with her status as the superstar of Drury Lane, and she used it to equip herself with even more ponies and maids, dresses, shoes, and perky hats—and of course quietly to pay down Thomas's ever-present debts. Despite the appearance of happiness, however, her wedded life had continued to deteriorate, and by 1779 she was living apart from her husband. Thomas moved in with a dancer from Drury Lane, while Mary used her earnings to lease a gorgeous house in the Great Piazza of Covent Garden. Then she began consorting with the first in a long list of famous lovers, including politician Charles James Fox; Sir John Lade, heir to a brewery fortune; and several other noblemen who wished to take her under their "protection"—a covert way of offering money in exchange for becoming a long-term bedmate. She turned down many offers (even one from the Duke of Rutland for six hundred pounds per year, a better-than-comfortable seventy-thousand-pound salary today), but she accepted and adored, without remorse, other men, since she'd been "ill-bestowed upon a man who neither loved nor valued me."

Bolstered by gossip columnists and a flurry of cheap, easily accessed caricatures that praised her and her sensuous figure, by the time she was twenty-one Mary Robinson had become the most popular actress in London. Yet even as she played lead characters in some of the most famous and important shows of her day, her biggest role didn't come until her third year at Drury Lane, when, after opening the season with more Shakespeare

(*Hamlet* and *Richard III*), she played Perdita in Garrick's version of *The Winter's Tale.*

It was December 3, 1779, when the royal family came to see the show. Both the king, George III, and queen were present—at stage right, which Mary noticed with "a strange degree of alarm"—as was their teenage son, George (later George IV), who at this point hadn't yet become the infamous blubberous rake of Jane Austen's lifetime. He was known instead for his fondness for gentlemanly pleasures and for a sweet generosity that pervaded despite his fondness for wine and women.

As Mary sauntered expertly through her lines in a hip-hugging milkmaid's outfit with red ribbons, it was Prince George's obvious attention to her character, Perdita, that people were talking about: George stared at her intently during the entire performance with near-rabid desire. While Mary had little idea what was happening—she remained focused on her acting—the end of the performance brought a swift realization: "Just as the curtain was falling, my eyes met those of the prince of Wales; and with a look that I *never shall forget,* he gently inclined his head . . . I felt the compliment, and blushed my gratitude."

The day after Prince George spotted Mary, he broke up with his girlfriend via post and announced his intention to pursue another, the bright actress from the evening before, "Robinson . . . the greatest and most perfect beauty of her sex." He then composed another letter, this one to Mary (the first of many), expressing his infatuation and requesting an interview with "Perdita," signing as her onstage lover in *The Winter's Tale,* "Florizel." Mary was flattered to know that "the most admired, and most accomplished prince in Europe was devotedly attached," but she was unsure how to proceed: What would she do if, after a few weeks of fun, he cast her out? Were they to engage in this affair, the publicity would be oppressive and unmerciful, but the prince was adamant that his "inviolable affection" and "enthusiastic adoration, expressed in every letter" could never lead him to do anything rash. Yet these were just words, and Mary had been burned before. She held steadfast until she received the proper assurances: "A promise of the sum of twenty thousand pounds [over two million pounds today], to be paid at the period of his royal highness' coming of age . . . signed by the prince, and sealed with the royal arms." This veritable fortune was finally enough to send Perdita flying to her Florizel: Mary relinquished her career on the stage and became a full-fledged courtesan to England's heir apparent.

A few clandestine meetings were followed by a raucous consummation in the royal servants' quarters, cocktails, and then repeated revelry until three or four in the morning, gifts of jewels, miniature portraits, flowers, and sweets. It was all a blissful blur, but Mary never lost track of the reality of her circumstances: "How would my soul have idolized such a *husband!* Alas, how often, in the ardent enthusiasm of my soul, have I formed the wish that that being were *mine alone* . . . often I have lamented the distance which destiny has placed between us."

In July 1780, the *Morning Post* reported that the two were seen at the theater making eyes at each other, and that "a certain *young actress* who leads the *Ton* [England's high society] appeared . . . with all the grace and splendour of a Duchess, to the no small mortification of the female world, and astonishment of every spectator." A few days later the same paper marveled at this woman, Mary Robinson, noting how she'd made "a conquest in the heart of a young and illustrious personage, at the very moment when he was surrounded by all the beauties of the British Court, vieing with each other to captivate and ensnare him." Some loved her, others despised her for having snatched up so mighty a mate, but whatever their feelings, she was still unquestionably famous:

> *Whenever I appeared in public, I was overwhelmed by the gazing of the multitude. I was frequently obliged to quit Ranelagh [Gardens], owning to the crowd which staring curiosity had assembled round my box; and, even in the streets of the metropolis I scarcely ventured to enter a shop without experiencing the greatest inconvenience . . . I cannot suppress a smile at the absurdity of such a proceeding.*

Day after day, George paraded Mary on his arm all over the city. They were *the* power couple of their time, their every movement a public event, and Mary at the center of it all. She was seen in clothing of the highest fashion and finest quality—at parties and concerts, in her own box at the opera house, and driving around St. James's Street and Pall Mall in one of her several lavish phaetons, usually on her way to visit other ladies in their sumptuous, stylish homes.

Yet it wasn't long before these indulgences turned into bad publicity, the flirtation brought scandal, and the passion elicited blind rage. The press was having a field day with Mary Robinson and her ungoverned lifestyle, and soon her ability to ignore the criticism collapsed under the strain. The "hourly augmenting torrent of abuse" had become downright ruthless, as we can see in this nasty letter from "Dramaticus" in the *Morning Post.* Reacting to her having leased her own theater box, the author seethes with animosity and proclaims Mary as nothing more than a prostitute:

> *The audacity of Mrs. R—, who was an actress last winter, and whose situation and character is certainly not improved since her resignation from the stage, is beyond example or excuse . . . I know of no rank of prostitution that can either lessen the crime or disgrace of it; and, however profligate the age may be, I believe that the greatest libertine of our sex would revolt at the idea of handing a wife, sister, or daughter, in to a box where they were certain of being surrounded by public prostitutes. The managers owe it to the public, they owe it to themselves, to preserve the side-boxes for the modest and reputable part of the other sex.*

Her defenders responded in kind, paying tribute to her qualities as an actress and suggesting that those who had trouble with her were merely feeling the creeping hand of envy clench around their unfashionably clad throats, but the damage was done, and Mary Robinson started to crack; humiliation and anger now simmered below her elegant surface, and given the right spark, she would fly off the handle and into a defamatory rage. One particularly embarrassing incident occurred at the theater, where she came upon her estranged husband canoodling with a young girl. Mary yanked him into the lobby by the hair and then expended her animosity "in blows and reproaches to the complete entertainment of a numerous auditory." The prince, annoyed by the news of this mess, responded with great displeasure: Mary was becoming a liability.

His father, George III, had been pressuring him to end the affair, and now, with so much bad press surrounding the couple, the prince complied. He had lost interest in Mary anyway and had already turned his attentions to Elizabeth Armistead, another actress (who, coincidentally, had also played Perdita, in an earlier production of *The Winter's Tale*, and would be the eventual wife of Charles James Fox, Mary's friend and lover). Mary was hurt and shocked when she received George's brief letter—"*we must meet no more!*"—but she wasn't prepared to end the relationship without first cashing in on the prince's promise. With the power of the press at her disposal and desperation lurking around the corner—it must be remembered, she'd abandoned her profession to be with George and had long given up living within her means—Mary puffed herself up and spat out her bottom line: the prince would provide her and her daughter with a settlement, or she would publish his love letters.

The latter was something to be avoided at all costs. Any private royal conversation aired in public could be disastrous, but considering how many letters there were (scores, from an almost daily correspondence) and their very personal content, this was a particularly powerful threat; George was finally driven to the negotiating table out of fear of exposure. After months of back-and-forth, Mary was awarded five thousand pounds in exchange for the letters and a further five hundred per year in lieu of the full twenty-thousand-pound bond. Though the lump-sum payment didn't even cover her debts, which were extensive, her annuity remained one of the prince's largest outgoing payments.

(His next highest, in 1787, was in the amount of three hundred pounds for musicians, far and away beyond the cost of his other bills, such as thirty-one pounds for Humphreys the rat catcher and twenty-five for his coach and its accoutrement.) It should also be noted that poor George III had to *borrow* the money to pay his son's settlement, so for one astonishing moment, Mary Robinson's sexual powers were so immense that the King of England himself was at her mercy.

By 1783, Mary was twenty-five years old and still the hottest thing about town. Since the split with the prince, she'd enjoyed a string of illustrious lovers and ratcheted up her fame through more luxuries and overexpenditures—clothes, carriages, and a pink satin bed rumored to be "the most superb and elegant piece of furniture in Europe." She'd also become friends with Marie Antoinette, after their meeting in Paris, and upon returning to London ignited a frenzy in the fashion world with her many new acquisitions: a headdress that set the "standard of taste," as the *Morning Herald* reported (purple and white feathers festooned with flowers, diamonds, and bows), and a white satin gown that, in combination with her daring jewelry, brought the *ton* to its knees at her first public appearance. More shocking still was her *chemise de la reine,* a simple white muslin gown tied with a ribbon under the bust that—gasp!—was worn without the usual panniers or bodice and instead allowed the body's true form to become apparent. Such a "naked" dress led to national scandal in France when Marie Antoinette posed in one for a portrait in 1783 (it was, at the time, as if she were posing in her underwear), but Mary wasn't thrown. She embraced the *chemise* without fear, and together with the Duchess of Devonshire popularized dresses that heralded new trends in fashion—higher, looser waists; flowing fabrics; less structure and adornment: the kinds of dresses Jane Austen and her characters would be lucky enough to wear before the Victorian era snapped all the cinching, bones, and hoops back into place.

Beyond her chic fashion sense, Mary was also becoming known as a lady of extraordinary intellect, a woman apart from the rest of the quivering masses who'd come to worship her—and *this,* not her style or fame, would turn out to be her most important and lasting quality. Many reporters took note of her sparkling, opportunistic intelligence, including one at the *Morning Herald* who saw in her eyes a mind capable of much more than she was putting on: "The *wit* of the *eye.* I have seen an eye full of rhetoric and elocution full of invitations and forbiddings.—I have spoken to a woman with an eye of such *wit* that has struck me *dumb* with a repartee flash, without the assistance of a single word.—Look at *Mrs. Robinson's eyes!*" On top of all her celebrity, intellectual and otherwise, she'd become involved with a British war hero from the American Revolution, Colonel Banastre Tarleton, who would be her on-and-off lover for the next sixteen years. She was also carrying their child.

In July of 1783, though, this rosy life took a turn for the worse. Seven months into her pregnancy, she drove to Dover in a flustered rush at two in the morning to prevent Tarleton from fleeing England. His debts were severe enough to spur a quick departure for France, but unbeknownst to him, Mary—desperate to be with him as their baby's arrival neared—had borrowed the eight hundred pounds he needed. The details of this fateful summer's eve will never be fully understood, but Mary's daughter claims the problem began with a fever contracted after "an imprudent exposure to the night air, when, exhausted by fatigue and mental anxiety, she slept in a chaise with the windows open." She ended up in bed for the next several months, and as winter approached, her sickness grew steadily worse until she was in the throes of "a violent rheumatism which progressively deprived her of the use of her limbs . . . in the pride of youth and the bloom of beauty, was this lovely and unfortunate woman reduced to a state of more than infantile helplessness." Sometime during those terrible months, the unborn child was lost, which has led modern scholars to wonder whether a miscarriage wasn't the catalyst for the near-total ruin of Mary's health. It is suspected that she bled out in the chaise and developed an infection, causing the fever that led to her paralysis; or that hypothermia, or even a stroke, was the culprit. Regardless, we know she never recovered full use of the lower half of her body. From here on out she was so weak that she often had to be carried between rooms and to her carriage, and after losing Tarleton's child, she never became pregnant again.

So, very ill, Mary was forced to retreat from society and focus on getting back her strength. She toured Europe in search of a cure, trying the baths at Flanders ("receptacles of loathsome mud"); the sunshine at Villefranche, near Nice; and the many spa treatments in Aachen, near the Belgian-Dutch-German border. And when she wasn't overwhelmed with pain—she frequently used opium to offset it, much like Samuel Taylor Coleridge and his daughter Sara would do—she consoled her understandably low spirits with writing. Bedridden, it was "to the more assiduous cultivation of her talents" that she now turned her attention, not only as a fix for boredom, but also as her new profession.

In 1788 she returned to England and settled with her mother and daughter at 45 Clarges Street, just two blocks from Georgiana at Devonshire House, and devoted herself to writing. For several months she used a pseudonym in an attempt to shake off her past as Perdita once and for all, remaking herself as "Laura" or "Laura Maria" for her first attempts as a professional authoress. In this endeavor at anonymity she did extraordinarily well—her readers had no idea that the composer of such *"vastly pretty"* poems was in fact the famous (and infamous) Mrs. Mary "Perdita" Robinson. Even the ladies of Elizabeth Montagu's exclusive Bluestocking circle came to admire her work and to recite it among themselves, which, considering Mary's reputation and her long list of extramarital lovers, would likely never have happened had they known the identity of the author behind the verse.

Accustomed as she was to the limelight, Mary soon grew tired of the deception and dispensed with it once the French Revolution gave her an opportunity to write, confidently, on a subject she felt drawn to. Like Charlotte Turner Smith and Helen Maria Williams, she was radical, cosmopolitan, and so devoted to the Revolution—one can't help but wonder whether being thrown over by the Prince of Wales fueled her belief in the righteousness of the cause—that her participation in the chorus of its early enthusiasts was a given. To the "revolutionary debates," she contributed a small pamphlet of poetry called *Ainsi va le monde* ("Thus Goes the World"), and immediately garnered the highest praise from the pickiest of reviewers, who this time knew exactly whose pen was responsible. "This poetic address . . . gives us a favourable opinion, in a general view, of the literary abilities of the fair writer, Mrs. Robinson," said one, in *The Monthly Review*. *General Magazine* went further, praising her "very refined sensibility" and her "correctness of taste." Mary, it seems, no longer cared about separating herself from Perdita—after such acclaim, why would she? *Ainsi va le monde* went into a second edition right away and was quickly translated into French—because how could the Parisians not identify with words like these?:

> *WHAT is the charm that bids mankind disdain*
> *The Tyrant's mandate and th' Oppressor's chain;*
> *What bids exulting Liberty impart*
> *Ecstatic raptures to the Human Heart;*
> *Calls forth each hidden spark of glorious fire,*
> *Bids untaught minds to valiant feats aspire;*
> *What give to Freedom its supreme delight?*
> *'Tis Emulation, Instinct, Nature, Right. . .*
> *See! From her shrine electric incense rise;*
> *Hark! "Freedom" echoes thro' the vaulted skies.*
> *The Goddess speaks! O mark the blest decree,—*
> *TYRANTS SHALL FALL—TRIUMPHANT*
> *MAN BE FREE!*

A year later, after she'd again published on the Revolution—in another pamphlet, entitled *Impartial Reflections on the Present Situation of the Queen of France*, she implored the public to rethink their violence against her old friend Marie Antoinette—Mary Robinson found her voice. She'd tiptoed onto the literary stage, discovered public approbation "beyond her most sanguine hopes," and would now endeavor to earn herself an income. She would compose a novel.

Seventeen ninety-one saw both her *Impartial Reflections* and a second volume of verse hit the shelves and become instant hits, but compared with her next work, they were mere blips on society's radar. Her first novel, *Vancenza; or the Dangers of Credulity,* sold out in a single day. The second printing was gone twelve days later, followed by the third the next week and two more before the public was satisfied. It was the single most popular novel written by a female in England to date, and among the top 5 percent of the best-selling novels of the late eighteenth century.

Much like Charlotte Turner Smith's heroine in *Emmeline* and Charlotte Brontë's famous Jane Eyre, the main character in *Vancenza,* Elvira, is a paragon of grace and intelligence with a lonely past. She's "the animated portrait of her mind; truth, benignity, pure and unstudied delicacy" with nothing wanting—she is impeccable, "everything fancy could picture." Elvira's charms notwithstanding, like Emmeline, she knows little of her parentage and spends most of the novel trying to figure it out. Gothic misadventures ensue: Elvira falls in love with Prince Almanza, a friend of the family who is injured while hunting near her home, and over a series of back-and-forth displays of affection, she decides to accept his marriage proposal and live happily ever after. Then, during the wedding preparations, Elvira finds a hidden casket and, within it, a letter from her dead mother, the haunted

Madeline Vancenza, whose story of seduction sounds an awful lot like Mary Robinson's (at least from Mary's perspective):

> *I considered the Prince as my friend, and my protector: he availed himself of those confidential titles to cover the blackest purposes; and under the mask of friendship obtained my esteem—esteem ripened into affection. He marked the weakness of my soul, and triumphed over that honour he was bound to protect, by all the laws of truth and hospitality.*

Would that she'd never opened that casket! For, tragedy comes as a result of the letter: Elvira discovers that her mother's seducer is her fiancé's father, and that she is engaged to her own half-brother. She is horrified and immediately falls into a melancholy stupor. And here, at this particularly cringe-worthy moment, Mary's authorial bravery takes hold. Instead of offering Elvira a chance to redeem herself, like Adelina in *Emmeline* (who, amazingly, gets to marry the father of her baseborn child), and as the Gothic style commanded, she commits to the sad truth that within this social system there simply can be no happy ending—despite perfect virtue and beauty, a sullied woman is a dead woman, and Elvira is given no other out but the sweet relief of death.

Vancenza is skillfully, poetically written, if not a little verbose. Even so, a modern reader will find the novel a bit absurd. It drips with Gothic attributes (creaking doors, untold secrets, attempted murders and kidnappings, unidentified people, unexplained events) and takes place in a quaintly crumbling castle where everything, even breakfast, is an event shrouded in mystery. It is a decidedly melodramatic work written in an outmoded style. Yet, as a commentary on the plight of women in the eighteenth century, on the lack of options for them (especially those who shirked societal norms), *Vancenza* is a triumph. Its opinions on the aristocracy have inspired scholars to call it "nothing short of revolutionary." Anticipating Mary Wollstonecraft's radically feminist treatise, *A Vindication of the Rights of Woman,* and Charlotte Turner Smith's *The Old Manor House,* Mary Robinson's novel opened the floodgates with this discourse on the senselessness of imbuing a mere child with feudal power:

> *Little and contracted minds are apt to envy the possessors of exalted titles and empty distinctions.* IGNORANCE *only descends to bestow admiration upon the* gew-gaw *appendages of what is commonly called* RANK; *it fancies it beholds a thousand dazzling graces, dignifying and embellishing the varnished form of artificial consequence. To the abject sycophant, who eats the bread of miserable obedience, poisoned by the breath of adulation, the* baubles *of greatness are objects of veneration; the imbecility of childhood is amused with every toy:—but the* ENLIGHTENED MIND *thinks for* itself; *explores the precepts of uncontaminated* truth; *weighs, in the even scale of unbiased judgement, the rights and claims of* intellectual pre-eminence; *exults in the attributes of* reason; *and opposes, with dauntless intrepidity, every innovation that dares assail even the* least *of its prerogatives.*

Given a rant like that in England's pro-Revolution atmosphere, reviewers were falling all over themselves to assert *Vancenza*'s greatness: "[A] record of domestic woe, extremely interesting and pathetic, has been decorated by the pen of our fair enchantress with peculiar taste, elegance and variety"; "The richness of fancy and of language, which the fair author had so successfully displayed in her poetical productions she has also transferred to prose narration"; and "Considering the number and the variety of her productions, we are disposed to think that she has more successfully climbed Parnassian heights than any female votary of the muses which this country has produced."

SUCCESSFUL THOUGH SHE WAS, THE LAST EIGHT YEARS OF Mary Robinson's life were more turbulent than anyone would've liked. Living with Tarleton had ruined her finances, what with his high-stakes gambling and proclivity for imprudence, and after sixteen tumultuous years, the couple finally split, leaving Mary many thousands of pounds in debt—there was barely enough money for rent, let alone rent on a fancy abode. It was a new, simpler life, then, for her.

Her social calendar discarded, she could now become the independent lady of letters she seems to have, at some level, always wanted to be. In such circumstances, inspiration was quick to ignite. Living first in a modest house, 14 St. James's Place, and then moving in with her daughter at a cottage near Englefield Green, Mary was freed from distractions and abuzz with ideas. She quickly cranked out a second novel, *The Widow, or a Picture of Modern Times,* another volume of poetry, and a play called *Nobody,* and then returned to Gothic romance with *Hubert de Sevrac,* set amid the French Revolution, and *Angelina,* a work that Mary Wollstonecraft found particularly fine, praising it as "just, animated, and rational": "The sentiments in these volumes . . . breathe a spirit of independence, and a dignified superiority."

Strengthened by acclamation from such a progressive icon of female power—a person to whom she swore adoring fealty—Mary continued with her radical novels (*Walsingham; or, the Pupil of Nature; The False Friend; The Natural Daughter*) and tackled the antifeminist atmosphere of 1799 with a bold retort, *A Letter to the Women of England, on the Injustice of Mental Subordination*, which, published during the storm of controversy surrounding Wollstonecraft's *Memoirs*, was so daring that Mary (who, it will be remembered, adored the spotlight) decided to avoid the inevitable attacks on her character by using a pseudonym.

Mary also wrote actively for the *Morning Post*, filling the paper with treatises on the high life in London in pieces such as "Modern Male Fashions" and "The Gamester," an allegory on the dangers of gambling. She also opened some witty discourse on relationships in "The Ingredients Which Compose Modern Love," and addressed all manner of favored themes in her serialized "Sylphid Essays": the subjugation of female genius, fickle fashions, "adventurous" women, and the problem with self-importance. (The *Morning Post* was the same paper that had published "Dramaticus's" caustic rant against her fifteen years earlier, and thus, her decision to contribute to its pages leaves one wondering how circumstances with its publishers had evolved in the interim. Unfortunately, little is known about her perceived change of allegiance; perhaps it is due to Daniel Stuart's acquisition of the *Post* in 1795 from its previous editor, John Bell, or, as is more likely the case, to Mary's need for a consistent source of income between books.)

At the end of 1799, she replaced Robert Southey, Sara Coleridge's paterfamilias (see chapter 5), as the *Post*'s poetry editor. Her additional responsibilities included the selection and editing of other poets' work and frequent visits to the newspaper's offices, which is how she befriended Samuel Taylor Coleridge. He was engaged to write political articles at the *Post,* which at this point had become a Tory newspaper, and in the process, came to greatly admire Mary: "She is a woman of undoubted genius . . . I never knew a human Being with so *full* a mind—bad, good, and indifferent, I grant you, but full, and overflowing." So enraptured was he with the aging invalid—"Ay! that Woman has an Ear"—that in 1800, just months before her death, Coleridge showed her the draft of one of his most famous and lasting legacies, *Kubla Khan,* a poem written under the influence of opium. His friend and fellow essayist Thomas De Quincey was also experimenting with the drug, to counteract an unknown physical ailment (as De Quincey would later recount in the best-selling *Confessions of an English Opium-Eater*), but it was Mary Robinson's experience with it that led Coleridge to confide in her: After one particularly painful day in the medicinal baths, Mary swallowed almost eighty drops of opium and awoke in the same kind of poetic fury Coleridge found so inspiring. She then composed her own *Kubla Khan,* before Coleridge ever dreamed of it, a work originally titled "Insanity" and retitled "The Maniac" when it was published:

> *AH! WHAT ART THOU, whose eye-balls roll*
> *Like* Heralds *of the wand'ring soul,*
> *While down thy cheek the scalding torrents flow?*
> *Why does that agonizing shriek*
> *The mind's unpitied anguish speak?*
> *O tell me, THING FORLORN! and let me share*
> *thy woe.*

That Mary was using opium so readily was a sign of her failing health, and despite her best efforts to recover, she was in rapid decline as the fall of 1800 approached. Coleridge was very concerned, and wrote to author, and mutual friend, William Godwin (who was himself reeling from the loss of his wife, Mary Wollstonecraft, three years earlier): "Have you seen Mrs. Robinson lately? How is she?—Remember me in the kindest and most respectful phrases to her." Very sick, and aware of her impending death, Mary spent the last few months of her life in a state of constant production: *Lyrical Tales* came first, with its inventive diversity of metrical style reflecting William Wordsworth's own *Lyrical Ballads*; followed by a pile of poetry for the periodicals; and finally her *Memoirs*, which she placed in her daughter's hands "with an *injunction* that the narratives should be made public . . . *Promise* me that you will print it!" Maria Elizabeth of course agreed, and as the winter closed in, Mary sank into a stupor and died the day after Christmas in 1800, at age forty-two, "pressing to her heart her daughter, who knelt by her bedside."

Public interest in the Prince of Wales kept Mary Robinson's name in the papers long after her death, as "Perdita . . . The Mistress of Royalty," who always incited the "most refined and elegant conversation" with her "capacious, intelligent mind." The prince himself would not be remembered so fondly, however, especially after he ascended the throne in 1820. By that time, his arranged marriage to Caroline of Brunswick was in shambles; he was addicted to opium, extremely fat, and notorious for his alcoholism, laziness, and predilection for dropping outrageous sums on harebrained fun. He spent £155,000 renovating his cherished home in Brighton, the Royal Pavilion, and £75,000 annually on jewels, plate, and upholstery alone (values that today would come to around £10,020,000 and £4,840,000 respectively).265 Despite his faults, he was "a great admirer" of Jane Austen's novels and requested, much to her dismay, that *Emma* be dedicated to him. Jane recognized the inadvisability of refusing the king of England and complied, but hated the experience, which one of her biographers, Claire Harman, perfectly describes as "being patronized by nincompoops." George IV survived Mary Robinson by nearly thirty years and fathered several illegitimate children, but his private letters extoll Mary above all other women as the true love of his life.

Mary also left an indelible impression on the world of fashion, even as she withdrew from it later in life. That soft, unstructured *chemise de la reine* was nicknamed the "Perdita chemise" and became universal among the chicest women—*Lady's Magazine* couldn't help but notice that all females "from age 15 to 50 and upwards . . . appear in the white muslin frocks with broad sashes" under the bust—along with the "Robinson hat" (featuring a wide ribbon that doubled as a veil when pulled down), the "Robinson hat for Ranelagh" (a big white one decked out in flowers), the "Perdita hood," the "Perdita handkerchief," and the "Robinson gown," of chocolate poplin with red cuffs. She also popularized wearing a riding habit in the morning, and standardized the look with her own interpretation of it: pearl-colored with yellow accents, or dark brown with a scarlet vest. As she appeared to do her whole life, she started the trend, and the *ton* trotted along behind her "with flattering avidity."

Mary Robinson was *the* toast of the town: an independent lady with lovers aplenty, a friend to many in high places, and an ingenious, prolific wordsmith. Because everyone—those in the worlds of fashion and the stage, her publishers, the gossip columnists, her mother, her daughter, and a flock of followers—always wanted a piece of her, Mary's public persona was a somewhat calculated one. Even her *Memoirs* were packaged in a way that presented her in the manner she deemed most gratifying: a guiltless victim of circumstance where her failed marriage was concerned; an active, cultivated intelligence otherwise, even despite her frivolous lifestyle. The real Mary Robinson was complex, and a bit self-defeating in her approach: Her self-promotion and scandalous behavior won money and fame—all things she wanted, unapologetically. However, they brought with them a reputation for indecorum that, as Victorian-era morality took hold in an England increasingly obsessed with the Romantic style of Wordsworth, Byron, Keats, and Coleridge, led to her, and her writings', gradual disappearance from the popular consciousness.

Still, while she lived, no woman was more notorious, more frequently caricatured, or more easily (and rightly) recognized for her talent and sheer force of will, than Mary Robinson.

four
CATHERINE CROWE

[*c.* 1800–1876]

On the evening of June 12, 1850, preparations for a momentous event were under way at William Thackeray's house in London's Young Street: Charlotte Brontë! Jane Eyre herself! Coming to dinner! Thackeray was no slouch in the literary world, having just published in serial form his scathing and hilarious novel *Vanity Fair*—but Charlotte? This was *big.* The famous "Currer Bell" had been unmasked only a few months ago, and once the world heard who she really was—"the smallest creature I had ever seen (except at a fair)," reported Harriet Martineau, who'd met Charlotte back in December—all of London was clambering to get a look at the provincial parson's daughter whose second edition of *Jane Eyre* was selling like crazy across England.

Yet because Charlotte was shy, countrified, and opposed to aggrandizement in all its forms, a certain amount of planning was needed to ensure her comfort. Of course all the best china was brought out, and a most beautiful dinner ordered, but Thackeray, concerned that the people surrounding Charlotte should be the *right* kind of people, also handpicked the guest list, which featured some of the most inspiring and learned, yet kindest, citizens in his circle. Thomas and Jane Carlyle, a troubled but sweet couple with literary accolades aplenty; Charlotte's publisher, George Smith; socialite Mrs. Proctor and her daughter Adelaide; Thackeray's own daughter, Anne, a future authoress who was then just thirteen years old; and a smattering of his most cheerful friends, including a Miss Elliot, a Mrs. Brookfield, and a Miss Perry.

Thackeray paced fussily as the moment of Charlotte's arrival edged closer, all in a tizzy to get the evening just right, and when she finally stepped down from the carriage, he and the guests just stared. Here was "a tiny, delicate, serious, little lady," as young Anne Thackeray remembered: timid and fretting, wearing a drab green dress and a mismatched hairpiece. She crept in silently, hands mittened, and Thackeray foolishly introduced her as Currer Bell, to which she responded grumpily that "she believed there were books being published by a person named Currer Bell . . . but the person *he* was talking to was Miss Brontë." The evening was looking gloomy, and unfortunately, it would not improve: Charlotte Brontë was more of a loner than Thackeray had anticipated, and any conversation beyond whispered prattle with Anne's governess, Miss Truelock, was beyond her abilities. That brilliant discourse everyone expected never began; the only words she spoke audibly, in fact, were in answer to Mrs. Brookfield's simple question "Do you like London, Miss Brontë?"—to which she responded, cryptically, "Yes and no," before sinking back into silence.

Charlotte departed, Thackeray scuttled off to his club, and the remaining literati gaped at one another in wonderment. They'd come to meet "the great *Jane Eyre* . . . the unknown power whose books have set all London talking," but instead of insight and cleverness, they'd found only dim chitchat and prickly retorts! Mrs. Proctor announced with amusement that it had been one of the dullest evenings of her life, and Anne, as she later wrote, was so bored that an extra dish of cookies would've been enough to improve the evening.

But no matter. These literature devotees would easily have been able to transfer their adoration for Charlotte Brontë to another woman, for as G. H. Lewes correctly noted in his anonymous (and offensive) article "Flight of the Authoresses," London was full of "female horrors with inky thumbs." There were plenty of lady writers to love.

By the mid-nineteenth century, you couldn't swing a petticoat without knocking over authoresses young and old. Newcomers such as Mary Russell Mitford and Frances Milton Trollope were doing well; there were Charlotte and Emily, of course, and the other Victorian greats George Eliot (Mary Ann Evans), Harriet Martineau, Elizabeth Barrett Browning, and Elizabeth Gaskell; and also a few hangers-on from the previous century who still pumped out novels and poetry, Fanny Burney and Maria Edgeworth among them. With so many successful women writers saturating England's marketplace, men like Lewes were starting to get rankled: "They spoil my market . . . Is this fair? Is it ladylike? Is it endurable?" However annoyed he was at the "sunk capital" of the male author's life, though, even pouty Lewes had to accept, begrudgingly, that some of these women were quite talented. He specifically mentions Fraulein

Fanny Lewald, "not only an authoress but a *German* authoress," and Geraldine Jewsbury, a chain-smoking redhead who "plays with paradoxes" and "paints characters in a [single] phrase . . . *These* women, and some few others have claims."

The next lady he describes, one of these "others," is also the person who, after Charlotte Brontë, likely garnered the most attention in Thackeray's living room once the awkwardness had simmered down. Catherine Crowe was one of the most popular, most prolific writers of the day, and by 1850 she had eight best-selling books, a healthy file of periodical and newspaper contributions, and a committed circle of readers begging for more. She's the only authoress Lewes admitted to flat-out envying—"if her story had not been so good, the *Leader* would have printed mine"—and one of the few Victorian writers who enjoyed a run of success paralleling those of her more famous contemporaries such as Eliot, Dickens, and Thackeray. Edgar Allan Poe emulated her, Charles Dickens betrayed her, and *everyone* knew her name.

Mrs. Crowe was also the one person at Thackeray's party with whom Charlotte Brontë really should have made an effort, not only because of the many things they had in common, but also because Charlotte had just weeks earlier been associated with Catherine in print, and to her great benefit: "How many of us can write novels like Currer Bell, Mrs. Gaskell, Geraldine Jewsbury, Mrs. Marsh, Mrs. Crowe, and fifty others, with their shrewd and delicate observation of life?"

Catherine Crowe was a dynamic personality and a natural hostess, conversationalist, and storyteller, but in her early days you would never have known it. She was as innocuous a child as they come, inactive in a way that other authoresses were not: no juvenilia or letters have surfaced; nor is there any record of her doing anything noteworthy until much later in life. This ordinary youth makes Catherine's early history tricky to extract, even down to her birth. Some place it in Kent, in 1790, while other research leans toward 1800, or even 1803, but for our purposes, it will suffice to say that she came into the world sometime around the year 1800, while Helen Maria Williams was climbing the ranks among the Paris elite and Mary Robinson was saying her final good-byes.

Catherine's father, John Stevens, was the proprietor of one of Regency London's most fashionable establishments. Stevens's Hotel was where Lord Byron and Sir Walter Scott came to take their brandy surrounded by hordes of dandy soldiers, and according to one Captain John Gronow, it was no uncommon thing to find "thirty or forty saddle-horses and tilburys [sporty carriages]" outside the place, waiting for their drunken charges, and that any poor soul not in a uniform would be stared at by the servants and turned away, "very solemnly assured that there was no table vacant." Because of this dedicated clientele, John Stevens was able to afford lodgings in London's Mayfair for himself (where he'd stay for a few days each week to handle his business matters) and a family home in the Kentish hamlet of Borough Green. Catherine was comfortable in both places, it would seem, because her books show a practical knowledge of London alongside a deep appreciation for the countryside. It can also be surmised that, despite all this back-and-forth, she was given a decent education at home: she was fluent in German and had the basics of French, and she played the harp; in short, she achieved in abundance the accomplishments expected of a gentleman's daughter.

In 1822, after living for ten years with her family at 36 Clarges Street—coincidentally, just a few doors down from the apartment Mary Robinson occupied when she first started writing—young Catherine Stevens met and married Captain John Crowe. He was a tall, attractive Irishman who'd fought with distinction at the Battle of Waterloo, but he was older than she, and without much care for domestic life—though it must be said that Catherine probably wasn't very interested in it, either. Considering she may have had as many as thirty-two candles on her birthday cake that year (if we are to believe she was born in 1790), it stands to reason that Captain Crowe's offer of marriage was a now-or-never kind of situation; she may have felt compelled to find someone, *anyone*, to keep her from dreaded Victorian spinsterhood (see chapter 6 for more on that). Yet even if she was closer to a more "normal" age for matrimony—twenty-two or even nineteen, by some estimates of her year of birth—we know, based on her letters and subsequent separation from her husband, that whatever courtship she and John Crowe had was short-lived and less than thrilling. For the moment, though, Catherine had done her duty.

After her wedding in Chichester Cathedral on June 6, she and Captain Crowe departed for Corfu, to live among the regiment and their families (the Greek island was under British control during the Napoleonic Wars). Catherine also duly delivered her own baby, John William Crowe, on July 6, 1823, and continued life as another wife and mother among many.

Then, three years later, disaster struck. Her husband was put on half pay and summarily tossed out of his regiment—and because he was on the wrong side of forty, too old and crotchety for another tour, in a blink John Crowe Sr.'s military career came to a screeching halt. To his deep regret, he and his family had to retreat from their life abroad and start anew in the spa town of Clifton, near Bristol. It must have been a gigantic blow for a veritable military hero with a shining record of service, but for Catherine, it was a whole new beginning. In Clifton, the seeds of her future career were sown.

Why a seasoned veteran with a penchant for excitement chose sleepy, suburban Clifton for retirement isn't known, but perhaps, like the pensioners who flock to Florida, John Crowe was in the mood for the kind of pleasures Clifton could provide. He wasn't alone; the town's cheap rents, mild winters, pretty vistas, ample hot springs, and other soothing diversions were attractive to so many ex-captains of the queen's army that the area was known as "a colony of half-pay notables," as A. B. Graville wrote in his *Spas of England*. Full of men with proud lineages but little money, Clifton could at least provide Captain Crowe with a decent society of sympathetic friends with whom to commiserate.

For Catherine, too, life wasn't so bad among the military has-beens. Her row house in Lower Harley Place, near the River Avon, was well situated for rambles in the woods and among the amenities of Clifton Green, and the homes of her neighbors afforded some excellent socializing. Mrs. Ellen Sharples and her daughter Rolinda, painters who'd both exhibited at the Royal Academy, lived next door, at 2 Lower Harley Place; and from Rolinda's diary we know the two families were very much involved with each other.* They all took their evening tea together,

* Mrs. Sharples was an exhibitor in 1807, and young Rolinda was featured on three separate occasions, in 1820, 1822, and 1824.

often with Mrs. Crowe providing musical entertainment on the harp; strolled to church arm in arm each Sunday; and found all manner of other interesting ways to keep themselves happy in their dull little town. One summer night, for example, Rolinda and Catherine took a donkey cart joyride out on the heath and spent hours dissolved in laughter. The Sharples were both furious overachievers; Rolinda, especially, was engrossed in project after project, and Catherine likely found her company as stimulating as it was riotously fun.

Through the Sharples, Catherine came into contact with another intellectual, Sydney Smith—"the Smith of Smiths," as Lord Macaulay described him—who by this time had several literary feathers in his cap. He'd founded his own periodical, the exalted *Edinburgh Review,* and along with acting as one of its main contributors, he'd also authored multiple books on religion and philosophy. (*A Letter on the Subject of Catholics* and *A Letter to the Electors upon the Catholic Question* are among his most famous.) In Clifton, as a newly elected member of the senior clergy at Bristol Cathedral, Sydney Smith became a regular addition to the Sharples-Crowe circle. His attendance at their dinner parties ensured lots of jocose commentary and observations—and as Catherine sat surrounded by people of wit and industry, something powerful must have shifted inside her. She essentially drops off the map in the ten years between 1828 and 1838—we have little in the way of details about this time by the time she reappears—but considering the magnitude of change that had come to her life, we can only assume she'd taken a good, hard gander at the path laid out before her and found it wanting. We do know that her father's death, from an unknown cause, in 1833, granted her financial freedom, and that her friendship with Smith supplied a big dose of courage and directed her as to what to do with it. (She later described her first acquaintance with this luminous man of letters as the defining moment in her transformation.) However it had happened, by 1838 she'd separated from her husband and moved to Edinburgh to start her literary career. Her marriage was over, and she had money to spend: Catherine Crowe was *free*.

EMERGED FROM HER CHRYSALIS SO LATE, CATHERINE BARreled headlong into her new situation with the confidence of someone who'd been planning her escape for a while. Quickly, and with panache, she raised the curtain on the second, and much fuller, half of her life. She drew on her inheritance to set herself up in a manner befitting a freethinking woman just loosed from her leash: she purchased a gorgeous Georgian-style town house with tall windows in Darnaway Street, Edinburgh; hired a staff; and wasted no time in collecting a spectacular group of socialite friends to adorn her parlor. Sydney Smith had given her a leg up in this regard, by supplying her with a letter of introduction to Lord Francis Jeffrey, the celebrated literary critic with whom Smith had founded *The Edinburgh Review* in 1802, and through Jeffrey she instantly began to sashay among Scotland's finest. In his lavish drawing room at Craigcrook Castle, she came to know Charles Dickens, Sir Walter Scott, and chemist Dr. Samuel Brown, along with the famed phrenologist George Combe, whose *Constitution of Man* and other works she'd read voraciously and of whom she considered herself a disciple. She was already nursing a profound interest in paranormal happenings and the mysteries of the human psyche, something that would later change her life dramatically, so this connection with George Combe was probably particularly exciting.

Socializing aside, now that she was so free and unencumbered, it was to fiction that she directed most of her energies. Again, it must be mentioned that evidence supporting a penchant for writing prior to this moment has never been found, but considering how well even her early works were executed, it stands to reason that she had tried her hand at it before 1838 (and that, somewhere, tantalizingly, her first attempts are waiting to be uncovered). However, as a new writer on the scene, she likely had no idea what would sell, good quality or no, and her first book feels a bit like a tiny toe dip in the waters of wordsmithing: *Aristodemus*, a verse-form tragedy meant for the stage, has been called "forgotten and forgettable" by modern scholars because of its tired structure—unsurprisingly, it didn't sell well at all. That mistake notwithstanding, her verses burst with the germinating seeds of literary excellence. Take, for instance, these lines on the differing values of young and old:

> *Old men live long; they're chary of the life*
> *The younger squander. Life is their dear treasure,*
> *More worthless, more esteemed. The gallant'st*
> *youth*
> *Would dastard [stupidly] turn, and fly one half the*
> *ills,*
> *That these same greybeards cling to.*
> *Life's but the means with us—the bark that floats*
> *Us on to glory or to pleasure, which*
> *We oft-times wreck in the pursuit.*

With *Aristodemus* we can also see another of the rare cases where "By a Lady" can work for the benefit of the authoress. Sales were disappointing, but since no one knew who'd penned the work, Catherine could easily shrug it off and soldier on, name unsullied—which is exactly what happened. She went back to her desk to consider how she should proceed, and within two years she'd produced her answer.

WHEN EDGAR ALLAN POE'S STORY, "THE MURDERS IN THE Rue Morgue" was published in 1841 (in an issue of the Philadelphia-based *Graham's Magazine* dated April 20), the reading world was agog. There were crimes, detectives, false suspects, plot twists—and the end, wow! It was all so new and exciting, and indeed, "Rue Morgue" has long been considered the very first "modern" detective story. Yet though the work was fabulously forward-thinking, "The Murders in the Rue Morgue" had a number of precursors. The title character of Voltaire's novel *Zadig*, published in 1747, is considered a possible inspiration for Poe's C. Auguste Dupin; scholar Lucy Sussex points to William Godwin's *Things as They Are; or, The Adventures of Caleb Williams*, published in 1794, and to the 1827 anonymous novel *Richmond: Scenes in the Life of a Bow Street Runner*, which both have detectives as major characters; and to Ann Radcliffe's *The Mysteries of Udolpho*, also from 1794, for the influence its suspense and intrigue had on the emergence of the female sleuth in literature. Even Jane Austen's *Northanger Abbey* can be taken as a piece of the proto-crime pie, what with its protagonist's impulsive clue-sniffing escapades; it's usually, and rightly, considered part of the Gothic genre, but Catherine Morland's passion for investigation could perhaps be considered an embryonic antecedent to future female characters with magnifying glasses in their pockets, such as Catherine Crowe's Susan Hopley.

Published in January 1841, preceding "The Murders in the Rue Morgue" by just months, *The Adventures of Susan Hopley; or, Circumstantial Evidence* features exactly the kind of plot points Poe would come to favor: a murder or disappearance followed by a detection drama, all wound up in a complex narrative skein that is unraveled only at the end. And since it was written with nigh-unbelievable skill and fluidity (considering it was only Catherine's second book), *Susan Hopley* was exactly the kind of thing Poe wished for: a supertriumphant best seller. Everyone bought it, most loved it, and much of later nineteenth- and twentieth-century crime fiction would come to emulate it. "It is powerful, beyond all question," said one reviewer. "When we had read the first twenty pages, the book was not again lain down."

The plotting of *Susan Hopley*, riddled with coincidences and details that are later revealed to be less trifling than one is led to suppose, is a feat of cunning. In a flash, the story flips from one point of view to another, and soon it becomes clear that Susan isn't a customary *Jane Eyre*-type lead; rather, she's a particularly bright thread in a tapestry of people and events. Here she is, our unlikely heroine:

> *Worthy, excellent Susan! Methinks I see her now, in her neat, plaited cap, snuff-coloured stuff gown, clean white apron, and spectacles on the nose, plying her knitting needles, whose labours were to result in a comfortable pair of lamb's-wool stockings for my next winter's wear, or a warm waistcoat for poor old Jeremy; or in something, be it what it might, that was to contribute to the welfare and*

> *benefit of some human being; and I believe, if it had so happened that the whole human race had been miraculously provided to repletion with warm stockings and waistcoats, that Susan, rather than let her fingers be idle and not be doing something for somebody, would have knit jackets for the shorn lambs and blankets for the early calves.*

She's wrapped in a plain, self-sacrificing package, yes, but Susan is a daredevil. Through the narrative of her employer, Harry Leeson, we learn that many years ago, before this quiet, honest, benevolent girl came to warm his hearth by serving tea "sweetened exactly to my liking," along with pleasant chats, she was the principal detective in a series of investigations that led, each time, to capture of the guilty and vindication of the innocent. She and her brother, Andrew, were first under the employ of Harry Leeson's adoptive father, the good Mr. Wentworth, and together with Wentworth's daughter, Fanny, they lived in gilded glee. However, Fanny's fiancé, Mr. Gaveston, will stop at nothing to attain Fanny's *and* Harry's shares of the Wentworth inheritance. Gaveston first tries to drown young Harry (but is thwarted by Andrew's exceptional swimming), then dear Mr. Wentworth is found with his throat slit. And when Andrew is found missing along with a lusty servant girl, Mabel, it is swiftly determined that he must have murdered Mr. Wentworth and escaped abroad.

Susan is unconvinced. Sensing a deception, she immediately resolves to "go over to the house that had been the scene of the catastrophe, and inspect every part of it herself." She has no training, yet she still manages to find an important bit of evidence: "a pair of little studs united by a chain, with a bit of coloured glass in each; on one was inscribed W.G.... the initials of Mr. Gaveston." However, a clue though she has, she's just a servant girl, and one with a lot to gain from her brother's exoneration; she can't step forward without having her motives questioned, so she heads for London, where she and her "unhappy story" are less well known, to start a new life for herself.

In the city, as she bounces from job to job, it becomes clear that her forte is the Sherlockian arts. One of her employers is accused of stealing, and Susan proves her innocent; one has a daughter who marries an Italian count, and Susan is the first to suspect (rightly) that he's not actually a count; and later, when she's accompanying the bride on her Continental tour, Susan recognizes Mabel, the servant who supposedly ran off with her brother after he allegedly murdered Mr. Wentworth. Mabel has changed her name and married a French nobleman—and she has no idea what happened back in England all those years ago, because villainous Mr. Gaveston lured her away before the crime occurred. Astounded at the turn of events, she joins forces with virtuous, estimable Susan and a cadre of other detectives to track down the guilty parties. Finally, all is made right:

> *Mr. Gaveston, when he left the court, seeing that all that remained for him was a life of infamy or a disgraceful death, fled with all speed to Brussels; where, after making a will . . . he retired to his chamber in the hotel, and blew out his brains.*

Catherine Crowe was criticized for this and other dark moments in the novel (which, after all, features cold-blooded murder and condemnation of innocent folk). Yet despite its macabre qualities, *Susan Hopley* sold wildly among all classes of society. Crowe's dexterity at weaving the narrative threads into one neat conclusion left reviewers in awe. "We hardly know what to say of this book," said one, "it perplexes us extremely . . . Incidents, at first minute and carelessly thrown in, grow up by degrees into matters of great importance and elaborate art." And Susan, "through all the intricacies of the story," wrote another critic, "winds her way with preternatural ease" toward the conclusion as "the *Dea Vindix* [avenging goddess] who unties all its knots."

Amazing though it was, some found this new style of writing a little grating. Mrs. Gaskell considered it good only for those "in certain states of mind in which one is too lazy for thought or any high feeling, and only *up* to being a bit occupied by scenes passed before you without much connexion, like those unrolling views we show children." Catherine's friend Sydney Smith needed a little convincing, too, and wrote that the incidents in the novel were overly improbable—"A boy goes on board a frigate in the middle of the night, and penetrates to the captain's cabin without being seen . . . Susan climbs into a two-pair-of-stairs [i.e., second-story] window to rescue two grenadiers . . . and so on"—but ultimately he thought very highly of it and praised Catherine's ability to carry the reader eagerly to the end.

It was this skillful storytelling that propelled the work forward even with its perceived flaws; the novel became impossible to ignore, and then it went to the stage. The theatrical version of *Susan Hopley* opened in London at the end of May 1841 and, after a run of three hundred nights there, found similar success in America and Australia. It's unlikely Edgar Allan Poe was ignorant of the novel, and in fact he could have been exposed to it *before* writing "The Murders in the Rue Morgue": Buoyed by the successful transatlantic voyages of Isambard Kingdom Brunel's and Junius Smith's steam-driven ships in 1838, Samuel Cunard launched his British and North American Royal Mail Steam Packet Company soon thereafter, initiating regular mail runs between the continents. Attaining a copy of the book, and the newspapers reviewing it, would have been simple. This historical fogginess notwithstanding, it's clear that, considering how much of Wilkie Collins's early work reflects Catherine's techniques, the significance of *Susan Hopley* was far-reaching and profound.*

BACK IN EDINBURGH, CATHERINE CROWE CELEBRATED HER success quietly—by settling down at her desk to write more books. She produced *Men and Women; or, Manorial Rights*, another work of mystery, using the same themes and meticulous structure; the first of her five brilliant books for children, *Pippie's Warning*; and *The Story of Lilly Dawson*, which, of all her novels published in the years after *Susan Hopley*, amassed the greatest praise—critics commended its "admirable psychological ingenuity" and hailed her characterization of Lilly Dawson's friend Miss May Elliot as "perhaps one of the ablest in fiction." Catherine also published short stories, including one that appeared in an 1846 issue of *Hogg's Weekly Instructor* titled "A Story of a Weir-Wolf."

---

* Wilkie Collins, friend and protégé to Charles Dickens and author of *The Woman in White*, borrowed from Catherine Crowe on two occasions. His first crime story features a maidservant detective bearing a strong resemblance to Susan Hopley, and his later novel *No Name* reuses one of her plot devices: "Identifying a criminal by cutting, unobserved, a scrap of cloth from their clothing, then producing it, like a jigsaw piece, in evidence." See Sussex, "Detective Maidservant."

Catherine's circle of friends was rapidly expanding along with her literary output, and by 1848 she'd made the acquaintance of many celebrities. A close friendship with Thomas De Quincey, author of *Confessions of an English Opium-Eater,* developed during the course of her salon parties at Darnaway Street and at Lord Francis Jeffrey's late-night soirees. She also lavishly entertained the American writer and lecturer Ralph Waldo Emerson, and he in turn introduced her to the Carlyles of London—the same Carlyles who would accompany her to Thackeray's Charlotte Brontë soiree in 1850—who became great friends of hers. (Their works of philosophy, history, and mathematics, and their books of letters are recognized today as some of the greatest of the nineteenth century.*) In 1846 she even stopped in for dinner at Rydal Mount, home of the Wordsworths.

Catherine also came to know her illustrious neighbor Robert Chambers, who with his brother William founded *Chambers's Edinburgh Journal* and W. and R. Chambers Publishers, two of the most successful literary enterprises in Edinburgh. Chambers was a formidable author in his own right: he'd just published, anonymously, his extraordinarily popular *Vestiges of the Natural History of Creation.* It was an important, though somewhat misdirected, precursor to Darwin's *On the Origin of Species,* and speculation about its authorship ran rampant throughout the decade. Some attributed it to female mathematician Ada Love-

* Jane Carlyle was principally known as a letter writer, but she's also been cited as the inspiration for her husband's writings. Of Thomas's works, there are many to reference: His *On Heroes, Hero-Worship, and the Heroic in History* defines the modern theory of history (most especially the Great Man Theory); *Sartor Resartus* directly influenced Emerson's transcendentalism; and the Carlyle circle, a circle by which to solve quadratic equations, is used every day in thousands of classrooms.

lace, and others even suspected Prince Albert as its author, but there were more than a few who felt that Catherine Crowe, described by Scottish journalist Alexander Ireland as a "very clever, eccentric person" with "the reputation of dabbling a little in science," was the obvious culprit. Catherine was definitely enthusiastic about *Vestiges*, but as to its origin, she was as clueless as the rest of them. One night over dinner she was even accused of having written "that naughty book" in front of the author himself:

> *The situation was delicious. As the talk went on, the consciously guilty ones exchanged furtive glances, and were scarcely able to maintain the gravity required . . . "I have a strong suspicion," said the questioner, "that my vis-à-vis Mrs.—[Crowe], is the author . . . Come now, confess. You cannot deny it." To our surprise and infinite amusement, the lady did not deny "the soft impeachment." She hesitated and looked embarrassed, but said nothing, only shaking her head and laughing in a sly significant way,—as much as to say, "I can keep my own secret when I choose, and I will not have it forced from me by this rude fellow." The incident was a source of much amusement when recalled in after days, and afforded many a hearty laugh to the chief-conspirator and his confederates.*

If only they knew just how eccentric Catherine had become. In the years following *Susan Hopley*, her interest in the paranormal had grown beyond the bounds of mere "dabbling." She was obsessed with phrenology, mesmerism, somnambulism, and the supernatural, and after publishing a translation of German poet and medical writer Justinus Andreas Christian Kerner's *Seeress of Prevorst: Being Revelations Concerning the Inner-Life of Man and the Inter-Diffusion of a World of Spirits in the One We Inhabit,* she was absolutely full-up on spiritualism and the many questions surrounding it: is there a whole other dimension, a spirit world, existing here alongside us?

In this thinking, she wasn't alone. During the first half of the nineteenth century, as England underwent rapid, unregulated industrialization, a niggling sense of unease was developing amid all the change. Human muscle was being replaced by iron and steam; science and technology were becoming the powers behind all forward motion; industry and productivity were the gods of the land. Within this obsession with materialism, the philosophical climate grew extremely prejudiced against anything one couldn't measure with science, and accordingly, even with the many millions of dollars the new trade markets poured into industrialized England's economy, there was a pervading sense of emotional and intellectual dissatisfaction. Gray, smoky cities and clacking machines just couldn't be the answer to everything.

Thus the Spiritualist movement gained steam in both the United Kingdom and the United States, and with it a renewed interest in trying not only to prove the existence of a world outside our perceived one, but also to reach it, communicate with it, move around within it. In 1848, American sisters Kate and Margaret Fox made headlines when they claimed to have initiated conversation with a spirit via "rappings" (table tapping or, in this case, finger snapping). They snapped, challenged the ghost to snap back, and, as reported by Sir Arthur Conan Doyle in his *History of Spiritualism,* were "instantly answered." Even though the girls had no special training, and the apparition was (it was assumed) just a regular guy, "the spiritual telegraph was at last working . . . [It] was the supreme sign of a new departure." With that, the cult of Spiritualism spread like wildfire, and soon London was filled with people calling themselves mediums; dinner dates turned séances became more common, and you could now have your fortune told or speak with a dead relative after your evening port and cigar.

Many met this wave of paranormal babble with skepticism and suspicion, but those searching for truth amid the dogma of science and technology welcomed these strange communications with open arms—and Catherine Crowe, already a confirmed expert on the occult and known for her ever-eager, excitable temperament, was one of the latter. Inspired by *The Seeress of Prevorst* and George Combe's research, she'd spent the previous few years contemplating dreams, ghosts, presentiments, spectral lights, and haunted houses—she was sure there was one near her childhood home in Kent—obsessing over accounts of doppelgängers and sprites, and continuing to question, with seriousness, why centuries-old spirituality, rather than religion, could not be reintroduced to England under the umbrella of reason. Given time and research, she believed, the two could be blended—"Extend the bounds of nature and science, till they comprise within their limits all the phenomena, ordinary and extraordinary, by which we are surrounded," she wrote. And in proving this union of the supernatural and science, it seems Catherine was determined and adventurous. At an 1848 dinner party hosted by Dr. James Young Simpson, who just months later would discover the anesthetic properties of chloroform, she and another guest drank ether, turned to their neighbors, and "laughed with open, dead, eyes." She enjoyed herself, but fellow guest Hans Christian Andersen, of fairy-tale fame, was thoroughly shaken; he recounted in his diary that the experience was "uncanny . . . I had a feeling of being with two mad people."

Catherine's cogitation on the supernatural culminated in what would become, and remain, her most famous work. *The Night-Side of Nature; or, Ghosts and Ghost Seers* has been classified as a collection of ghost stories, but it is in fact a cogent, dynamic treatise on the value of an open mind superimposed over tales of trances, stigmata, apparitions, and other wonders. Using a huge collection of historical and contemporary examples, Mrs. Crowe calls for a nonjudgmental approach to the possibility of an "other" world and attacks those who would deny its presence outright. Could people accommodate a reality more encompassing than the one industrialized, mechanized, for-profit science provided? She thought so:

> *Somewhat of the mystery of our own being, and of the mysteries that compass us about, are beginning to loom upon us . . . and, in the endeavor to follow out the clue[s] they offer, we have but a feeble light to guide us. We must grope our way through the dim path before us, ever in danger of being led into error, whilst we may confidently reckon on being pursued by the shafts of ridicule—that weapon so easy to wield, so potent to the weak, so weak to the wise—which has delayed the birth of so many truths, but never stifled one. The pharisaical skepticism which denies without investigation, is quite as perilous, and much more contemptible than the blind credulity which accepts all that it is taught without enquiry; it is,*

indeed, but another form of ignorance assuming to be knowledge.

During the Middle Ages, Catherine claims, "nobody thought of seeking the explanation of the facts they witnessed in natural causes." Anyone, therefore, who arose as a witch or sorcerer could only be assumed to have been cursed by God, rather than afflicted by some natural cause, and in the ensuing persecution, men, women, and children were killed as an offering to what she calls "the demon of superstition." Now that this kind of action was considered barbarous and unjustifiable, society's opinions had become fully the reverse of that of the ancients: "From believing in everything, they ceased to believe anything . . . man's spiritual nature was forgotten; and what the sense could not apprehend, nor the understanding account for, was pronounced impossible."

Catherine was convinced that things were improving, though. In spite of the materialists and their get-rich-quick schemes, the machines, the smoke, and the new obsession with productivity, "the wise men of the world will, ere long, be obliged to give in their adherence to Shakspere's [*sic*] much quoted axiom, and confess that 'there *are* more things in heaven than are dreamt of in their philosophy' . . . Thank God! We have lived through [it]."

This friendly tone, so cordial and accepting, in combination with her philosophy of tolerance, rallied people to the cause and sold thousands of books: sixteen editions of *The Night-Side of Nature* were issued over six years, all over Europe and in America, to a public eager to revel in Crowe's "shadowy borderland," as one reviewer described it, "where the eye dwells on a swarth canopy of clouds, and the ear catches stray cadences of ineffable speech, and the feet stumble on dark mountains—there, on the Night-Side of Nature, loves Mrs. Crowe to pitch her tent." The reviewer goes on to repent his earlier belief in the ways of materialism—"the ordinary vice of such as fancy themselves wiser than their neighbors"—and lauds Catherine for her ability to address a subject many found beyond comprehension with a voice "so positive and real . . . her readers are commonly moved to go some way with her." Indeed, Catherine's voice was the first in what would soon become a literary chorus against dehumanizing technology. (In Bram Stoker's *Dracula,* for instance, published at the height of the Spiritualist movement, Dr. Van Helsing sarcastically laments our "enlightened age, when men believe not even what they see.") *Night-Side* was widely read and oft quoted, substantiating Catherine Crowe as a pioneering figure in the study of the unknown. Yet its popularity eventually came to overshadow her other achievements; her works of fiction fell into obscurity even while she lived, and her mind, so full of the paranormal, began to unravel.

BY 1852—FOUR YEARS AFTER *NIGHT-SIDE* HAD MADE HER AN icon in the social, artistic, literary, and now scientific life of Edinburgh and beyond—Catherine had published six novels and started a seventh; compiled a volume of short stories and novelettes, issued as *Light and Darkness* in 1850; and contributed more than three dozen articles to the periodicals. Robert Chambers's *Edinburgh Journal* printed a number of her works, and in 1850, Charles Dickens ran her story "The Loaded Dice" in his newfangled magazine, *Household Words* (though he deemed it "horribly dismal" and instructed the editor to delete some of the darker, more morbid material, especially "that part about the sister's madness"). On top of this, her son, John William, had resigned his commission in the Eighty-Third Regiment and come to stay with her at Darnaway Street. That October, he was married to Phemie Menzies, daughter of a Scottish army officer, and within a year Catherine Crowe was a grandmother. Domestically and professionally, she was likely overwhelmed.

Her studies of the occult had continued, however, and were now bordering on manic. Day and night she pored over texts and diaries, obsessed over theories, and felt with increasing intensity the desire to prove or disprove humankind's ability to commune with spirits. She wanted desperately to publish a second installment of *The Night-Side of Nature*, outlining her ideas on the subject, but she was uncomfortable doing it without more evidence. So, seemingly undeterred by her diabolical schedule, she spent a great deal of time traveling between Edinburgh, London, and the Continent to attend séances and demonstrations, documenting her observations all the while and thinking of little else. Yet Catherine was not young—she was somewhere between fifty-two and sixty-four at this point—and it was only a matter of time before all this physical and mental effort took its toll.

The traveling might also have been part of a plan to distract herself, because by February 1854, nearly everything around her looked grim. Her newest novel, *Linny Lockwood*, hadn't done as well as her others, and she was also growing frustrated with her lack of progress in untangling the knotty world of Spiritualism. None of her hypotheses had yet been proven, and as she finally confessed to the American publisher who'd agreed to issue her *Night-Side* sequel, printing would have to wait—there was still "much that is most perplexing connected with the phenomena."

In need of friendly environs, she decided to travel back to Edinburgh for a visit with Robert Chambers and George Combe, but it being February, the trip was grueling, and when she finally got settled, she was thoroughly ill.

Her morale was low, her body was weak, her mind a-jumble with undone tasks and baffling speculations, and soon her condition reached its nadir. On the night of February 26, Catherine was discovered by Robert Chambers in what he later called "a terrible condition of mad exposure"—naked in the streets of Edinburgh, muttering, believing herself to be quite invisible. As the story goes, she was promptly bundled up and taken inside on the shoulders of her concerned friends, but she'd drawn a great amount of attention to herself in the process. Before long, Edinburgh was abuzz with the tale of the wandering naked authoress.

Writer and actress Fanny Kemble heard about it a few days later, recounting with further detail, whether or not accurate, that Catherine had had a vision of the Virgin Mary and Jesus Christ, "both of whom commanded her to go without any clothes on into the streets" for a walk, with just one addendum: "She received the assurance that if she took her card-case in her right hand and her pocket-handkerchief in her left, her condition of nudity would be entirely unobserved . . . [and] under the influence of her diseased fancy, Mrs. Crowe accordingly went forth." Rumors being rumors, Fanny's version was just one of a tittering, jittering mass of gossip, and however inaccurate it was becoming, a story so sensational just couldn't be stopped. Charles Dickens joined in the laughter, too, and assiduously padded the tale with some of his characteristically off-color flourishes. "One of the curious manifestations of her disorder," he wrote, "is that she can bear nothing black. There is a terrific business to be done, even when they are obliged to put coals on her fire . . . she is now in a mad-house and, I fear, hopelessly insane."

We don't know exactly how it happened, but the reality of the situation was probably far less dramatic. It's true that some kind of psychological mishap occurred as a result of her mental and physical strain, and that there was a resulting intervention by Robert Chambers, but it's more feasible that, rather than hauling a naked Catherine up the stairs over his shoulder, he simply provided for her while she lay in abstraction. (Also, considering the weather in February in Scotland, a nude midnight constitutional seems downright silly, even for someone who was mentally ill.) It is also known that five or six days later, she was in London at Hanwell Asylum under the care of perhaps the greatest authority on insanity then, Dr. John Conolly, whose diagnosis was reassuring: she was suffering from the effects of stress, he said, and the fact that she'd been enmeshed in ghosts and ghouls for too long without a break wasn't helping. Catherine was told to rest for a few months, and went home delusion-free.

She quickly wrote to the papers explaining as much, but the damage was done. It was all too easy for those with prejudices against women, who were already notorious for fainting spells, dizzy fits, and in the worst cases, "hysteria" (which, incredibly, was believed to be caused by the uterus wandering about the body of its own volition), to use her story to protest the new, more-prominent place of the fairer sex in society, and to denounce Spiritualism as fraudulent hoo-hah. There was simply too much fun to be had at Catherine's expense; so, from mouth to mouth, her story went. It began in the papers, first with an anonymous paragraph in the *Times* and two more, on separate occasions, in *Zoist,* which also printed Crowe's retort and another from one of her friends (though, apart from its willingness to show both sides of the story, *Zoist* was by no means nice about it*). She also appeared in the works of artist William Bell Scott, and in the diary of popular novelist Mrs. Archer Clive. Then there were the countless letters and notes passed around England, most notably by rumormonger Charles Dickens—"she is now under restraint, of course!"—and Lord Robert Lytton. In plain terms, poor Mrs. Crowe had become Lady Godiva.

Charles Dickens's reaction was typical, for there *was* a fierce (though not wholly unexpected) backlash against Spiritualism and the ideas its followers were promulgating. Yet, in fairness to Catherine, and considering the calamitous price she would pay for this indiscretion, it's worth mentioning that Dickens acted particularly callously. She undoubtedly considered him a friend, and he most certainly thought highly of her work, as seen in his review of *Night-Side*: "The authoress of 'Susan Hopley' and 'Lilly Dawson' has established her title to a hearing whenever she chooses to claim one. She can never be read without pleasure and profit, and can never write otherwise than sensibly and well." Though he ultimately used his review to protest her philosophy, worrying about the "common fault of trying

---

* "If [she] went naked into the streets, exposing her exquisite and hitherto unseen and unappreciated beauties of shape and hue, she must to my poor apprehension have been mad . . . and very fit for Dr. ———, who, perhaps, sent her away . . . both because she was *no longer mad* and moreover was *very disagreeably disagreeable* . . . I hope [Mrs. Crowe] will give the results to the scientific world of her investigations into the recondite and doubtful matter of true science: and when she writes to me again will not aim at surpassing the very pretty little bit of Christianity which closes her epistle." From *Zoist,* April 1854.

to prove too much," he was in support of her literary efforts and had been for years. After the Edinburgh incident, though, he publicly rejected Crowe and dismissed her as "a medium, and an Ass," a pretty nasty jab from someone with whom she had shared, and enjoyed, so many evenings. It says a lot for her personality, however, that Dickens was the only friend she lost: George Eliot and Harriet Martineau were both sympathetic from the start, applauding her bravery for standing up to the editors at *Zoist,* and Sydney Smith, Robert Chambers, and George Combe were all completely on her side.*

Though she was surrounded by attentive friends, this upheaval was still a professional catastrophe of the worst order for Catherine. The second installment of *Night-Side* was permanently shelved, and the only other book she would publish on Spiritualism would be short and "obviously troubled." Yet she did continue writing, albeit in a simpler, less taxing form, directed at children. She penned two ingenious versions of *Uncle Tom's Cabin,* one for elementary ages and another for young adults; *The Story of Arthur Hunter and His First Shilling*; and *The Adventures of a Monkey,* among others. She was able to live comfortably off the profits for the remainder of her life, but seeing how her other works have languished in obscurity for more than one hundred fifty years, it's unfortunate that such a severe breakdown befell her—today, the incident would quickly have been eclipsed by another outrageous display from another celebrity,

* George Eliot, whom she met in 1852 in Edinburgh, and Harriet Martineau were both correspondents of Crowe's. Their letters are filed with Special Collections at the University of Kent.

but in a Victorian England, bound by the laws of decorum and respectability, to rebel so rashly meant career suicide.

This is not to say that her life after 1854 was all sackcloth and ashes. On the contrary, she found her strength again with the enviable gusto she'd always displayed. As soon as she was well, Catherine joined her son, granddaughter, and daughter-in-law in Belgium for some spa hopping and companionship just as the summer was winding down; she even ran into William Thackeray, who after four years away from her, described, as a good old friend would, "that cheery, good-natured Mrs. Crowe." An excellent linguist, she traveled frequently over the next decade, as the 1860s approached—her time in Greece as a newlywed was still in the back of her mind—relishing her sunset years in Europe and England, with friends or as a solo vacationer. She rented a house with her son on Lake Windermere, and for a while wrote letters from Paris and Boulogne, and from Dieppe, where, after encountering her in the same hotel, she dined several times with the famous Elizabeth Gaskell. Soon after, she settled with John William and Phemie at 22 Sandgate Road, in Folkestone, Kent, and died at a ripe old age in 1872.

Though Catherine Crowe lost many fans near the close of her career (and consequently, the attention of today's readers), she was one of Victorian England's most talented and varied authoresses. Her literary abilities never went unnoticed by the critics, especially her fondness for combining unlikely situations with simple, understandable, even homely characters and dialogue: "The writer, in a word, has the art of *reality*," as one reviewer put it. She was also praised for her depiction of women and their predicament, how they were seen as men's accessories rather than human beings in their own right, and were thus unprepared for adult life; how ignorance and parental apathy led to horrible marriages; and how a lack of education made women tremendously vulnerable in England's changing society. Catherine wrote women as she wished they could be: resourceful, industrious, lionhearted; and in so doing, she offered an early challenge to the ideals the Victorians demanded with increasing intensity over the coming years. "The circumstances of her heroines . . . would possibly have been condemned by writers of Miss Austen's school as hopelessly vulgar," English writer Adeline Sergeant wrote in 1897, "but Mrs. Crowe's way of treating these characters and their surroundings bears upon it no stamp of vulgarity at all . . . One is conscious of a note of hard common sense and a power of seeing things as they really are."

five

SARA COLERIDGE

[1802–1852]

When Sarah Fricker Coleridge,* her husband, Samuel Taylor Coleridge, and their four-year-old son, Hartley, first arrived there in 1800 (around the time of Catherine Crowe's birth and Mary Robinson's premature death), the beauty of Greta Hall was a welcome sight for Mrs. Coleridge. After a tiring journey of more than three hundred miles, she confessed herself "most delightfully situated," once she'd settled into the simple yet comfortable house. It had crisp white lines, yet it wasn't elegant: the place was shoddily built, every stick of furniture in

* There are a great many "Saras" and "Sarahs" to keep track of among the Lake Poet families. Mrs. Sarah Fricker Coleridge (that's Sarah with an *h*) was Samuel Taylor Coleridge's wife, and sister to Edith Fricker Southey, who was married to Robert Southey. Sara Hutchinson was Coleridge's lover, and our Sara Coleridge was Sarah and Samuel Taylor's daughter. Significantly, Samuel Taylor asked that his daughter's name be spelled without the *h*, to reflect not his wife's spelling, but his lover's.

it was second- or thirdhand, the walls were bare, and its position upon a grassy swell meant bone-chilling, window-rattling drafts in the winter. (Robert Southey called it the "Palace of the Winds.") Yet with the town of Keswick just moments away, Skiddaw's towering bulk almost abutting the back of the house, and the family's dear friends William and Dorothy Wordsworth nearby at Grasmere, Greta Hall was perfect. From its lower-floor windows visitors enjoyed a panorama of St. Johns-in-the-Vale, a picturesque Lake District valley, and from upstairs, a peek of Derwentwater and its small clutch of islands. Samuel Taylor Coleridge found the place so arresting that he had trouble shaving with his mirror opposite the window: "Some Mountain or Peak is rising out of the Mist, or some Slanting Column of misty sunlight is sailing across me . . . I offer up soap and blood daily, as an Eyeservant of the Goddess Nature."

These days the drama of the horizon has been replaced by the banality of modern buildings, but inside Greta Hall, things are much the same as they were during the early nineteenth century. Both the kitchen and the main hallway still have their original flooring, and several cast iron fireplaces have been preserved. The second-floor study, with its broad windows and yawning ceiling, is most certainly the grandest room of the house. It was the favored haunt of Robert Southey after he and his wife moved in with Mrs. Coleridge, but today it serves as a family library. The house originally came well stocked with more than five hundred books—one of the other advantages of relocating here for Southey and Mr. and Mrs. Coleridge. And nowadays, the antique volumes have been joined by others: modern works on the Lake Poets.

Three of those poets, Robert Southey, William Wordsworth, and Samuel Taylor Coleridge, have all been anthologized extensively; they've been the subject of biographies on multiple occasions; their swarm of correspondence has been published again and again; and their works have rarely been out of print. A smattering of titles addressing the wives, daughters, and sisters of these eminent men have also appeared (a notable example is Kathleen Jones's *A Passionate Sisterhood*), but however important these women were to their male counterparts, their own contributions to literature have been marginalized, or condemned as "minor."

Sara Coleridge, born at Greta Hall, has unfortunately suffered the latter fate. Living in the colossal shadow of her father, Samuel Taylor Coleridge, and burdened by Victorian England's strict code of female conduct, even percipient young Sara, who by the age of twenty-two had published two books and acquired the full use of *six* languages, couldn't escape the overarching demands of womanhood. Her work correspondingly reflects a person beleaguered by interruptions. It's not epic or grandiose, like that of George Eliot or Charlotte and Emily Brontë, for that would have required exactly the kind of long, undisturbed hours she *didn't* have. Instead, Sara Coleridge's writings consist mostly of essays, translations, introductions, appendices, and poetry—things that could be written in short bursts during her off-hours—as opposed to novels. (The one novel she did write, however, would become her most lasting contribution.) Many weren't even original: she spent eighteen years of her life editing and repackaging her father's work.

Sara lived in a time of postrevolutionary political conservatism—as opposed to the more rebellious days of the

Wollstonecraftian yesteryear—and at first glance, she appears even to have *embraced* the values of the patriarchy. She has given us no forceful depiction of or any obvious attack on the crushing cultural mores with regard to women; she never joined in any chorus against this injustice or that exploitation. For these reasons, it appears, she has been ignored—she's too conventional, too restrained to warrant much regard.

A second glance at Sara Coleridge, however, reveals not only an intellect worth studying, but also a woman who took an especially clever and calculating path to publication. Her work was crucial in establishing her father's legacy as a philosopher and poet, and through these efforts she was also able to (if subtly) assert her own literary prowess. She could be a writer while *appearing* subservient, switching, at a whim, between the two roles of "Angel in the House" and "Virago of the Press"—the latter of which she used to describe Harriet Martineau—without visibly breaking any rules. She lived what was essentially a double life, and she lived it amid a constant stream of impediments. Even as she battled depression (nervous "hysteria") and an ugly drug dependency, she continued to apply herself to scholarship and to the great task of "putting in order a literary house"—that of her father, whom she barely knew—and to producing a novel that would later be recognized as the first of its genre in English.

While digging through Samuel Taylor Coleridge's great mass of papers and letters, Sara found occasional references to herself, "a remarkably interesting Baby; with the fairest possible skin, and large blue eyes—and she smiles as if she were basking in a sunshine as mild as moonlight, of her own quiet happiness." As she continued this work through the last years of her life, before she died of breast cancer in 1852, it became clear to her that while she played on the floor of idyllic Greta Hall, the family was anything but happy.

Samuel was away in Wales, amusing himself with his lover, Sara Hutchinson, when his wife gave birth to their daughter, alone, on Christmas Day 1802. He came home to meet the baby—"[a] GIRL! I had never thought of a Girl as a possible event"—and with that, his participation in raising her ended. By New Year's Day he'd unceremoniously departed once again, without recording Sara's birth on the frontispiece of the family Bible, as he had for each of his three sons: Hartley, Berkeley (who died of consumption in infancy), and Derwent. In daughter Sara's mind, this oversight was "an omen of our lifelong separation, for I never lived with him for more than a few weeks at a time."

Samuel's absence from his family, combined with his opium addiction and wandering eye, kept his marriage in a constant state of strain. Finally, after years of torment for both husband and wife, he left for good, and Mrs. Coleridge's brother-in-law Robert Southey (who would soon become poet laureate) took over the care of Greta Hall and its inhabitants. It was a decided improvement having good Uncle Southey and his children around, and Sara thrived. Living in proximity to his genius and her mother's doting attention, she blossomed into an avid thinker. She relished her studies; she was dedicated, focused, and enthusiastic about all things literary and linguistic. Over the next few years she even managed to outdistance her brothers, who were enjoying formal schooling at Ambleside and later at Oxford: "[She] has received an education here at home that would astonish you," as Southey reported in 1815, when Sara was thirteen years old.

"She is a good French and Italian scholar, a tolerable Latinist, and is now learning Spanish. She has begun music also, and is said by those who are competent in the subject to display most extraordinary talents for it."

By Sara's own account, the remaining hours of each day were spent happily, on the whole, despite her father's absence; she played and danced, caught anemones in the coastal village of Allonby, and adventured outdoors. Southey was regularly pulled from the comfort of his second-floor study to scramble up one of the Lake District's many mountains with Sara and the other children, or to carry a picnic to Walla Crag. When the weather was bad, there were kittens with names like Hurlyburlybuss, Baron Chinchilla, Pope Joan, and Arch Duchess Knurry-murry-hurry-purry-skurry to play with—Southey recorded the many "cat-astrophes" at Greta Hall in an essay called "Memoirs of Cats Eden," published later in his prose collection *The Doctor*—and of course there were lots of things to read. Southey wrote personalized stories for Sara and the other kids, the most famous of which is *The Three Bears,* and for this and all his love, Sara worshipped him (and when it came time for her to marry, in 1829, it was Southey, not her father, who gave her away).

Southey was also responsible for setting Sara to work on her first real literary enterprise. He had originally presented Martin Dobrizhoffer's *Historia de Abiponibus* to her brother Derwent for translation as a way to offset some education costs, and Sara had agreed to assist, but Derwent soon abandoned it when he zipped off to Cambridge. Left to her own devices, Sara charged forward, and at age nineteen, she saw her book, *An Account of the Abiphones, an Equestrian People of Paraguay,* published by John Murray. This in itself was an amazing accomplishment: John Murray's desk was piled up to the proverbial ceiling with submissions from authors trying to get in with the man who had published Lord Byron, including one from Jane Austen—Murray printed *Emma* in 1815, with that grudging dedication to Prince George—thus his interest in Sara spoke very highly of her abilities. Even with Murray's fame, reception for the book was muted, but it was still complimentary of Sara's skill and scholarship. "How she Dobrizhoffered it all out, it puzzles my slender Latinity to conjecture," wrote Charles Lamb, poet and author of a popular children's version of Shakespeare's tales. He couldn't get enough of it:

> *Yes, I have seen Miss Coleridge, and wish I had just such a—daughter. God love her—to think that she should have had to toil thro' five octavos of that cursed (I forget I write to a Quaker) Abbeypony History, and then to abridge them to 3 . . . at her years, to be doing stupid Jesuit's Latin into English, when she should be reading or writing Romances. Heaven send her Uncle do not breed her up [to be] a Quarterly Reviewer!*

Charles Lamb had placed great faith in her talents (and with good foresight, for she *would* become a critic for the great literary periodical *Quarterly Review* later in life). Others were a little put off by her exuberant, sometimes hurried style, but any unfavorable reviews were easily forgotten once she received a banknote from John Murray for the sum of £113, which would be more than £8,900 today. It was her little slice of success. And though she may not have cared about her father's opinion after he finally got around to reading it, ten years later, his belated comments must've been gratifying nonetheless: "My dear daughter's translation of this book is, in my judgment, unsurpassed for pure mother English by anything I have read for a long time."

Sara was indeed a prodigy, but a career in writing was always out of the question. The expectations placed upon her were no different from those that burdened most young women of her day: her enthusiasm for writing did not preclude eventual abandonment of it as she came of marriageable age. Like all young women, she was enveloped in day-to-day preparations for marriage (music lessons, dancing lessons), and was just as clueless about wedded life as the rest of her peers, for in this strict society it was difficult to get information about the minutiae of a marriage. Novels were miserly in their descriptions of what happened after the vows were exchanged and the fun honeymoon was had in Brighton, and apart from the opaque insinuations of the moralizing conduct literature that was still widely read, or the occasional letter from a married friend, girls had no idea what to expect beyond the altar. It's surprising, considering that marriage was the single most important event in a woman's life, and what with the innumerable measures taken to prepare young women to become wives. Yet it must be remembered that, as questions of feminine morality (and, ipso facto, the sanctity of a man's property and progeny) increasingly dominated English discourse (as they would continue to do under Queen Victoria, who ascended the throne in 1837), purity reigned as *the* desired female virtue. Information on sex was accordingly kept under strict lock and key, to preserve a girl's chastity—for it was felt that if she were brought into contact with any such worldly information, her innocence would certainly suffer. Thus, having been enshrined in their bubbles, and with almost zero understanding of their own anatomy (let alone that of their husbands), an untold number of virgin brides found their wedding nights utterly terrifying. Despite the obvious difficulties resulting from such prudish concealment, even the medical community was complicit in its continuation. One doctor, when asked how to prepare a young woman for matrimony, responded, "Tell her nothing, my dear madam, for if they knew they would not marry."

Sara Coleridge had little practical understanding of life after marriage, but she was sufficiently aware of the inevitable lifestyle changes to find the prospect rather bleak. So when she accepted her cousin Henry Nelson Coleridge's 1823 proposal at the age of twenty-one, it was with the understanding that she wouldn't be walking down the aisle for a very long time. Henry agreed—he needed time, too, to forge a career in the law—and Sara threw herself into her projects with a new sense of urgency.

Southey suggested the memoirs of a sixteenth-century French soldier for her next translation, which John Murray gleefully snapped up and published as *The Right Joyous and Pleasant History of the Facts, Tests, and Prowesses of the Chevalier Bayard, the Good Knight Without Fear and Without Reproach.* It was shorter than the Dobrizhoffer work, but far more difficult to translate, and as Sara puzzled it out, Mrs. Coleridge noted her daughter's energetic bustling, her bouncing back and forth from the desk to the bookshelves: "She is never weary of turning to books of reference, Dictionaries (of which this library furnishes several in old french) &c. Many of the Chevalier's exploits were acted in Italy so that she has immense folios of Italian Histories to look into, all of which is an amusement and a thing for which she seems to have a passion." After she completed the work, Sara powered directly into a third translation, "Memoirs of Jean de Troye," but it would never find its way to press. By 1826, a year before her wedding, Southey began to insist that she write only for fun, without the stress of deadlines and printers, suggesting that her literary labors would distract her from honing "those duties which she will have to perform whenever she changes from the single to the married state." She'd known it was coming, but she was not adept at her new occupation—"I have a great deal of sewing to do at present, and alas! I am slow with my needle"—and characteristically, she had no interest in learning by observation. She went straight to the books instead: "You once mentioned to me a publication intended for the instruction of young housekeepers—I believe by Mrs King—," she wrote to her friend Elizabeth Crumpe. "[D]o you think it contains much that is not to be found in Mrs Rundell?" Her friend responded in the positive, and Sara traded theology and philosophy for recipes.

Yet cooperative though she was, on the inside Sara was bucking against the injustice of it all. This final clampdown on her mental pursuits left her wistful and glum, as she confessed to her brother Derwent:

> *I should have been much happier, with my tastes, temper & habits, had I been of your sex instead of the helpless being that I am. The thing that would suit me best in the world would be the life of a country Clergyman—I should delight in the studies necessary to the profession, & I am sure I should not dislike nor shrink from the active duties of it . . . I would not marry.*

Her work, the only part of her life over which she reigned—and the part that was unfailingly stimulating, exciting, full of possibility—was fast coming to an end, and she grieved for its loss as she might have mourned the passing of a friend: "I regret that I cannot make more use of this noble library while I still have the advantage of it . . . there is so much that I should like to do & to see and to copy and to transcribe before I lose the opportunity for ever!" As the wedding came and went, Sara sank into a state of deep depression. She loved Henry—part of her even welcomed the abrupt transition her marriage afforded. (Just before the wedding, she wrote to her husband-to-be that she could not help but be sentimental about Greta Hall and her old life, but she knew and felt this change "to be infinitely for the better.") Yet at what cost? More and more during the first year of her marriage she was barely able to get out of bed, and as her health deteriorated, she began to search for ways to dull the nervous, nauseating ache of the whole business of womanhood.

IT IS NOT KNOWN WHEN SARA STARTED EXPERIMENTING WITH laudanum (a tincture of opium mixed with alcohol), but because her first mention of it, in 1825, indicates a certain familiarity with the drug, it's likely she was already in the beginning stages of a habit that would, over time, become a torturous dependency. She'd seen enough of her father's legendary struggles with opium—watching, stunned, as he was "half reduced to idiotcy [*sic*]" after his daily dose—to know that her own involvement with narcotics was unfortunate. However, as she explained to her brother, she didn't expect any difficulty in stopping, and so she continued, seemingly unfettered by worry, to quash her frazzled nerves with the "black drop," as laudanum was known: "It has done me much good & no harm," she wrote, even though by this time she was already unable to sleep at all without it. "I might exclaim with Mrs. O'Neil [a popular poet], 'Hail lovely blossom that can'st ease the wretched victims of disease.'"

The trouble was that Mrs. O'Neil's "lovely blossom" had a history of snatching its own "wretched victims" despite their best efforts to avoid the trap. A laudanum user would first feel euphoric and docile before drifting off into a deep sleep, but they'd awaken in a worse condition; depression, dull-wittedness, and slurred speech were very common, along with restlessness and agitation, and the only antidote was another dose. Laudanum didn't cause dependency in everyone—Southey used it for occasional insomnia and hay fever, Charles Lamb for colds, Percy Shelley for headaches, and many thousands of women for menstrual cramps; it was even used by the spoonful to hush fussy babies. However, those who succumbed to its powers too frequently and then tried to quit would experience withdrawal symptoms such as immobilizing muscle and abdominal aches, nausea, and diarrhea. These, in combination with the side effects of the drug itself (horrific constipation, itchy skin, dry mouth, and difficulty breathing), only added to whatever problem had prompted use of laudanum in the first place.

Sara's "disease" was surely more indicative of deeply rooted discontent than of some physical malady, but before the advent of psychology, it was impossible to understand the relationship between body and mind, let alone between society's choking structure and female "sickness." To her, it was obvious that her endless forays into "derangement" were caused by a childhood accident, when she'd fallen into a river and nearly drowned;

she never speculated that her compulsory metamorphosis from maiden into matron was the problem. Yet, as the years went on and the corset of female protocol was tightened around her, she experienced a congruent decline in health: After the birth of her first child, she was weak and "despair[ing] of being entirely healthful and strong;" and after the second, she slept only every third night and lost so much weight that her menstrual cycle stopped entirely. Her use of laudanum greatly exacerbated these troubles, but at the same time the drug gave her a socially acceptable escape from a harsh truth: had her beloved years of study been in preparation for a monotonous, subservient existence, one that awarded her the greatest freedom attainable within the bounds of female propriety while simultaneously taking away any liberty she'd had for protest?

STILL, SHE HAD NO CHOICE; A WOMAN'S PURPOSE WAS MARriage, and Sara was determined to fulfill hers well. With resignation, she confirmed again and again in the run-up to the event her readiness for the shift: "My childish and girlish castles in the air are now exchanged for others which have you for their object—to contribute to your daily comfort and pleasure—this is the earthly goal toward which all my hopes and wishes are turned." The gravity of the occasion notwithstanding, Samuel Taylor Coleridge did not attend the marriage ceremony—apart from two short visits in 1822 and 1826, he hadn't seen his daughter in almost twenty years—but his wedding gift was thoughtful: William Sotheby's translation folio of Virgil's *Georgics, Georgica Publii Virgilii Maronis Hexaglotta,* a book to "mark the Talent and Industry that have made her Mistress of the Six Languages."

The newly married couple set up house at 21 Downshire

Hill, in Hampstead, which was then well on the outskirts of London proper. Henry, by now a fully fledged lawyer, caught the omnibus to work every Monday and stayed at Lincoln's Inn until his end-of-the-week return. Sara's mother worried about the distance, concerned that her daughter had moved "from a *too* bustling family to one of utter loneliness," but Sara was just fine with it. She busied herself with volumes of theology, scribbled a bit of poetry, and pored over her studies, and soon her leisurely studies were traded for motherhood. Baby Herbert was swiftly followed by Edith, but Sara was so consumed with bitterness at losing herself, and time *for* herself, that just being near the young ones left her choking with heartache. By her mother's account, Sara would "sit in a Carriage (wh[ich] we hired by the hour to drive on the Heath with the children and the nurses) and never speak one word to the poor babes the whole time." In spite of her numerous, violent breakdowns, pregnancies and births would continue to plague her; she would conceive seven times over the course of ten years, miscarrying often, and twice going to full term only to deliver sickly infants who died shortly thereafter.

To find relief, Sara drowned herself in laudanum and lay in bed with her books for days at a time, soaking up every last second of seclusion and serenity before duty called again; this, she discovered, was the easiest way to get some time for study. Within the span of these precious hours, she kept up with the literary world. She was enamored with—and some might say, even a little envious of—several female writers of the day, including Hannah More, dramatist Joanna Baillie, Felicia Hemans the poet (though she thought her "over-rated"), and, in accordance with her taste for obscure literature, "the delicate mirth, the gently hinted satire, the feminine, the decorous humour of

Jane Austen, who if not the greatest is surely the most faultless of female novelists."

She also began a long-standing relationship with the works of Harriet Martineau, who shared Sara's opinion on educational methodology. Henry seemed to favor sermons for teaching little Herbert and Edith, but Sara knew better: "Children mark what you *do* much more, and what you say less, than those who know them not imagine." After one of her more debilitating stints of infirmity, she endeavored to apply herself to teaching her kids through something she could *do*: write poetry. She wrote hundreds of poems for "Herby" and "E" on a variety of schoolhouse subjects such as geography, history, and languages; and in 1834, upon the approval of her doting husband, she collected a few of them and published *Pretty Lessons in Verse for Good Children.* She wasn't overly excited about the book; dinky poems on spelling and vocabulary, like this one, were meager fare for a mind such as hers:

"O, sister! You've spelt the word wrong:
In chestnut there's surely a t."
"No t does to chestnut belong,
As you in my lesson may see."

Or this one on the merits of staying in bed:

The Tiger, confined in a cage,
No doubt is a little bit sullen;
His new English den, I'll engage,
The Lion considers a dull one.
But they can submit to their fate;

'Tis seldom they kick up a riot;
And Herbert must lay down his pate;
I'm sure he has nothing to cry at.

Still, *Pretty Lessons* gave her a pretty income. The new market for children's literature—one of the few authorial niches that could be occupied by a lady without too much rebuke—had stood ready and waiting for a work like this; the book went through five editions in as many years and was still in print as late as 1927. It was also compiled during some of Sara's worst years, amid infant deaths and depression—but you'd never know from the lilting, finger-wagging lessons like this one:

When Herbert can say all his nouns
And likewise the four conjugations
How much it will please his Papa
His Aunty, and all his relations!

Other poems of hers from this time, the ones she chose *not* to publish, offer a far clearer depiction of her dark state of being, and her rising bubble of resentment:

I envy the beasts that are seeking their prey
And the vile slimy reptile that crawls in my way,
Yon carolling bird makes his joy be heard
Ah! Now he's falling! —he carols no more!
His sporting & singing and soaring are over
Yet I envy him still as he falls on his nest
With the sharp pointed arrow stuck deep in his breast.

Temporary relief from this cycle of good health and vigorous industry followed inevitably by guilt, lassitude, and "madness" came at the end of July 1834, when Samuel Taylor Coleridge's final illness ended in his death. Sara had never really known her father, but through his writings, she'd come to revere his ideology and to cherish, however distantly, the rare gem of his character, which shimmered in the pages of his work—the death of his philosophy caused her grief, and the "extinction of [his] light" left her deeply affected. She did not have another nervous episode at the news of his passing, however, because she'd unearthed a golden opportunity from it:

> *There was everything in the circumstances of his departure to soothe our regret[,] and we feel happy in the hope that his writing will be widely influential for good purposes. All his views philosophical and theological may not be adopted, & the effect of his posthumous works must be impaired by their fragmentary condition, but I think there is reason to believe that what he has left behind him, published and unpublished, will introduce a higher & more improving mode of thinking . . . immediately popular they can never be—but their exposition of truth may mould the opinions and tinge the feelings of hundreds.*

Samuel's death had given his daughter a new reason for living: she would repackage and promote his intellectual genius, and defend his philosophy against those who didn't agree with it (or, as was the case more frequently, understand it). But why Sara? Why would it be she, the least loved of his three surviving children, who suddenly jumped to her father's aid? In describing her reasons for shouldering such a task, she frequently uses the words *duty* and *responsibility* and points to her humble desire to "enlighten the world" with her father's genius. Even though some of that may have been true, her unexpected and sudden move to stake claim to the Coleridge legacy speaks volumes about her intentions. It can be inferred that Samuel Taylor's death gave Sara the chance not only to be a good, dutiful daughter by protecting and promoting his work, but also to assert her own genius—by way of his authority, she could establish herself in the literary world without censure. It is known that Sara's health and spirits made a full recovery at this point, and that, considering her productivity over the coming years, she set about her new task with the same vigor she'd applied to the intellectual pursuits of her single life. "STC's works must be reissued," she wrote to her husband, "[but not] disjointed and unaccompanied. Let them be set forth . . . with the complete scheme of arguments which convinced his own mind. Then let them be taken to pieces and examined grain by grain . . . if they are true they will prevail in the end."

The first of her responsibilities was to correct the rampant misrepresentations then hitting the periodicals in response to Samuel Taylor's recently published *Poetical Works*. Thomas De Quincey's four-part tirade in *Tait's Edinburgh Magazine* was at the center of Sara's crosshairs, due in large part to its distortion of her mother's character, but there were others to address as well. To her, J. A. Heraud's *Fraser Magazine* write-up had a reckless heartlessness, and John Wilson's piece in *Blackwood's* was unaccountably bad: "[Wilson] is a fool to speak of my Father's *master* . . . Wordsworth the master of Coleridge indeed! This is gross flattery of the living Bard." Feisty yet focused, she directed her efforts not toward a vulgar battle of words in the papers, but to creating a new reputation for her father via the careful refashioning of his writings—and just like that, Sara was busy at her studies again. When she wasn't caring for her children, she worked with Henry on a new edition of Samuel Taylor's *Table Talk,* collected notes for what would become the four-volume *Literary Remains,* and began work on her own long-form prose tale in a completely new style, *Phantasmion,* which would be published in 1837.

Table Talk was only the first in a projected series, and even though Sara enjoyed the work (and the full-bodied physical and mental health that came spryly along with it), she began to realize that editing was a thankless undertaking. Because of the escalated discomfiture in society surrounding female authorship—a hurdle set higher than ever due to the increased political and social conservativism of early nineteenth-century England—Sara Coleridge's efforts on *Table Talk* went unattributed in the book. And considering there was so much yet to do for Samuel's writings, this situation was one Sara could likely expect again and again. As her diary later indicated, she was nearly at a breaking point when *Table Talk* went to print:

> *No work is so inadequately rewarded either by money or credit as that of editing miscellaneous, fragmentary, immethodical literary remains like those of STC . . . It is something to myself to feel that I am putting in order a literary house that otherwise would be open to censure here or there. But when there is not mere carelessness but*

a positive coldness in regard to what I have done, I so sometimes feel as if I had been wasting myself a good deal.

THE FLU CAME TO DOWNSHIRE HILL IN THE SPRING OF 1836, and Sara, already weakened by burdensome social mores and the expectation that she must live entirely through other people, predictably suffered the worst of the household. Her editorial work was pushed aside and her children hustled out of the room to play with their nurses while Sara lay weeping. How infuriating it was! She slept, she read, she used laudanum to forget herself and, as autumn neared, the trip to Henry's family home in Ottery St. Mary that she'd managed to sidestep all year was imminent. She did not want to make the journey, but Henry insisted, and after a five-day trip in "great misery" and several weeks of illness at Henry's parents' house, thirty-four-year-old Sara finally played her ace. She set off for London on October 14, with her children and their nurse, but on the first day of travel, she had the coach pulled over at Ilchester and announced that she was too ill to continue. The children went back to Ottery with the nurse while Sara sat down to set the scene for Henry, who'd had some business in the opposite direction and was now, conveniently, unable to come collect her:

> *Your feelings will be sad when you hear that I cannot proceed with my journey. God in heaven, to whom I fervently pray, knows that I cannot. I was much worse after arriving yesterday—in hysterics[,] frequently had no sleep last night, and in attempting to set out today found I could not do it . . . I never suffered as I have done for 24 hours.*

> *Judge kindly of me my beloved, & write to me at Ilchester. Indeed I would go if I could. I would suffer pain[s]—but their terrors are too dreadful and my prostration too great. If I am now quiet I shall gradually recover but if I proceed I never shall . . . This is dreadful—the separation from you[,] but it cannot be helped.*

Sara checked herself into a cozy inn and stayed there, sequestered in her upper-floor room, for the next five weeks. Letters from this time are numerous and revealing, especially in the varied amount of physical complaints she offers—one day she'd be improving, and the next, "infected" and "shattered," or in the throes of "vaginal shock." The appearance or disappearance of her symptoms was dependent on Henry: they would instantly return whenever he set a date for her departure, and slacken after she'd convinced him to let her stay on. It can never be known whether she was actually malingering during these weeks, but the broader implications are clear as day: Sara's dissatisfaction had been severe enough to lead her, consciously or not, to seek an escape from *all* her responsibilities—her husband and children, her home, her mother, all of society. Once she arrived there, in her private space, she was well.

Each morning, she would write to her husband to beg for further respite, sometimes with pouty dejection—"Life is blighted . . . how can I live here?"—other times apologetically, with guilt about the money spent on her accommodation and "the misery of causing so much affliction," and once, in a moment of shields-down honesty, with pure, boiling rage: "Now he holds me down upon the ground in his horrid gripe: I am even yet struggling for breath & liberty: if I ever get alive out of his clutches I will drive the monster away and when he comes near me again he shall be received on the prongs of a pitch-fork"—she speaks of the metaphorical "black vulture" of this trip brought down upon her at Henry's insistence, thus implying that it was all his fault. After she finished her daily installment of scene setting and sympathy rallying, she would have a quick breakfast in her room and settle down to the real business of her stay, *Phantasmion*.

THIS "BURLESQUE CHILD'S TALE ON THE SUBJECT OF THE Insect," a novel-length "wondertale" crammed with fantastical characters and plot lines, was in first draft form when she arrived at Ilchester. By the time she left, it was completely revised and ready for the press. *Phantasmion* wasn't going to be a best seller, though, and the way it was published went a great distance to ensure it *never* would be. A tiny print run of just two hundred fifty copies, with no illustrations, no author's name—confound it!—and an expensive nine-shilling cover price meant *Phantasmion* had little chance to strike it big. Those who did get hold of a copy received it either warmly, praising "the power, the grace, the refinement of her mind," as John Duke Coleridge, Samuel Taylor Coleridge's great-nephew, wrote in the preface to a later edition; or with jaded indifference, like this critic from the *Quarterly Review*: "It is . . . a Fairy Tale, the last, we suppose, that will ever be written in England, and unique in its kind. It is neither German nor French. It is what it is." This reviewer agreed with the majority of English literary society in their opinion that the fairy-tale genre had long overstayed its welcome. Starting in 1823, with Edgar Taylor's titillating collection of Brothers Grimm tales, *German Popular Stories*, London quickly became flooded with fairy-tale books, pamphlets, and periodicals, and their corresponding revamps in the theater and in ballet. The public was full-up on fairies, and Sara knew it: "To print a Fairy Tale is the very way to be *not read,* but shoved aside with contempt . . . works of this class are wholesome food [though], by way of variety, for the childish mind."

Indeed, upon its 1837 publication, *Phantasmion* was easily dismissed as just another work from a worn-out genre. Yet modern academics argue that, dispersed throughout Sara Coleridge's framework for a typical fairy-tale story—a hero in search of an object, after meeting many trials, returns home victorious to get married or become king—are the seeds of what we now know as fantasy literature.* Unlike stories that take place "once upon a time" or "east of the sun, west of the moon," *Phantasmion* is meant to be *believed;* the physical aspects of the land and the people in it are recognizable, even though they exist completely apart from our own world and are often imbued with magical powers. Furthermore, the setting is never just in some character's imagination, but here, now. (This, for J. R. R. Tolkien, was what disqualified Lewis Carroll's *Alice's Adventures in Wonderland* as "fantasy"—as it was labeled at the time—because Alice wakes up in the end and discovers she's only been dreaming.) Indeed,

---

* The definitions of fairy-tale and fantasy literature are a matter of debate, but most scholars agree that the main delineating factors are: believability, the nature of the hero, and whether the world is somehow connected to our own (via a magic door, wardrobe, dream, etc.). There are potential subcategories that may come into play in our future—fantastic-uncanny and fantastic-marvelous among them—along with the overarching question of origin: did fantasy arise out of fairy tale, or should fairy tale be considered part of fantasy? Suffice it to say, there is no consensus yet. For more information, see *The Greenwood Encyclopedia of Folktales and Fairy Tales,* ed. Donald Haase (Westport: Greenwood, 2008), or Michele Eilers's essay, "On the Origins of Modern Fantasy," *Extrapolation* 41, no. 4 (2000): 317–37.

Sara Coleridge worked hard to delineate the fantastical events of her hero's journey as specifically *not* imaginary. In its decidedly un-*Alice*-like final sentence, her triumphant hero Phantasmion looks upon his bride:

> *Phantasmion looked round in momentary dread, lest [his wife] should have proved a spirit and vanished . . . but there she stood, her face beaming bright as ever in full sunshine, the earnest that all he remembered and all he hoped for was not to fade like a dream.*

It's all real, and it all happens to ordinary, imperfect people.

Before breathing in this final moment of peace, Phantasmion trudges through years of violence and despair, much of which has been brought down upon him by his own ill-conceived actions—this is another departure from traditional fairy tales, whose heroes are inherently perfect. Phantasmion displays a wide variety of characteristics, both heroic and not. He saves a baby from certain death just after eavesdropping on a delicate exchange between a queen and a mermaid, and he pursues justice for all; but he's utterly ruthless with his enemies (at one point, consumed with fury, he turns into an earth-burrowing insect and leaves an entire army "crushed and mangled, with broken arms, legs, ribs, and sculls, some over their steeds and some under them . . . kicked and plunged and trode"); he also chases after women. Although, when Iarine appears, with her rounded arms "dazzling in whiteness" and a neck so graceful that art cannot hope to imitate it, he remains devoted to her for the rest of his life. Phantasmion is, like the rest of us, a mixed bag of light and dark. He's a real person.

The most startling aspect of Sara's writing here is her uncanny, and unprecedented, attention to worldbuilding. Palmland has its own geography, its own history, and a unique ethnography (its people are "given to agriculture, and had never acquired that skill in arts and manufactures"; this proclivity leads to conflict with the neighboring nation). Their world exists entirely apart from our own. Though other writers were experimenting with paracosmic settings such as this (the Brontë sisters' land of Angria and E. T. A. Hoffmann's doll world in *The Nutcracker and the Mouse King*, the book behind the ballet), Sara's Palmland is detailed in the extreme. From its conflicted history to its people and their system of logic that allows magic and prophecy to be weighed equally alongside knowledge and experience, Palmland was created consciously from the ground up, piece by piece.

Its details and intricacies aside, the grander purpose of *Phantasmion* was, for Sara, simply a matter of introducing her readers to an inspiring place in their minds; here, surrounded by "tissues of unrealities . . . the poetical beauty of things is vividly displayed, truth is exhibited, and thus the imagination of the youthful reader is stimulated to find truth for itself," as she described it in a letter to her brother Derwent. She further elucidates her philosophy in this short poem, scribbled in the front cover of her own copy of *Phantasmion*:

Go, little book, and sing of love and beauty,
To tempt the worldling into fairy-land;
Tell him that airy dreams are sacred duty,
Bring better wealth than aught his toils command,—
Toils fraught with mickle harm.

But if thou meet some spirit high and tender,
On blessed works and noblest love intent,
Tell him that airy dream of nature's splendor,
With graver thought and hallowed musings blent,
Prove no too earthly charm.

Her message, unfortunately, did not translate universally. For some readers, the very few who obtained a copy, *Phantasmion* was way over the top; so much description was akin to "a bellyful of macaroons . . . what begins very pleasantly is ended with disgust." However, once it landed in the hands of the transcendentalist movement in America, the work started to gain some footing. It was complex, no doubt, requiring great patience on the reader's part, but *Phantasmion* was an important landmark in literature and deserved to be read. The *Boston Quarterly Review* saw to this in 1840, with an extraordinary "literary notice" in the form of a fictitious conversation that acted as both an announcement and a rave review:

REV. MR. N. [reading]—"Phantasmion."

PROF. P.—By Coleridge's daughter . . .

REV. MR. N.—And she is the wife of Henry N. Coleridge.

PROF. P.—I believe so. A family apparently of not unequal relations. This revolution of double and triple stars in the heaven of thought, is an apparition as rare as it is beautiful.

REV. MR. N.—Well! we cannot hope to get true [commentary] in the seclusion of our little obscure village. I think I have heard the book ridiculed as unintelligible, and even silly.

Prof. P.—Nay . . . the imagination is now so little exercised, and the mind's natural [state] so tyrannized over by the understanding, that a work of poetic character like this is not received [all] at once . . .

Rev. Mr. N.—Is it a fairy tale then?

Prof. P.—It uses fairy machinery, but with a human significance. It is the old but never worn out subject of the progress of a young mind from innocence to virtue, from perception to knowledge. The forms of the insect world are borrowed to facilitate this progress, so that Phantasmion flies where others creep.

Rev. Mr. N.—Is this meaning obvious, or am I indebted for it to your own ingenuity?

Prof. P.—It is not brought forward with the stiff, good sense of English allegory, nor can you find it if you hunt in every fold of the narrative. [Instead] you will find much painting for the pleasure of painting . . . it is the spontaneous melody of solitary hours, the vision ever ready for the eye, which looks out with ardor and purity into nature. Read a got-up book made for profit and fame, as too many are now, and then turn to this genuine record of the life of the mind, and you will feel the difference.

For these two fictional readers, and those who now recognize *Phantasmion* as Sara Coleridge's greatest contribution, that five-week stay in Ilchester was well worth her time. Henry disagreed; by the time he came to collect her on November 17, his patience was at an end. Nevertheless, it was a significant moment. Away from the life of self-denial she led as a mother, wife, and daughter, Sara was able to step into a new self-asserting role as authoress, and intellectual. This seemed to give her the confidence to reevaluate her role as an editor. Samuel Taylor's works were *her* legacy, *her* task; she would now take control of the situation and publish as she saw fit, with proper attribution. And, soon, Henry's death would give her total freedom to do it.

By 1842, Sara had been engrossed in full-time literary labors for five years. Together she and Henry had worked tirelessly on the four volumes of Samuel Taylor's *Literary Remains,* publishing one a year between 1836 and 1839, and she'd begun a systematic reread of her father's writing that required full familiarity with his theological and philosophical predecessors—this was a bear of a project to complete all by itself, but it was necessary in order to bring to fruition her plans for new editions of *Aids to Reflection, The Friend,* and *Biographia Literaria.* She'd also spent the entirety of 1836 to 1840 in one stage of pregnancy or another, suffering three miscarriages and, finally, in 1840, the last of her infant deaths with one-week-old Bertha Fanny Coleridge: "Our loss, indeed, has been a great disappointment, and even a sorrow; for, strange as it may seem, these little speechless creatures, with their wandering, unspeaking eyes, do twine themselves around a parent's heart from the hour of their birth . . . [but] it was plain that the little darling was not for this world."

In the midst of all this, Henry's health was failing. Eighteen forty-two saw him hopelessly bedridden, thereby revoking Sara's right to self-imposed invalidism and leaving her in charge of her husband's many household responsibilities. It was now her task to provide the income and to sort out Henry's affairs as he strode solemnly to the grave, and for the first time, she was forced to confront a new domestic arrangement and the very real possibility of her husband's death.

Henry expired the following January, from a degenerative nerve disease, and Sara did mourn, but not for the loss of a *husband*, for it was in marriage, engulfed in society's expectations, that she'd lost much of herself and what could have been. Instead, she grieved at the loss of a partner with whom she'd spent the last twenty years and weathered many storms. "No two beings could be more intimately united in heart and thought than we have been, or could have been more intermingled with each other in daily and hourly life," she wrote, ". . . [but] my sorrow is not greater than I can bear, for God has mercifully fitted it to my strength. While I was losing my great earthly happiness, I was gradually enabled . . . to be content to part with [it]." Eight months later, after having taken time to process her emotions and not once suffering one of her nervous collapses, Sara seemed downright peppy in the midst of her widowhood:

> *I have cultivated cheerfulness as I never did before . . . Now I crave to see fine works of art, or the still more mind-occupying displays of nature. I try to take an interest in the concerns of my friends, to enter into the controversies of the day, to become intimate with the mood of mind and character of various persons . . . I do not brood miserably over my loss, or sink into an aimless, inert despondency; I have even an upper stratum of cheerfulness in my mind.*

She was out in the world a great deal after Henry's death, much more than before, and over the next few years she gathered around her many of London's most famous literati: Henry Crabb Robinson, poet Aubrey de Vere, and soon-to-be prime minister William Ewart Gladstone were among her correspondents, along with authoresses Joanna Baillie and Anna Jameson. She also enjoyed an exchange with Elizabeth Barrett Browning on how to deal with their mutual dependency on laudanum, which in the last years of Sara's life required her taking a huge dose of straight morphine every other night to help her sleep. It was a drastic measure, certainly, but she was at least able to control her addiction well enough to live and work normally.

And work she did. In the year of Henry's death, she published a new two-volume edition of her father's *Aids to Reflection*, which included her useful essay "On Rationalism," to further explicate Coleridgean reason. This was followed by editions of *Biographia Literaria; Notes and Lectures Upon Shakespeare; Essays on His Own Times;* and *Poems of Samuel Taylor Coleridge*—all three bear her mark in one way or another, either in a lengthy introduction (the one in *Biographia* fills nearly an entire volume) or as an appendix to further qualify her father's thinking. It was an enormous task, but her investment in and labors for Samuel Taylor Coleridge kept him in print and at the forefront of the public imagination; oddly, this "minor" authoress helped her father avoid the same crippling designation. When she wasn't busy with that, she was a critic for *The Quarterly Review*, mother of two—Herbert was at Eton, and Edith was studying with Sara at home—and a prolific essayist on poetry, philosophy, government, art, and education.

When Sara Coleridge died at age fifty, she left a mass of unpublished papers along with the beginnings of an autobiography (later finished and published by her daughter) that revealed her happy childhood at "dear Greta Hall" and a time of great mental productivity, followed by marriage and motherhood, and her corresponding ill health, despondency, and drug use. These last were a tragedy, and Virginia Woolf lamented them greatly. In 1940, Woolf responded to an early (and somewhat misdirected) biography on Sara with an essay in memoriam to the forgotten authoress, the "chequered dappled figure flitting between a vanished radiance and the light of every day," whose capabilities were undermined by societal strictures: "She meant to write her life. But she was interrupted."

six

DINAH MULOCK CRAIK

[1826–1887]

CONTRARY TO THE BELIEF OF MATRONS LIKE JANE AUSTEN'S Mrs. Bennet, a single man in possession of a good fortune wasn't always in want of a wife, for he had lots of other things to occupy his time. A career, most likely military, religious, or political; or the upkeep of his estate; or theater hopping, pub crawling, gambling; or hunting, fishing, and rambling with his friends. Life as a man was varied and busy. Of course, for the fairer sex, things were different. A single woman, even if she *was* in possession of a good fortune, was constantly on the hunt for a husband; financial independence might give her some freedom (and the right to be choosier), but until she found a man, her true destiny in the eyes of society remained unfulfilled. Her purpose was unrealized, her very being in stasis until a match was made and the wedding vows exchanged. As Miss Iremonger put it in *Dear Miss Heber,* a collection of eighteenth-century correspondence, "we are always *to be* married till we *are!*"

Even so, matrimony wasn't necessarily guaranteed—and spinsterhood was becoming an increasingly common fate, though rarely by choice. In the sixteenth century, 5 percent of upper-class girls never married; during Jane Austen's lifetime, it was up to 25 percent. Just thirty-four years after Austen's death, the 1851 census revealed that an astounding 42 percent of women age twenty to forty were unwed—as was Dinah Mulock Craik, who was, by then, twenty-five years old—and that, including widows, two and a half million English women were single and self-supporting. This sudden and alarming excess of unattached females caused a storm of speculation in the media. In an 1862 book-length essay, *Why Are Women Redundant?,* writer and social commentator W. R. Greg determined that these unfortunate single women, who, "in place of completing, sweetening, and embellishing the existence of others," had "an independent and incomplete existence," were as such because of male profligacy: men were shirking their responsibilities to the women of England, preferring "luxuries and shadows" to boring old monogamy and perpetuating an "unwholesome social state . . . both productive and prognostic of much wretchedness and wrong."

In reality, the problem was much more complicated. Amid the rapidly changing political, social, and economic landscape of the nineteenth century, the traditional state of blissful matrimony was becoming much harder to attain due in part to a tilted ratio of men to women in the English population. As far back as the Plague years, morbidity rates had favored women,* and this, combined with the many thousands of men who immigrated to North America, New Zealand, Australia, and South Africa—those whose wages weren't keeping up with the cost of living or who, like many in the years following the Napoleonic Wars, were unemployed—created a major demographic discrepancy. By 1851 there were 365,000 more women than men in England. New opportunities for gaining material wealth also seem to have compounded the problem by creating a greater desire for it in society, thus heightening the expectations of a newly married gentlewoman: she now presumed to receive not just a home upon marriage, but an "establishment" resplendent with lady's maids and servants, the finest in crystal and lace (for entertaining in style, as middle- and upper-class Victorian wives did often), and a monthly spending allowance to maintain her at a level of luxury to which she'd grown accustomed. Within this home, she would spare little expense in creating an insulated, protected space in the new Victorian fashion, one designed to safeguard her husband and children from what was now viewed as an entrepreneurial, yet corrupt, external society: carpets, curtains, wall coverings, lamps, portraiture, and a seemingly endless list of housewares and furniture were now required not only to

---

* Sharon N. DeWitte's 2010 research has revealed that the risk of death during the Black Plague was likely higher in men due to a stronger prevalence for frailty and physiological stress. See Sharon N. DeWitte, "Sex Differentials in Frailty in Medieval England," *American Journal of Physical Anthropology* 143, no. 2 (October 2010): 285–97. DeWitte has also shown the continuity of this trend beyond the Middle Ages—in seventeenth-century London, women were still outliving men despite the dangers of pregnancy and childbirth—and that since at least the mid-nineteenth century, women in European populations have lived on average two to three years longer than men.

further adorn this harmonious environment, but also to keep the man at home and out of the pubs. (One contemporary book of advice, *The Practical Housewife,* reminds the reader that men "have so much liberty of action, so many out-door resources if wearied indoors, that it is a good policy . . . to make home attractive as well as comfortable.")

The few marriageable men who remained in England were understandably hesitant to enter into such an expensive arrangement, and many more found it entirely unthinkable: younger sons, typically living on just a small annuity, would have to scrimp and save over a period of decades if they ever hoped to have enough to marry on. So, unless he was very wealthy or extremely enterprising, a man could easily be into his fifties before considering a walk down the aisle, and even then, he was still hamstrung by a maze of social niceties when it came to courtship. W. R. Greg's "luxuries and shadows"—those dark distractions that, in his opinion, it will be remembered, were the real source of England's marital woes—may have amounted to a man's evasion of duty, but they were far easier and cheaper to attain.

Yet despite the practical hurdles, women were still honed for marriage (and marriage *only*) with an unrelenting single-mindedness. According to society, an unwed woman had no function; along with a growing number of her sisters, she was doomed forever to feel "as a kind of excrescence on the surface of society," as John Stuart Mill put it, "for all women who are educated to *be* married, & what little they are taught deserving of the name 'useful,' is chiefly what in the ordinary course of things will not come into actual use, unless nor until they are married." Since the only escape from this endless assault was to find a husband, *any* husband, the marriage market soon turned into a frenzy of desperate manhunters. A fictional letter in *The Lady's Monthly Museum* paints a telling picture of this fanatic search for matrimony:

> *My papa and mamma have been trying for the last three years to match me, and have for that purpose carried me from our country seat to London, from London to Brighton, from Brighton to Bath, and from Bath to Cheltenham, where I am now, backwards and forwards, till the family carriage is almost worn out, and one of the horses is become blind, and another lame, without my having more than a nibble, for I have never yet been able to hook my fish. I begin to be afraid that there is something wrong in their manner of baiting for a husband or in mine of laying in the line to catch him.*

It sounds bizarre, but in the words of an almost-spinster in Samuel Butler's *The Way of All Flesh*, "What else could she do? Run away? She dared not." Bolting for the exit was an extreme solution, truly, but the other options for an unmarried lady of genteel birth—ladies like Dinah Mulock Craik, whose father's family was of minor Irish gentry—weren't much more appealing. Since finding employment (as a governess or a teacher) was, for a high-born lady, unthinkably humiliating, her choices were more about finding a surrogate household to serve than attending to herself. She could move in with a family member and become "a star of promise and of hope through the homes of her kindred and friends," like one Dear Aunt Mary in *Good Words* magazine. She could also most certainly stay home and care for her aging parents (as many youngest daughters of large noble families were expected to do, regardless), while busily throwing herself into local charity work: arranging teas and fund-raisers, making soup for poor neighbors, and stitching crafts for a bazaar could be her raisons d'être forever, or until she received that hoped-for proposal. Yet if she was sure no suitor would ever come calling, and if there was none who might benefit from her assistance, a gentlewoman spinster could join a convent and pray for "permanent freedom from the weariness of a self-centered existence," as Anne Judith Penny outlined in her well-intended though admittedly harsh work *The Afternoon of Unmarried Life*: "At your age, you should be able to accept, with full assurance, any of the *certainties* of faith . . . this knowledge will be a great consolation when you feel too miserable to pray for yourself."

If none of these options was acceptable, as a last resort a single woman could discard her family heritage altogether, pack up, and head for the colonies, where wife shortages were rampant—surely then a successful proposal would come! So obviously effective was this final solution for W. R. Greg (of *Why Are Women Redundant?* fame), that he devised plans for a Great Spinster Debarkation: hundreds of thousands of unwed women would be deployed overseas (in modest numbers, of course, to ensure appropriate chaperoning), whereupon their reason for living would at long last be realized. (We scoff, but even so, many despairing ladies took Greg up on his offer. Thanks to well-publicized rhetoric surrounding "matrimonial colonization" and the broad acceptance of women's perceived moral authority, thousands of unwed females of all classes were enabled to resettle overseas using agencies such as the Family Colonization Loan Society and the British Women's Emigration Association.)

Each fix was more ridiculous than the next, and each ignored the more intimate scope of emotional needs of a woman for whom spinsterhood loomed: being "redundant" was a painful experience, an outward sign of failure as a female. Everywhere she went, a spinster was mocked and derided, "every article of dress, every word, every movement . . . satirized," as Nelly Weeton remembered, and her dependence on the generosity of others never quite forgiven. Since this turn of events could potentially befall anyone, suddenly it is quite understandable that Mrs. Bennet is so desperate to marry off her daughters in *Pride and Prejudice*; or that Charlotte Lucas, at age twenty-seven, is keen to accept Mr. Collins, who is "neither sensible nor agreeable" and whose attraction to her "must be imaginary." However degrading it is, Charlotte solves her larger problem—she will be married, and freed from ridicule. With little money and few physical charms, she really "felt all the good luck of it . . . he would be her husband." And as is obvious to Elizabeth and everyone else in the novel, Charlotte isn't exactly thrilled about having to throw herself away on so unworthy a match; it is "a most humiliating picture!" Yet inner torment wasn't something Jane Austen was keen on dealing with directly; nor was it much spoken of in society.

Solutions to this problem were as strange and paradoxical as the problem itself. What to do when a woman who, by no fault of her own, was husbandless in a society where marriage was imperative yet near impossible? Florence Nightingale and fellow activist Barbara Bodichon, for example, figured that the best course of action would be to demand freedom from marriage altogether, along with equal female participation in the workforce. Conservatives obstructed this idea by stepping up their alarmist attempts at making independence look as unappealing as possible—"wasting life and soul, gathering the scantiest subsistence, and surrounded by the most overpowering and insidious temptations." Yet no proposed fix was successful at averting the crisis, because, at least in part, the emotional issues at hand were never addressed; women remained at fault for something they couldn't control and for not obtaining what was often unwanted in the first place.

A DRASTICALLY DIFFERENT, MORE PERSONAL APPROACH WAS needed to help single women find their place in the world, and it was in this that Dinah Mulock Craik would really shine. Her essay series on the subject, later published as *A Woman's Thoughts About Women,* quashes self-pitying despondency and prescribes a new, more practical, more rational program based on education and self-reliance. It was simple, Dinah thought: Do not adhere to the false pretense that helplessness is sexy—"We *must* help ourselves . . . by the full exercise of every faculty, physical, moral, and intellectual." In doing so, a young woman would discover her inner fortitude and the power of her being, with or without a husband, and become a paradigm of modern womanliness, "foot-sore and smirched, but never tainted; exposed, doubtless, to many trials, yet never either degraded or humiliated . . . young girls, trust yourselves; rely on yourselves!"

Along with her straightforward guidance for dealing with depression—"This lot is probably the hardest any woman can have to bear . . . [but] there is no sorrow under heaven which is, or ought to be, endless"—Dinah also emphasized that this situation was not a result of a woman's inherent flaws or frailty, but rather of a culturally supported mishandling of girls. They were crippled, she wrote, for they'd been taught to believe they were to be wives or nothing at all. As a result, young ladies were selling themselves to the highest bidder without regard for passion or future happiness, embittering their souls and cheapening the experience of love into a meaningless search for "evening-parties, dresses, and gloves, a fine house, and blue-and-silver curtains." This should not, and would not, stand:

> *Every girl ought to be taught that a hasty, loveless union stamps upon her as foul [a] dishonour as one of those connexions which omit the legal ceremony altogether; and that, however pale, dreary, and toilsome a single life may be, unhappy married life must be tenfold worse—an ever-haunting temptation, an incurable regret, a torment from which there is no escape but death. There is many a bridal-chamber over which ought to be placed no other inscription than that well-known one over the gate of Dante's hell: "Lasciate ogni speranza, voi chi entrate." ["Abandon hope all ye who enter here."] God forbid that any woman, in whose heart is any sense of real marriage, with all its sanctity, beauty, and glory, should ever be driven to enter such an accursed door!*

Instead of encouraging them to enter this barbaric melee—one that echoes the married lives of Charlotte Turner Smith, Mary Robinson, and Sara Coleridge with surprising accuracy—*A Woman's Thoughts About Women* proclaims singles as independent citizens in need of free access to work and education; "withdraw[ing] from public inspection" into "channels of private beneficence and quiet zeal," per Judith Penny's advice—this did not have to be a spinster's fate. No, Dinah Mulock Craik knew from experience that a practical approach to life was more beneficial, and that there were other reasons for living besides the wifely kind.

DINAH MULOCK CRAIK WROTE *A WOMAN'S THOUGHTS ABOUT Women* in 1857, when she was thirty-two years old and still unmarried. Like the many thousands of self-supporting Englishwomen documented in the 1851 data previously cited, she'd been working her whole life, paying her own way for as long as she could remember, living by her own rules and on her own dime. She was, and remained throughout her life, the living embodiment of the successful female she presented for consideration in *Woman's Thoughts*—resilient, cunning, independent to the core, hard-pressed to accept defeat. Born in 1826 to Thomas Mulock and Dinah Mellard Mulock, Dinah experienced a childhood that went a long way toward instilling these values of autonomy and fearlessness. Often she would go out onto the green behind her house in Newcastle-under-Lyme and stay there till sundown, running around in "groups of dirty, happy little rogues," playing ball with her brothers, roasting potatoes on a bonfire, digging holes in neighbors' gardens, and, in one particularly dangerous stunt that gave her "a degree of naughty satisfaction," sailing down the river on a chunk of ice with a stick to help her steer. (Afterward, one of the other sailors was obliged to take himself to bed not because of sickness, but because "the whole of his available wardrobe was hanging to dry by the kitchen-fire," Dinah later wrote.) Being outdoors all the time served a dual purpose of allowing her time away from a contentious, increasingly unstable home: her father showed symptoms of what we now recognize as bipolar disorder, and he spent much of Dinah's childhood in and out of incarceration.*

Her education was conducted at a cheap day school for cottagers' daughters, near her home, where no Coleridgean romance existed. Here, Latin and philosophy were set aside in favor of more pragmatic knowledge, such as science and math, and the books read erred toward "good general knowledge" instead of fantasy. "Literature was very limited," Dinah later wrote in *Chambers's Edinburgh Journal*, "for we were not rich, we had no large domestic library, nor did we live in a reading community . . . the treat of being read to was [also] quite impossible in our busy household." Yet even with this impediment, as she grew toward adolescence, Dinah developed a taste for books: a neighborhood bookseller generously shared his modest lending library with the family, and soon Dinah was neck-deep in Jane Austen, Edward Bulwer-Lytton, Sir Walter Scott, and the early installments of Charles Dickens. She even started scribbling prose in her own perfectly natural way—not with a Charlotte Turner Smith–esque book of poems or a heady translation, but with a tale called "The Party of Cats," in which her kitty, Rose, takes the neighbor's kitties to dinner in the rhubarb patch and a delightful time is had by all.

Happy enough though Dinah was in the country, posterity rejoices in her family's 1840 move to London, for it's through her

---

* Dinah's father has long been acknowledged as a difficult, quarrelsome man, but recent research has shown Thomas Mulock to be more of an abuser than first realized. He experienced bouts of great happiness followed by anger and dejection, and in one unusually violent moment, had to be forcibly removed from his wife and children with the help of the police. See Karen Bourrier, "Narrating Insanity in the Letters of Thomas Mulock and Dinah Mulock Craik," *Victorian Literature and Culture* 39 (2011): 203–22; and the Mulock Family Papers, on file at the Charles E. Young Research Library, UCLA.

letters to friends back in Newcastle that we can see the effects of her self-governance. She was already quite the adult at age thirteen, she fancied, fully capable of planning trips to Bath by herself, passing judgment on others less developed—"the present race of juveniles, gentlemen especially, are extremely foolish and stupid, with very few exceptions"—and offering her friends some sage philosophy on life's little bumps:

> *After all childhood is a very pleasant thing, only it is so soon over, and then come all sorts of vexations. Twelve months have made a difference in me. I do not think I am less cheerful than I was at Newcastle, but I have lost a great deal of my thoughtlessness, and it is all very right that I should.*

However adorable such words might sound coming from a youngster in braids, this personal confidence was to come in handy when, at age nineteen, just after her mother had died, Dinah's father deserted the family, and she was left to fend for herself in London. The reasons for such a sudden and spectacular departure from parental obligation are not known; regardless, it was brutal: he refused even to speak to Dinah as he packed up and moved out, leaving her without a penny in the world. The family solicitor back in Newcastle was summarily informed that the children were "entirely destitute . . . Mr. Mulock w[ill] have nothing to do with them," and Dinah sat down to consider her options. Very fortunately, her brothers were old enough to find work for themselves—but what could *she* do? Seek protection with an aunt or a cousin, as convention dictated? Enlist herself as a governess, like Charlotte Brontë's Jane Eyre, and slave away for a pitiable thirty pounds per annum? For this hardheaded young woman, these options must have all seemed preposterous. She does not appear to have been the type to take easily to being anyone's ward, eternally dependent on and subject to the munificence of others.

As early as 1841, Dinah had been dabbling in literature, the only vocation where women could meet men "on level ground," as she later wrote, "[and] often beat them in their own field." The *Staffordshire Advertiser* printed her first poem, a short one on the birth of Queen Victoria's baby girl, and it wasn't long before Robert Chambers, Catherine Crowe's dear friend, got wind of this sharp-witted young talent through his London scout Mrs. S. C. Hall; he then quickly published a slew of Dinah's early poetry in his *Edinburgh Journal*, starting in 1845, and by the following year, works by "D.M.M." were a regular sight all over England. She wrote and wrote—tales of down-and-out characters who slowly reveal their worth, stories about love and loyalty, and pieces long and short that turned around a central theme of hope, self-reliance, prudence, and functionality. She also took distribution into her own hands, energetically walking from one part of the city to another with copies of her work under her arm, dropping a poem here, a story there; making herself known by forging contacts; and showing herself, pluckily, to anyone willing to pay for her work.

This is how Dinah learned to dominate her trade. Each periodical catered to a different audience, she discovered, and writing these audiences would gain her more renown over a shorter period of time: *Chambers's Edinburgh Journal* was cheaper than others and therefore more attuned to working-class readers. So she gave them simple, realistic tales about the value of perseverance and the duty to one's family ("All for the Best," "Good Seed," "Minor Trials," "The Motherless Children"). *Bentley's Miscellany* and *Fraser's* were directed at upper-class people with spare half crowns to spend on magazines, so to them went stories with more imaginative, and less moral, circumstances ("The Self-Seer," "The Wife of King Tolv," "Hyas the Athenian"). And for those with the highest literary taste, who reached for Robert Chambers's premiere publication, *Papers for the People,* Dinah contributed long-form works with complicated plots and dialogue (an entire volume of *Papers* was dedicated to "The Half-Caste: An Old Governess' Tale"). Assessing the literary quality of these early short stories is a dicey prospect, mostly because they were either edited with a very heavy hand or, as was sometimes the case, expanded dramatically by a staff writer looking to fill pages. However, the evolution of her style between these contributions and her later work is telling. In that span of time, she learned how to manipulate language better, abandoning tangled, inverted diction in favor of the approach she would later be known for; she grew skilled at finding inspiration in daily life—from paintings, from folklore, and, as in "Miss Letty's Experiences," from people seen on the street—and at breathing life into her ideas; and she also honed the already well-developed creed driving her writing, which at its core preached hard work, economy, and familial affection for a successful life.

While writing for the magazines, Dinah also found time to publish a few children's books, *Michael the Miner*; and *How to Win Love, or Rhoda's Lesson,* in which a young girl must remember the needs of others; as well as *Cola Monti,* a piece about a painter who learns to be punctual and responsible by dint of dedication and practice—as the title page of *Cola Monti* reads, "God helps those who help themselves," a potent statement about the way she hoped to be perceived by her reading public.

It wasn't a lucrative living, but it paid for her little house in Camden Town and gave her a new level of confidence. She used to be self-conscious about her uncommon height ("I am quite a *giantess*") and her homeliness and thin frame, but as a professional authoress, it seems she felt more poised and coolheaded. Her friend and fellow writer Margaret Oliphant, who lived in the same "dreadfully shabby and out-of-the-way" neighborhood, where rents were cheap, remembered Dinah's singular personality:

> *She was a tall young woman with a slim pliant figure, and eyes that had a way of fixing the eyes of her interlocutor in a manner which did not please my shy fastidiousness. It was embarrassing, as if she meant to read the other upon whom she gazed . . . But Dinah was always kind, enthusiastic, somewhat didactic and apt to teach, and much looked up to.*

When, at age twenty-one, after nearly three years of toil in commercial work, she came into her mother's trust of four hundred pounds—the financial abundance of which can be gleaned by comparing it with Jane Eyre's pitiable thirty pounds a year as a governess—Dinah finally had enough money to take a few days off each month to enjoy her newfound (albeit modest) success. At some point she'd connected with a roommate, a Frances Martin—a girl even younger than she, who would go on to found the College for Working Women, a spinoff of the Working

Women's College founded by suffragist Elizabeth Malleson—and together they went about society "in the most independent manner," as Elizabeth Gaskell remembered, "living in lodgings by themselves, writing . . . such a phenomenon was rare, perhaps unexampled in those days." Unconventional maybe, but shrewd—the flourishing Dinah and Frances threw no-frills soirees from their home and invited everyone they knew in the business of letters: fellow *Chambers's* contributors Anne Maria Hall, Camilla Toulmin, and George Lillie Craik (Dinah's future husband's uncle of the same name); dramatist George Lovell; poet John Westland Marston; and Alexander Macmillan, who'd founded his publishing firm just a few years earlier. Dinah was always full of "wonderful vitality and high spirits," and unfailing enthusiasm for women's projects. Like Catherine Crowe, she also participated in the Spiritualist movement, even, on occasion, swapping literary discourse at her parties for a séance or two (though, it should be noted, her early writings reflect a mind unconvinced by mysticism; a character's unworldly experiences were always explained away after the subject realized it had all been a dream).

By age twenty-two, Dinah saw the profits from her magazine work paying the bills well enough to permit her a longer hiatus from month-to-month production, and for the first time, she began experimenting with full-length novels. Her initial attempt, *The Ogilvies,* attracted a fair amount of attention (unsurprising, given her keen understanding of the literary profession), but reviewers found it a little immature for their taste; the plotting was artificial, the circumstances improbable, the central plot tired and obsolete. (Dinah was drawing from the only novels she was familiar with: those from her 1830s secondhand lending library back in Newcastle.) She was a quick study, though, and her second try was far more demonstrative of her talents.

In *Olive*, we can see the style and quality she'd begun to cultivate in her early works flower alongside some forward-thinking philosophies. The main character, Olive Rothesay, is a hardworking young woman shadowed by the disadvantages of low birth and exterior flaws, but despite these impediments, she is a real gem on the inside. As far as Victorian disadvantage goes, Olive gets what could possibly be the worst of it. She's born disabled—"Hump-backed . . . poor thing, poor thing!"—and is consequently a terrible source of angst and torment to her parents: they know she'll never be marriageable, and thus she'll always be a burden. Because of their cruelty and coldness, Olive tearfully resigns herself to a philosophy of solitude in her youth that, over time, turns into self-hating denial of her need for happiness:

> *She had no maiden doubts or hopes, not one . . . Olive had ceased to dream about love at all. Feeling that its happiness was for ever denied her, she had altogether relinquished those fancies in which young maidens indulge . . . Scarcely was she even conscious of the happiness that she lost; for she had read few of those books which foster sentiment; and in the wooings and weddings she heard of, were none that aroused either her sympathy or her envy. Coldly and purely she had moved in her sphere, superior to both love's joy and love's pain.*

It was common for novels written by women to feature a disabled or maimed *male* figure. Hampered by their disability, these characters can't move about the world as freely as they would like, and instead are condemned to live and think in an enclosed space—like a woman. A disabled man could thus be endowed with feminine qualities, be gentler and more sensitive than a man with full use of his body or faculties, thereby making him more accessible to those who wished to understand his motives, nail down his affections, or simply control him: Linton Heathcliff in *Wuthering Heights,* "an ailing, peevish creature," is used as a pawn to gain Thrushcross Grange. In *The Mill on the Floss,* the only character able to perceive and appreciate the heroine's true worth is Philip Wakem, who has a recurring mental ailment and womanly "fits." Even virile Mr. Rochester must first be tamed via disfigurement and blindness before Jane Eyre can forgive his past transgressions, enabling them to marry. Yet disability in a female character acts as a double negative: she is granted freedom from the moral imperative to marry—marriage for a crippled woman was generally thought a hopeless cause—and is left to forge her own way in the world, independent. (Would that more eighteenth-century Englishwomen had been granted such autonomy!) This is how Olive is allowed to become a painter's protégée and to make a comfortable living for herself as an artist, conquering that self-loathing and shame in the process. She then is able to give her heart to a middle-aged widower debilitated by inner torment (again, disabled), and the two find respite within each other, "smiling, nestled . . . warm and safe in love."

Olive is an emotional work, giving voice as it does to all kinds of things no one wants to feel: rejection, loneliness, discomfort with the body. It was Dinah's commitment to frank openness, and her fearlessness in addressing uncomfortable truths, that made the book successful. Critics cited her ability to paint ordinary characters with color and flourish—the lowest, most pitiable soul in Dinah's work seems "heroic beneath the broadcloth of contemporary life." For its twenty-four-year-old creator, *Olive* was the impetus for an even greater confidence in her writing, and in her negotiation skills with editors. So, by the time she was ready to write her masterpiece, she was a literary force to be reckoned with.

In the two years following *Olive*, Dinah produced two more novels—*Head of the Family*, a country drama à la Eliot's *Middlemarch*, with a broad, dynamic cast of characters; and *Agatha's Husband*, a curious work chronicling the life of a newlywed couple through the ups and downs of jealousy and family pride, miscommunication and greed (though, of course, there is no mention of sex)—and for each of the four novels she had produced in five years, *Olive* and *The Ogilvies* among them, she was paid one hundred fifty pounds for the copyright (about fourteen thousand pounds in today's money). From the perspective of her publishers, Chapman and Hall, this was more than fair; they'd made a small fortune on Charles Dickens's work *The Pickwick Papers*, and had paid the author accordingly, but Dinah was no Dickens, and one hundred fifty pounds was still a little better than the going rate for a beginning writer. To them, she had no reason to complain.

She, of course, disagreed. Her works were selling well—very well, even if not Dickens well—and she figured she deserved more. New editions of her older novels were going out to great acclaim, and the profits were pouring into Chapman and Hall while she worked her fingers to the bone for scraps. Why couldn't she get a bigger slice of the pie? *Head of the Family* had gone into six editions; certainly there was some extra capital lying around. She appealed meekly at first:

> *Do you think that out of the profits of all that you could spare some addition to the one hundred and fifty pounds you gave me?—I know it is not a right—& yet it seems hardly unfair . . . [it is] important to me to gather up all I can—My head is tired out with having worked to hard.*

When their reply was in the negative, Dinah promptly walked away in search of a new publisher. Through Margaret Oliphant she was introduced to the directing publishers at Hurst and Blackett, and immediately entered negotiations for her newly finished novel, *John Halifax, Gentleman*. Still nervous about money, she also decided to reach out to her old friend Alexander Macmillan, for some additional employment while she awaited their decision. She wanted something regular, less demanding, "mechanical literary work—such as being a 'publisher's reader'—or the like—which w[oul]d give me a settled income . . . [that would] be a great blessing to me."

However wise a precaution this was, it showed itself to be unnecessary: Hurst and Blackett came back with a tantalizing offer for *John Halifax, Gentleman,* of three hundred pounds outright and an additional one hundred pounds after twelve hundred copies of the book sold. Plus she'd get half the profits on a second edition if the book were popular enough to warrant one—and it was, many times over. *John Halifax* was published in 1856, when

Dinah was thirty years old, and from then on, money was never much of a problem for her.

By applying to Macmillan for a side job, was Dinah demonstrating a latent uncertainty about her newest book? It seems an apt assumption; *John Halifax* was one of the first English novels to have a lowly tradesman as its hero, and Dinah must have worried about its reception. Yet no one should have been surprised that a work like this would come from her pen—it was exactly the kind of thing a seasoned, well-adjusted pragmatist with her finger on the pulse of literary culture would produce. And of course, it came at exactly the right time.

In the early 1850s, England was awash in the afterglow of the 1851 Great Exhibition, the most exciting show of technology and commerce that had ever been held. Items from all over the world were on display as part of some fourteen thousand exhibits in the specially built Crystal Palace: a hunting knife with eighty blades, Samuel Colt's repeat-action revolver, a leech-powered barometer, a steam-powered hammer. There was a galaxy of domestic and agricultural machinery to cut working time in half, such as Elias Howe's sewing machine, Cyrus McCormick's reaper, and devices for cutting stone, folding envelopes, printing, weaving, and cooking. Even the venue itself was a feat of engineering: the greenhouse-like glass-and-iron Crystal Palace was vast enough to accommodate four St. Paul's Cathedrals, not to mention the more than six million people who entered it during the five months of the Great Exhibition (on the busiest day, there were ninety-two thousand in the building at the same time, the largest indoor gathering ever at that time).

For all the wonders on display, the most revolutionary aspect of the Great Exhibition was the middle-class men present: those smiling proudly as their inventions were surveyed, those watching carefully to ensure the event they'd helped organize went off without a hitch, or those simply attending alongside their upper-class brethren, with whom, until now, they wouldn't generally have been allowed to mingle. Together, these men (and women) represented the new middle class, a group with a healthy commitment to industry and who, by taking risks a conservative aristocrat might have passed up in favor of the status quo, would shortly come to dominate the English economy. Here, at the Great Exhibition, they were also an embodiment of the social upheaval that had shaken up the marriage market: aristocratic roots no longer automatically equated to financial success. Instead, power was transferring from the landowners to the makers and distributors (farmers, bankers, merchants, manufacturers)—and the myth of the middle-class upstart was born.

How perfect, then, that Dinah should choose to use just such a person as her protagonist. John Halifax is the quintessential phoenix out of the ashes who, on account of his hard work and intrepidity, makes himself into exactly the kind of person on display at the Great Exhibition. And, reflective as he was of England's changing landscape, he had an instant mass following from the expanding middle class. When the novel opens, young John has taken shelter from a storm near the house of tanner Abel Fletcher and his puny son Phineas (another disabled character), the latter acts as the book's womanish narrator. John and Phineas lock eyes, and it is immediately determined that John is a noble being, that he doesn't belong in such a gritty life:

> *Thus he stood, principal figure in a picture which is even yet as clear to me as yesterday—the narrow, dirty alley leading out of the High Street, yet showing a glimmer of green field at the farther end; the open house-doors on either side, through which came the drowsy burr of many a stocking-loom, the prattle of children paddling in the gutter, and sailing thereon a fleet of potato parings . . . From a break in the clouds came a sudden stream of life. The stranger-lad lifted his head to look at it. "The rain will be over soon," I said, but doubted if he heard me. What could he be thinking of so intently? — a poor working lad, whom few would have given credit for thinking at all.*

Abel inquires emphatically, "Art thee a lad to be trusted . . . I say, art thee a lad to be *trusted?*" And John Halifax, who feels this moment is critical, conquers it by staring directly into Abel's eyes during the next round of questioning. "Shall I give thee [money] now?" Abel asks, and John replies sturdily, "Not till I've earned it, sir." So virtuous, so gentle, John Halifax is immediately taken off the streets and put to work in the Fletchers' tannery collecting animal hides for processing. It's backbreaking labor (and stinky beyond all reason), but John is grateful for it, of course: "I don't care what it is, if only it's honest."

Life goes on, and John becomes more and more the person he was meant to be. He teaches himself to read and write in his snug attic bedroom, with Phineas's assistance; he starts building model machines and shows a propensity for math; he saves two men from a sinking boat, but won't accept any money for his heroism; he leverages himself into a position of greater authority in the tannery, as a clerk, and marries his sweetheart, an energetic girl called Ursula; and finally, after years of work, he purchases his own mill and refits it with the latest technology. The Industrial Revolution is brought peaceably to the area, and John lives out the rest of his days in ease and amity as the neighborhood's benevolent leader.

Clean, self-directed, patient, thrifty—John is an absurdly upstanding citizen. He's so good, in fact, that the struggles and difficulties inherent in a hero's path are almost nonexistent for him: Every potential problem is solved before it comes to its full fruition. Women are perfectly invisible to him before he meets his wife. He never drinks, never overspends, never wastes time, never attends to any hobby or pursuit that isn't expressly useful. As a result of his near-ridiculous integrity, he gets everything he wants. Even after his mill is sabotaged by the wrathful Earl of Luxmore, an aristocrat representing a bygone era, John skirts around the problem by devising a new way to power the place (steam) and goes on to realize even greater success. He exemplifies the new middle-class morality, and the new, wage-driven husband women pined after; he is a common man of uncommon proportions, and for this, he is rewarded. Eighteenth-century-style characters such as Squire Brithwood and the earl, on the other hand, who binge-eat and -drink, embrace idleness, make coarse jokes, and hunt foxes like good patricians—they are doomed to be surpassed by John's enterprising purity (and to have very unsatisfying marriages).

By creating such a protagonist, one emblematic of her readers' value systems, and by reinforcing the newest modern social values in a well-constructed story, Dinah not only showcased her keen understanding of society but also made *John Halifax, Gentleman* impossible to ignore. It flew off the shelves. Four editions went out in two years with Hurst and Blackett, followed by other printings (cheap, illustrated, or otherwise) with eleven different English publishing houses and forty-five American ones. Readers gushed over Dinah's assertion that any and all professions were available to those who worked hard, and they lauded John for having done what they all wished they could do; they even swarmed by the hundreds to Tewkesbury to see where this Mr. John Halifax had lived and worked in so noble a way, perhaps wishing to carry some of his characteristics home in their pockets. "Miss Mulock," the saintly angel who had inspired them, was now famous: *John Halifax, Gentleman* was just behind *Uncle Tom's Cabin* in an 1863 list of popular titles, and Dinah's works became "more widely read than the productions of any other writer after Dickens."

The literati, on the other hand, were less enthused. To reviewers, John's squeaky-clean habits were irritating, and his ability to rise into financial success could not in itself make him worthy of gentry drawing rooms. He might be self-reliant, energetic, and kind, "but he would not—he could not, attain the bearing and manners of a fine gentleman; he could not by mere effort of self-culture attain the tone of good society." Still, what could bad reviews really do in the face of such broad success? The book was selling wildly and would likely continue to do so, regardless of the critical reception. Commentators just had to go with the flow:

> *Neither before nor after his successful incarnation was John Halifax to be weighed or measured. We know of no scales that will hold him, and of no unit of length with*

> *which to compare him. He is infinite; he outlasts time; he is enshrined in a million innocent breasts; and before his awful perfection and his eternal durability we respectfully lower our lance.*

DINAH HAD ESTABLISHED HERSELF AS AN AUTHORITY ON social causes, and consequently, editors now began to approach her for essays and didactic stories to further elucidate her position. This is when she wrote *A Woman's Thoughts About Women*, probably her most famous nonfiction piece; a new novel, *A Life for a Life*; and a serially published tale about female sisterhood across class differences, *Mistress and Maid*. She commanded big money for her work, too (as much as two thousand pounds per story), and eventually came to personify that troublesome, cantankerous businesswoman whom Victorian society found so nightmarish in Dickens's *Bleak House*.* Dinah, just like Mrs. Jellyby, would not allow others to control her professional dealings, and she was willing to break the rules of conduct to get what she knew she deserved. Margaret Oliphant wrote that Dinah's publisher Henry Blackett "turned pale at [her] sturdy business-like stand for money," and would tell others of the experience "with affright, very grave, not able to laugh."

Unlike Mrs. Jellyby, whose husband and children lived un-

* Mrs. Jellyby is so absorbed in her philanthropic efforts for African children that she pays no heed to the many domestic tasks a Victorian woman is expected to oversee: the servants are unruly, dinner is late and badly cooked, the children run naked and wild through the neighborhood, and her poor husband, Mr. Jellyby, is gravely neglected. Many who supported the woman's abandonment of all nonessential pursuits after marriage no doubt cited Mrs. Jellyby as the antithesis of a good wife.

washed and unfed among piles of forgotten domestic chores, Dinah had no one to look after—no husband and, after 1863, no brothers, either. Thomas Mulock's abandonment had inspired Dinah to reach for the stars to survive, but her two brothers had fared differently. Young Tom relinquished a promising career in art for a sailor's commission to make ends meet, and tragically met his end before the ship left harbor for its second voyage, after he fell from the mast and broke both femurs. Ben bounced from one profession to another for a long while, sometimes staying with Dinah at her rural Hampstead home, Wildwood Cottage, before dashing off to Australia to try engineering or to Brazil to photograph the new railways. Much like his father, he was unstable and volatile, "giving anxieties much grudged and objected to by [Dinah's] friends, but never by herself," as Oliphant remembers it, and eventually his mental derangement necessitated restraint in Dr. Harrington Tuke's asylum. Five days after his incarceration he attempted an escape and died from injuries sustained in the process.

Dinah was crushed at the loss of Ben, her one remaining near-and-dear relative, a man who had "given her affection for affection" even as his mind sank into melancholy. Cripplingly stunned, she was, for the first time, too sad to work, and wrote to her cousins of her plans to head for Scotland to recover:

> *All the funeral arrangements had to be made at once, and as quiet as possible, on account of the establishment. I sent for no one, for no one would help me . . . My poor boy—he suddenly came home to me on the 27 of Feb. [1863] and said, "Sister, I am going mad—you must take care of me"—and I did. And now he is at rest, and I thank God*

> *. . . Wildwood is let furnished till October, but I then give it up entirely. I shall never return to London any more.*

Wildwood was passed off to another single authoress, Eliza Meteyard (who would soon write her splendid *Life of Josiah Wedgwood*), as a mournful and distraught Dinah solemnly packed up her belongings and moved to a tiny town in Scotland near Glasgow, Wemyss Bay, where she had a small collection of friends. Considering how difficult it was to get there, her reasons for doing so require a bit of investigation. They seem centered on the loss of Ben and, maybe, if we were to guess, the need for removing herself from the environs of his painful and tragic mental decline. Yet upon further reflection, I believe there was another rationale for her choosing to reside near Glasgow and for staying as long as she did. Was it because her love interest was living there, too?

It's not known exactly when Dinah Mulock was introduced to George Lillie Craik the Younger; he may have accompanied his uncle to one of Dinah's parties, where the latter was often in attendance, or they might have met through another family member, James Craik, the minister at St. George's in Glasgow. However, while their first encounter was no doubt pretty standard, their second was completely unforgettable—it was "an extraordinary case of life imitating art." For Dinah, who took pride in defying convention, an ideal Victorian sexual relationship (as defined by the disability trope) suddenly and weirdly became reality: George was immobilized by an injury, she swooped in to care for him, and love blossomed in the light of her maternal purity (and without her indecently *seeking* him like a brash husband hunter). The sensational coincidence of it all led to a wide dissemination of the tale and, naturally, conflicting accounts of it, too, but it is almost certain that one version of their remarkable story is correct.*

George Lillie Craik the Younger was in business as an accountant in Glasgow, and he often went down to London to attend to his increasingly famous family. (The older George Lillie Craik's publications were numerous and pioneering, and George the Elder's brother Henry Craik, a pastor, was a well-known linguist.†) During one of these visits, in 1861 (by which time he'd apparently already met Dinah), George's train went off the tracks and crashed somewhere outside the city, summarily depositing George out onto the snow to bleed to death. His leg needed to be amputated—did he know anyone who could attend to him in his convalescence? As one report goes, he could only stammer "Miss Mulock" before passing out, and Dinah was swiftly summoned to his side. Another version recounts the train as having been smashed to bits very near her home at Wildwood and that,

---

* The details are fuzzy (neither George nor Dinah ever spoke of it publicly), but there is documented evidence that the train accident did occur: In 1861, Dinah wrote to her cousin with questions about the railway company's liability in the event of personal injury, and he responded with sympathy for her "very good and amiable actions." Additionally, when the 1861 census officer came around to Wildwood, George Lillie Craik was recorded as "visiting." See Reade, *Mellards*, 87; and Karen Bourrier, "Rereading Dinah Mulock Craik," *Women's Writing* 20, no. 3 (2013): 295n13.

† In her childhood, George Lillie Craik Sr.'s *The New Zealanders* was among the few books Dinah had before the arrival of her neighbor's lending library. His other titles included *The Pursuit of Knowledge Under Difficulties*, biographies of Francis Bacon and Edmund Spenser, and the coauthored *Pictorial History of England* (from which his *History of British Commerce* was extracted). George the Elder's brother Henry published *Principia Hebraica; or, an Easy Introduction to the Hebrew Language* and *The Distinguishing Characteristics and Essential Relationships of the Leading Languages of Asia and Europe*, among others.

upon seeing the mess, Dinah opened her doors to the injured. Yet another version places George at a hotel for his operation and Dinah on hand only by happenstance. However it shook out, George Lillie Craik somehow ended up on Dinah's couch short a leg, and soon, despite being far younger than his attendant—he was twenty-four; she was thirty-three—a flirtation developed. Dinah had scribbled to Ben of "inexpressible" feelings while George recuperated in the next room, where he remained for almost a year:

> *I do believe if he could cut himself up into little pieces for my sake he would do it—which isn't always the feeling of people one has done things for—generally very much t'other—nor is it always the result of people living constantly together for nearly nine months & consequently finding out all one another's weak points. They certainly are a most capital family—but the best of them all as they themselves agree, is George.*

In light of such a deep attachment, the motivation behind Dinah's flight to Glasgow after Ben's death seems rather more personal than professional. Also, even though two years had passed since the train accident, hers and George's love appears to have been as fresh as ever: After a few months in Scotland, Dinah found her spirit well on its way toward restoration. She was planning a new book that was, as she joked to her friend Mrs. Jolly, "a tale on a new plan, without an atom of love in it!"—this would be her *Christian's Mistake*—and she was able to offer strength and support in her letters to her other ailing family members. None of her friends, however, was informed of her impending marriage; she didn't wish to cause offense, but as thirty-five was then considered middle-aged, a fussy wedding seemed "perfect nonsense." Instead, she and George were married in the simplest fashion in Bath, on April 29, 1865, just days after her thirty-ninth birthday, and thereafter Dinah was so over the moon at the miracle of having attained him that she was able to make light of her longtime single status:

> *When people are happily married—they are so very happy! . . . I never alter my creed that a single woman may be perfectly happy in herself—if she chooses—and that the single life is far better than any but the very happiest married life . . . but oh—we are so happy!*

Meanwhile, Dinah's old friend Alexander Macmillan was on the hunt for a partner at his fast-growing London publishing house. George Craik was an experienced accountant; his new wife a potential gold mine of future publications—an excellent combination. The offer was made, and accepted, and less than two months after their wedding, George and Dinah Craik were back in London. He went to work for Macmillan, where he was well liked and respected, and Dinah, in the most unconventional fashion, stayed at her writing while in "the exquisite absorption" of her matrimonial home. She would not be abandoning her premarital projects as the conduct literature suggested; quite the opposite, in fact. She wrote five novels in the five years following her marriage (*Christian's Mistake, A Noble Life, Two Marriages, The Woman's Kingdom,* and *Hannah,* all modestly successful but less so than *John Halifax*) and serialized another, *A Brave Lady,* one of whose central themes was a woman's right to her own property. She also kept on top of her magazine work and children's books, experimented with translation, and helped George read manuscripts for Macmillan.

Soon the couple was building the home where they'd spend the next two decades. It was constructed in the middle of a rural panorama on Shortlands Road, near Bromley, outside London, and in a less-than-fashionable style—"We shall be Gothic to within an inch of our lives!" Nevertheless, it was warm, sturdy, and functional; a perfect reflection of its owners. "I built the house with *books,*" Dinah wrote, "which has entailed the hardest work I ever did, and it is not done yet." While nowadays the area has been suburbanized, the original grounds filled in and paved over, in its heyday the place was "very beautiful," as one of its numerous visitors remembered, with "books bedded in the recesses of the drawing-room, good paintings on the walls, and a sweet garden planned and planted by our hostess." It was here, in this haven of peace and companionship, that Dinah Craik stayed until her death eighteen years later, writing and writing, luxuriating in "the delicious retirement of dependent love" that life with George Craik turned out to be.

WHETHER IT WAS BECAUSE OF DINAH'S AGE, OR BECAUSE OF her husband's injuries from the train crash, or some other reason, the two would never succeed in bringing a biological child into the world. However, in a strange twist of fortune, Dinah *did* become a mother. At five o'clock in the morning on New Year's Day 1869, a nine-month-old baby girl was found frozen nearly to death on the side of the road, and Dinah, who was almost forty-three, marched straight down there and brought her home. The authoress must have felt an instant rush of pity for this "dainty little soul [with] big blue eyes" whose birth had been a tragedy for some poor woman. Even so, it's difficult to overstate the outlandishness of her actions. In a culture that valued blood ties and believed in hereditary personality traits, adopting an unknown baby was considered positively wacky—didn't she worry that the baby had been born out of wedlock, and that, consequently, the mother's loose morals would have been passed to the child? Victorian society as a whole couldn't shake this concern, and consequently there were virtually no options for orphans or illegitimates but to become wards of the state, a burden to their neighbors. Dinah didn't see it that way, however; the baby was a gift, a new treasure for a childless woman, and she was now their daughter. Dinah named her Dorothy, whose meaning in Greek is "the gift of God," and settled contentedly into a routine of raising her, making all her clothes, and loving every minute of being her mother. Her creative output was reduced during Dorothy's infancy, but Dinah didn't mind. Her new responsibilities were "twenty thousand times better than writing."

NOTHING DINAH WROTE AFTER *JOHN HALIFAX, GENTLEMAN* ever sold as well. Yet despite her declining popularity in a changing market—newfangled "sensation" novels were starting to take over, as you'll see in the next chapter—she wrote prolifically for the rest of her days. Ever the pragmatist, she continued working on social issues, especially those dealing with the "woman question" and the middle class. Her last full-length novel, *Young Mrs. Jardine,* entertained the idea that certain problems in marriage made a separation absolutely obligatory: "Drunkenness, dissoluteness, anything by which a man degrades himself and destroys his children, gives his wife the right to save them and herself from him." *King Arthur: Not a Love Story* attested strongly that adoption needed legal oversight (for, at the time, there were no laws regulating it). *Hannah* is about marriage with a dead wife's sister, an act that had been unjustly forbidden under English law since 1835. (This was parliamentary infringement on personal rights, according to Dinah, and it ruffled her feathers rather more substantially than some of the other social mores she addressed; she even traveled to Switzerland to celebrate the marriage of her dear friend William Holman Hunt to his dead wife's sister, Edith, then a patently illegal ceremony.) Her other works for children did well—*The Little Lame Prince* had particular success in America—as did her travel pieces, such as *An Unsentimental Journey Through Cornwall* and *Fair France*. In total, she published fifty-two books and countless articles, poems, and short stories before dying of sudden heart failure in October 1887, in the midst of preparations for Dorothy's wedding.

Dinah Craik always wrote directly to a middle-class audience, "novel-readers, pure and simple," as George Eliot put it, and as a consequence, she never had much of a reputation among intellectuals. Yet for this she was unapologetic. *The Mill on the Floss* and others like it, she responded, might be "as perfect as the novel can well be made . . . but . . . what good will it do? [Ask] whether it will lighten any burdened heart, help any perplexed spirit, comfort the sorrowful, succor the tempted, or bring back the erring into the way of peace; and what is the answer? Silence." It had to be acknowledged that women were whole people, that their selfless poise and delicacy were in many cases merely a polished exoskeleton built to protect their inner workings from scrutiny, and the outside world from the potential explosiveness of female frustration. With the coming of sensation fiction, however, women's humanity would soon get its day in the spotlight.

seven

MARY ELIZABETH BRADDON

[1835–1915]

HAVING WORKED ON THE STAGE WHEN ACTRESSES WERE seen as little better than prostitutes, Mary Elizabeth Braddon—like Mary Robinson—already had a long way to go in proving herself an authoress. Ultimately, however, her ground-breaking, utterly shocking novels punched clean through the ceiling of her publishers' best-seller records, and she became one of the wealthiest, most successful writers of the nineteenth century. Yet to understand properly the remarkable story, and work, of Mary Elizabeth Braddon, we must first explore the world in which she was living.

Every student of history knows that the Industrial Revolution wrought rapid change across the United Kingdom during the Victorian era, but as the cotton mills and colliery headframes sprang up like mushrooms, the literary landscape was also undergoing a dramatic reconfiguration. By the time George Eliot's last novel, *Daniel Deronda,* was published in 1876, her sophisticated style of writing had fallen by the wayside in the wake of the newest trend in women's literature, the "sensation" novel. Frequently scorned as an example of "feminine genius of this generation ha[ving] touched its high-water mark," sensationalist fiction meant death and danger; animalistic excitement and naked emotion; sensual secrets, tawdry surprises, roiling suspense—and, not to forget, a posse of unchaste female characters who may be villainous, or even murderous. It was everything George Eliot and our women of literature were not (at least, on the page); it was provocative, sexy, and shamelessly immodest.

Even though George Eliot was out of touch with the smashing modern phenomenon that was the sensation novel, she was not unaware of the social conditions that had brought its arrival. In *Daniel Deronda,* the crux of the matter is unambiguously stated:

> *We women can't go in search of adventures—to find out the Northwest Passage or the source of the Nile, or to hunt tigers in the East. We must stay where we grow, or where the gardeners like to transplant us. We are brought up like the flowers, to look as pretty as we can, and be dull without complaining. That is my notion about the plants: they are often bored, and that is the reason why some of them have got poisonous.*

Of course, female frustration was not a new problem, but the steadily worsening severity of society's chokehold on women was, by the 1860s, more palpable than ever. Whatever choices she made, a woman seemed to court condemnation. If she ended up without a husband, she was a social pariah; if she tried to seek one out, she was a jezebel. She should decorate her house, but not *too* well, because that would be vain; yet if she didn't decorate it well enough, she risked being a laughingstock to her more domestically inclined neighbors. Dress continued to be a platform for displaying one's adherence (or lack thereof) to a restrictive standard, and the means of judging yet another near-impossible female balancing act. Tighten the corset to show evidence of a "well-disciplined mind and well-regulated feelings," as one fashion magazine recommended, or keep it loose to show a commitment to a grander, godlier life, away from ornamentation and trends.

On top of all these exterior considerations was the growing aversion to women taking up space in public or displaying negative emotions. Despite the recent explosion of female-authored books, and an accordingly expanded place for women in society, ladies were still expected to be silent, gentle, ignorant nonentities, as Mrs. Ellis explains in *The Daughters of England*:

> *Woman, whose whole life, from the cradle to the grave, is one of feeling, rather than of actions; whose highest duty is so often to suffer, and be still; whose deepest enjoyments are all relative; who has nothing, and is nothing, of herself; whose experience, if unparticipated, is a total blank . . . in her inexhaustible sympathies [she] can live only in the existence of another . . . [her] very smiles and tears are not exclusively her own.*

This is where the sensationalists stepped in, depicting female characters throwing off the chains of passivity and *doing* something about their generations-long subservience. These fictional women ride horses in the moonlight unchaperoned and elope with their lovers "in fits of sensual passion," as an aghast Margaret Oliphant recalled. They approach their domestic torment not with quiet, selfless resignation, but with action: faking their own deaths, setting their homes on fire, changing their identities, murdering their spouses. They speak in slang, drink scotch, use their sexuality aggressively for their own ends, and even abandon their children if the occasion calls for it. Gone were the days of the vapid, helpless Gothic heroines; they'd been replaced with she-devils, "beautiful women of elegant figure and golden locks, whose fascinating exterior only hides a subtle brain and a pitiless heart."

IF THIS ULTRAMODERN STYLE HAD BUBBLED UP FROM A WOMAN'S nib in the earlier half of the century, societal and technological restrictions would likely have kept it firmly tamped down. Its author would have been slapped with a "she's gone *mad*!" designation and locked away, dismissed, and forgotten. Unfortunately for the ultraconservative Victorians, developments in publishing and distribution would rob them of the luxury of censorship by default. The shilling monthly magazine had smashed onto the scene just as stamp duties, paper duties, and other "taxes on knowledge" were abolished, and the resulting circulation levels made even the people behind established periodicals such as *Bentley's Miscellany* and *The New Monthly Magazine* stare in amazement. These established magazines were selling seven or eight thousand issues per year, but these new titles (cheaply produced thanks to advances in printing technology and railroad distribution) enjoyed circulation far and away beyond their numbers. One such magazine, *Cornhill,* sold *eighty thousand* copies in its first year alone. *Cornhill, Temple Bar, Macmillan's,* and other shilling papers were disseminating their lowbrow content all over Britain, and there was simply no way the older magazines could keep up. The reading public may once have been wealthy, educated, and leisured, their cravings for steady, didactic tales controlling the market, but now they were becoming the minority in Britain's expanding economy.

Naturally, the aristocracy bristled at this topsy-turvy turn of events, in which citizens with less money and less time to read were fueling the publishing business. High-minded littérateurs such as Dickens and Eliot could never survive in a world where the success of a book or magazine was "in the hands of a clever, pushing, semi-educated middle-class," as one rattled writer put it, with their aesthetic appetite hovering somewhere between that for "wall-furniture" and "soothing syrup for puling mediocrity."

The world hadn't really been taken over by a drooling mass of miscreants, as this critic supposed, but he wasn't entirely wrong, either. These shilling papers, and their "pushing" readers, *were* transforming the way stories were written, published, and marketed. Sensationalism was a mercantile venture; it was publishing as a *business,* with no pretense of high culture. Sensation novels were not destined to sit on some gentleman's library shelf, rebound in tooled calfskin to match the others, more likely to be admired (and bragged about) than actually read. Instead, they went straight to the lending libraries in cheap three-volume editions (and, later, slapdash one-volume versions, too) to be devoured by household servants, middle-class businessmen and their wives, and everyone in between. And because they were usually serialized, during the year or half year leading up to the first edition, the authors couldn't spin tangled webs of character interactions or create circuitous, leisurely plot lines. The central purpose of each monthly installment was to motivate the reader to buy the next one; there was no time for revision, and no need for it anyway, for as a nostalgic Henry Mansel, philosopher and Anglican theologian, wrote, "no divine influence can be imagined as presiding over the birth of this work beyond the market-law of demand and supply." These were tales of action and intrigue, of fizzy flirtations, crime, danger, and suicide; they were meant to titillate, not to incite introspection. And because this was exactly what the reading public wanted, they kept buying, and sensationalism kept growing.

This kind of writing could only be done by someone able to withstand the pressure of deadlines, and while it would seem logical that men might have the upper hand in this, accustomed as most were to a busy work life, it was quite to the contrary: the fairer sex represented a formidable competitor in this genre. They seemed invigorated by the breakneck pace of the new market—and, perhaps more important, excited to revel in the style. For, in sensationalist fiction, the inclusion of anything and everything not expressly forbidden was compulsory in order to sell more books. It was simply a matter of choosing which outrage, which injurious atrocity, to focus on first. So, in one delicious release after another, the women of Victorian society began to let their hair down. Through madness, illness (feigned or otherwise), divorce, bigamy, adultery, masked identities, flight, mayhem, and murder, female protagonists were escaping the tyranny of their families and heading for greener pastures, even if their creators could not.

Not surprisingly, female readers *ate it up*. They could readily identify with a protagonist who, much like them, had had it with a life in which she "sits at home and works sham roses in Berlin wool while her booby brother is thrust out into the world to fight the mighty battle." As such, sensation novels were a kind of shared fantasy. Within their pages, both women writers and readers were finally able to see their rage, hurt, and sadness play out without it jeopardizing whatever tenuous well-corseted existence they'd managed to find for themselves. Yet many found even the fantasy of an independent life too damaging, too corrosive to the moral infrastructure of England, to allow it. The backlash was predictably (and often, hilariously) ruthless.

One male critic lamented his lost serenity, for "the mixture of crime and crinoline . . . is enough to take away the breath of any quiet middle-aged gentleman." Be suspicious of girls who read, he warned: "The young lady who is kind enough to teach one's daughters French and music looks and talks like an ordinary being; but it is very likely, if we only knew all, that she has got a murderess in manuscript in her bedroom." Others drew attention to the corrupting nature of such unguarded passion, for it was thought that exposing oneself to "the machinations of ruthless schemers" would degrade inner morality, or, as one doctor claimed, "accelerate the occurrence of menstruation." The Right Reverend Francis Paget was so utterly paralyzed with spitting hatred for sensation fiction, the whole shameful lot of it, that he resorted to what has been called "a series of little orthographic explosions" in his parody *Lucretia; or, the Heroine of the Nine-*

teenth Century. He fumes, he seethes—these female blasphemers were ruining England! On purpose! Their wicked talk of fraud and crime was permeating the gentle spirit of his countrymen, leaving in its place a mass of brutalized, overpassionate individuals. And the *sex*! Paget was stunned that descriptions of it should come from the mind of a female:

> *No* man *would have dared to write and publish such books as some of these are: no man* could *have written such delineations of female passion . . . No! they are women, who, by their writings, have been doing the work of the enemy of souls, glossing over vice, making profligacy attractive, detailing with licentious minuteness the workings of unbridled passions, encouraging vanity, extravagance, willfulness, selfishness, in their worst forms . . . Women have done this,—have thus abused their power, and prostituted their gifts,—who might have been bright and shining lights in their generation;—who might have been an example to the young and inexperienced . . .* O *shame and misery to them, that they have put themselves in the lamentable condition of those to whom henceforth nothing can be pure, since even their mind and conscience are defiled! And* O *what a degradation it is, and what a sorrow it ought to be to us, that such books should find readers!*

AMONG THE LEADERS IN THIS DEBASED GENRE, HORRID EXAMPLES of womanhood though *all* its female writers were, Mary Elizabeth Braddon was the unquestioned front-runner, the absolute worst of them—at least according to critics of the day. Ellen

Price Wood, better known as "Mrs. Henry Wood," also found great success in the sensation market, perhaps most of all with her 1861 novel *East Lynne,* but she was generally regarded as less morally corrupted than Braddon; Wood's characters were always punished for their transgressions. It didn't help that Braddon personally thumbed her nose at convention by moving in with her married boyfriend and bearing six illegitimate children; she had no intention of living any other way than what *she* thought best, regardless of public opinion.

MARY ELIZABETH BRADDON WAS BORN IN LONDON IN EARLY October 1835, and as with so many soon-to-be-famous authoresses (including, significantly, nearly every writer featured in this book), her parents parted ways early in her life and initiated their daughter into a lifestyle far more transient than that of most girls. For Mary this meant multiple addresses during her youth, as she and her mother moved from London to East Sussex and back again; and then within London, to Kensington and Hampstead; and finally to Chiswick. Her education would be conducted sporadically, at multiple institutions, but again, like so many authoresses, what she lacked in constancy she gained in worldly skills and adaptability: bouncy little Mary ran all over each of her childhood neighborhoods, making friends with anyone who would join in her fun, including her mother's cook, Sarah Hobbs, who sang bawdy songs and kept a tame rat in the kitchen at Chiswick. And when she wasn't tearing her clothes or running off to the fair to see plays, she was reading the works of Charles Lamb, Sir Walter Scott, and Charles Dickens—*Nicholas Nickleby,* she reported, contained "not a dry page"—learning French, practicing the piano, and memorizing Shakespearean monologues (to entertain her neighbors) under the guidance of her mother, who until her death in 1868 was Mary's constant companion.

Writing was also part of her daily amusement, though not often to completion; much later in life, in fact, she reflected that "the interval between the ages of eight and twelve [had been] a prolific period, fertile in unfinished MSS." She remembered starting "a historical novel on the Siege of Calais"; "a story of the Hartz Mountains, with audacious flights in German diablerie"; and a work called "The Old Arm Chair," in which a stash of money is found tucked under the upholstery and conveniently snatches a poor couple out of the jaws of destitution. Her work was fleeting but ambitious, and her mother, a literary sort in her own right, supported the efforts of this precocious fledgling writer.

Mary was undoubtedly expected to wait patiently for a suitor to come a-calling, but it seems clear from the outset that this outgoing, curly-haired young woman would have none of the life society commanded of her. Instead, she took matters into her own hands and joined a touring actors' guild under the name Mary Seyton. Until age twenty-five, Mary traveled all over rural England for performances as a so-called walking lady, a minor actress, and at least once as a lead character: She played a major role in Tom Taylor's 1857 *Still Waters Run Deep,* at the Assembly Rooms in Beverley, Yorkshire. And in an amazing intersection of events, Mary also acted in George Dibden Pitt's stage adaptation of Catherine Crowe's *Susan Hopley,* which "ha[d] been applauded in London for upwards of three hundred nights, and in the provinces for many more."

Her exact role isn't known, but as she later hinted to friend and fellow author George Augustus Sala, she might even have played Susan Hopley herself:

> *I am glad you are [now] in Buckinghamshire, and not at Upton where Susan Hopley lived and everybody murdered each other. To a person of my theatrical experience there is always something rather awful in the sound of "Upton." I am sure you must have "my murdered brother, Andrew," walled up in your bedroom. Some day, when you are shaving or hanging up your coat, you will touch a secret spring in the wainscot, and he will come out with a back-fall, green and festering.*

She did well on the stage—her speaking voice was noted to be especially lovely. Yet, by her seventh season, Mary's attention was shifting away from her craft. After almost a decade of "omnivorous" absorption of every book she could get her hands on—"everything from Carlyle to Ruskin to Harrison Ainsworth and Fenimore Cooper," as her friend Adelaide Calvert remembered—she had begun experimenting with poetry and playwriting instead of learning her lines. ("She always managed to alight on the last three or four words correctly," so as not to throw off the other actors, but "half her speeches were impromptu.") While her acting suffered, her writing flourished. Thanks in part to the support of her first patron, John Gilby,*

---

* The waters surrounding Braddon and Gilby's relationship are deep and murky, and thus, conclusions about the nature of their dealings vary widely. Was there unrequited love on Gilby's side? A feeling of professional or personal competition with Braddon's eventual employer, John Maxwell? A sense of indebtedness from receiving,

in quick succession she papered the provincial presses with her short stories and poetry (later to be published together as *Garibaldi and Other Poems*); wrote her first novel, *Three Times Dead*; and penned a play, *Loves of Arcadia*. Through these small yet formative early triumphs, it soon became clear to Mary where her future lay. She said good-bye to her acting friends, bundled up her life, and headed back to London to seek her fortune as a writer—and what she found there was a market primed for her work.

During the next two years, Mary Elizabeth Braddon's meteoric rise to fame as a pioneer of sensation fiction was due in large part to the efforts of her editor, John Maxwell, and his publishing empire of shilling magazines. However, her writing style was so perfectly in tune with the public mood, so exactly what was wanted then, that her work likely would have been successful no matter where she chose to place it. The other factor driving the explosive appetite for sensation novels, and in turn shaping the aesthetics of the genre, was the proliferation of cheap newspapers, aided astronomically (like so many things) by the advent of the railway network. People were now able to read accounts of yesterday's real-life mayhem over their morning coffee and rolls—and because of another technological achievement, in the

---

on Braddon's side (or giving, on Gilby's), financial support early in her career? The rumors have swirled for decades, but the only truths we can glean are that Gilby was indeed her patron (though to what extent is not known) and that their relationship, whatever it was, ended very poorly when Braddon left for London. (In his final letter to Braddon, Gilby writes, "I can only feel a pity for you not unmingled with contempt, and wonder if you have one redeeming trait in your character.") See Jennifer Carnell, *Literary Lives: A Study of Her Life and Work* (Hastings: Sensation Press, 2000), 127.

glow of their very own bedside light.* Reports of sex scandals, murders, and other disasters—and the court cases that often ensued—attracted so many paying readers that serial fiction authors quickly adjusted their scope to match, for realistic characters were now far more intriguing to the buying public than the tired old protagonist tropes of years previous.

In the standard Gothic novel, it was always clear who the villain was—evil was branded onto his face and body, scorched into the very ground he walked upon. Villains were never without the physical marks of their character, such as "wild eyes" or "a cunning smile," dark hair or a foreign accent, or the "half-civilized ferocity [that] lurked yet in the depressed brows" of Heathcliff in Emily Brontë's *Wuthering Heights,* for example. Always full of secrets, villains lived in a perpetual state of scheming, in brooding darkness, waiting in the shadows to pounce on their prey. Yet, as the novices to newspaper reading were coming to find out, reality wasn't so neatly demarcated. Sometimes it was the golden-haired bride who drowned her children, or the sweet, kindly governess who pushed her father into the path of a moving train. And if the would-be destroyer of peace in the real world could be anybody, wouldn't it be more fun if fiction reflected that? Jane Eyre could be the antagonist instead of Bertha Mason, Marianne Dashwood

---

* Earlier in the century, gaslight had replaced candles in many parts of the house where open flames were inconvenient or dangerous (e.g., drafty hallways, nurseries, and kitchens), and as a result, if cost wasn't too much of a factor, more candles could be spared for nighttime reading. If money was tight, however, and reading was important, a gaslight could certainly be used in a bedroom for a fraction of the price of a candle, but it was dirty, smelly, and harmful to the lungs. See Flanders, *Inside the Victorian Home,* 203–10.

instead of John Willoughby, Dorothea Brooke instead of Nicholas Bulstrode!

After seven years as an actress, Mary Elizabeth Braddon knew precisely how to develop realistic characters, and immediately upon arriving in the city in 1860 she began to demonstrate this; she would have no more humdrum stories of the chased chaste. In "Captain Thomas" and "A Cold Embrace," for instance, her first short stories for the London papers, her male protagonists move, speak, act, and worry in the same fashion as any normal bloke. Jealousy threatens their relationships, and they work to try to make amends (to varying levels of success). The prospect of falling out of love both compels and frightens them; stubbornness creeps in and hampers their interactions. And money problems? They're a real, palpable thing (not just nebulous "debts"), and they're addressed with more detail than earlier novels might have dared. ("I—*I* had furnished this house!" yells one man in a jealous tizzy, ". . . and now I was told how happy [*he*] would have been in this house of my providing.")

Mary often relates this from a *male* first-person perspective—a very bold choice indeed—and with a well-developed Dickensian sense of humor. One man thinks to himself, "O how I hate the simpering hostess in her best gown!" before remembering that his mother-in-law paid for the wedding breakfast, his "sacrificial feast." Another remarks that his spoiled daughter, Frederica, would have "taken off her chenille net and pulled the hair-pins and the frizzy things out of her hair, . . . marched straight up to [a suitor], and said, 'I have gone mad, I love you, let me die!'—and there'd have been a situation for the father of a family!"

Mary also demonstrated her streetwise knowledge of the reading public in her choice of publication platform. After a period of deliberation, she'd settled on the *Welcome Guest,* one of the many papers owned by John Maxwell, who, by dint of a few well-timed acquisitions, had become a strong competitor in the penny and half-penny periodical market. His circulation was growing; his connections with London-area publishers were strong and profitable; and it would be a mutually beneficial relationship: Mary would get her writing into the hands of those who wanted it most (i.e., the middle-class sensation seeker), and Maxwell would keep his magazines in the black by stuffing them with her serialized literature, which cost him next to nothing to acquire.*

Soon, Maxwell and Mary were so invaluable to each other (she for the steady income, and he for the excellent content) that they were working almost exclusively together. Nearly everything Mary wrote in the next year was published by Maxwell or those connected with him, including her short stories "My Daughters," "My First Happy Christmas," "Samuel Lowgood's Revenge," and "The Lawyer's Secret," along with miscellany such as "London on Four Feet" (a compassionate ode to horses, donkeys, and other beasts of urban burden) and "How the Romans Supped." Also, with her stories in the *Welcome Guest;* a reissuing of her first novel, *Three Times Dead,* under a new title, *The Trail of the Serpent;* the staging of her play *The Loves of Arcadia,* at London's Strand Theatre; and the appearance of her *Garibaldi and Other*

* These early "penny dreadful" stories brought Braddon very little in the way of remuneration. We're not entirely sure why, but she was consistently paid half as much as Maxwell's other contributors, even after *Lady Audley's Secret* and *Aurora Floyd.* See Carnell, *Literary Lives,* 184n5.

Poems, Mary's work was poking out from practically every corner of London—and she'd been living there only six months.

BY EARLY 1861, JUST AFTER TWENTY-FIVE-YEAR-OLD MARY began working as Maxwell's assistant, the two were lovers and cohabitating at his home in Mecklenburgh Square. It was naturally a dirty, delicious scandal (and a perfect plot for one of Mary's dirty, delicious stories). Living together outside of wedlock was unscrupulous and lewd, and in this case the situation was greatly compounded by the fact that John Maxwell was *already* married, with five young children. His wife, Mary Ann Crowley, had suffered a mental breakdown after the birth of their last baby and moved home to Ireland. Yet, divorce laws being what they were—that is, in support of a dissolution only in the case of adultery (on the woman's side) or abuse—he'd been forced to stay married to her, even as his wife's health declined from what was defined at the time as "puerperal insanity" (the same condition Mary Braddon would inflict on her most famous lead character, Lady Audley). It was a hurdle for young Mary, no doubt, but not a roadblock, for in her eyes, rules and conventions were made to be broken. So, in June 1861, she and Maxwell became common-law man and wife, and they would remain so until 1874, when Mary Ann Crowley's death allowed them to marry legally. With newly found bliss (and, on Mary's part, newly pregnant queasiness), they settled down to their next task at hand: writing and publishing one of the greatest successes in the then-history of the novel.

HOW *LADY AUDLEY'S SECRET* CAME ABOUT IS A TREMENDOUS story in itself, because it almost didn't happen at all. Amid all the domestic change of 1861, Maxwell had started a new periodical, and from the beginning it was rife with shortcomings despite its all-star editorial staff.* *Robin Goodfellow* limped along in its earliest stages and during the content acquisition process, and as the publication date for the first issue approached, it became clear that getting it off the ground was going to be even more difficult than Maxwell originally supposed. It was soon to be advertised in the *Athenaeum*—"Another new journal? Why not! The world is wide[,] and there is room enough for every one to elbow his way to the platform"—but the planned lead story had collapsed, and Maxwell was forced to consider delaying the magazine's publication until the kinks could be worked out. *London Society* writer Joseph Hatton takes it from there in his 1888 lifestyle piece "Miss Braddon at Home":

> *The day before a decision was necessary Miss Braddon heard of the difficulty and offered to write the story.*
>
> *"But even if you were strong enough to fill the position," was the publisher's reply, "there is no time."*
>
> *"How long could you give me?" asked the aspiring authoress.*
>
> *"Until to-morrow morning."*
>
> *"At what time to-morrow morning?"*
>
> *"If the first instalment were on my breakfast table to-morrow morning," he replied, indicating by his*

---

* *Robin Goodfellow* was to be edited by novelist/historian Sir Frederic Charles Lascelles Wraxall and Dr. Charles Mackay, father of novelist Marie Corelli (who would go on to outsell most of her male contemporaries) and author of a history of public frivolities, *Extraordinary Popular Delusions and the Madness of Crowds*.

> *tone and manner the utter impossibility of the thing, "it would be in time." The next morning the publisher found upon his breakfast table the opening chapters of "Lady Audley's Secret."*

Robin Goodfellow rolled off the presses in early July 1861 with the first chapters of what was to become Mary Braddon's most famous work, but the magazine's troubles became too much for Maxwell to offset, and he was forced to scrap it. *Lady Audley* was, fortunately, then transferred to another of his new publications, one with far greater prospects, *Sixpenny Magazine.* And for the next few months, all of London was in raptures over Mary's baffling heroine, the blue-eyed beauty who, in the interval between being reduced to trembling in a storm and arriving home with an apron full of flowers, tosses her husband down a well. Inspired as it was by the real-life horrors of an infamous and widely disseminated court case—one in which a young, well-bred lady named Constance Kent was (correctly) suspected of murdering her three-year-old half-brother with a razor blade, cutting his throat nearly clean through—the reading public simply couldn't get enough of *Lady Audley's Secret.* Issues of *Sixpenny* sold like hotcakes; piles of letters arrived at Maxwell's office begging Mary to keep writing, and to reveal the secret (one letter was from the actor J. B. Buckstone, who would later nickname his blue-eyed daughter Audley); even other papers, such as the *Court Journal,* pronounced themselves enchanted by this "very exciting tale" that had left them wondering "whether the heroine has or has not been the perpetrator of a most revolting murder." During the following summer, after the serialized story had concluded, William Tinsley bought the publishing rights from Maxwell and produced eight editions in three months.

The brilliance of the novel is in Mary's commitment to the voguish ideology of a mysterious, shockingly persuasive heroine with a perfect exterior, the kind of woman who came to define the sensation novel: Lady Audley is blonde and fragile, a domestic goddess, the nicest girl around. She's smart, accomplished, "amiable and gentle . . . lighthearted, happy and contented under any circumstances," not ambitious or scheming in the least. It's precisely these innocent characteristics that make her so dangerous, because in becoming the perfect Victorian female—by indoctrinating herself into a society that by its very nature requires secrecy and underhand action—she, like Constance Kent, becomes a villainous, deceitful fiend of a woman.

Still, since the thrilling mystery of the novel hangs on the construct of Lady Audley's good character, the reader must first be left without a doubt that, yes, on the outside, she is ideal:

> *Every one loved, admired, and praised her. The boy who opened the five-barred gate that stood in her pathway, ran home to his mother to tell of her pretty looks, and the sweet voice in which she thanked him for the little service. The verger at the church, who ushered her into the surgeon's pew; the vicar, who saw the soft blue eyes uplifted to his face as he preached his simple sermon; the porter from the railway station, who brought her sometimes a letter or a parcel, and who never looked for reward from her; her employer; his visitors; her pupils; the servants; everybody,*

high and low, united in declaring that Lucy Graham was the sweetest girl that ever lived.

Little do they know that "Lucy Graham" is just one of many aliases Lady Audley has used to cover her tracks. Three years earlier, Helen—that's her real name—was abandoned by her gentleman husband (in much the same way the real-life murderess Constance Kent reported being deserted by her newly remarried father) when he departed to prospect for gold in Australia. Being the kind of woman who would never stand for such rejection, she responded by ditching her young child, faking her death, and taking up work as a governess under a new name. A little while later, and very luckily for her, an old local widower, Sir Michael Audley, becomes enraptured by those "soft and melting blue eyes" and that "drooping head, with its wealth of showering flaxen curls," and she is spared the life of a governess. They court, he proposes, and she accepts, happily and unapologetically intent on bigamy (and, not coincidentally, fully aware of the fortune she is about to step into—"I cannot be blind to the advantages of such an alliance," she says in a state of laughing agitation, "I cannot, I cannot!"). They marry, and our heroine takes up residence at Sir Audley's noble manor. Then, one day not long after the wedding, Helen's first husband, George Talboys, shows up at Audley Court and meets his untimely death at the bottom of a well—or *does* he?

A long investigation ensues, at the hands of Sir Audley's nephew, Robert Audley—a character with a distinct and obvious similarity to the real detective inspector in the Constance Kent case, Jack Whicher—and a number of other crimes are committed by Lady Audley to cover up her first, before the truth is finally pieced together: they've all been duped by this dolly of a heroine. The great Newfoundland dog at Audley Court had always known, as dogs do; as had Sir Audley's grown daughter, Alicia, who from the first moments suspects Helen of being "a practiced and consummate flirt . . . not contented with setting her yellow ringlets and her silly giggle at half the men in Essex." Everyone else, though, is appalled, and in response to the whole wicked affair, an exhausted Robert Audley goes on an enormous antifemale tirade while sitting at dinner:

> *Who ever heard of a woman taking life as it ought to be taken? Instead of supporting it as an unavoidable nuisance, only redeemable by its brevity, she goes through it as if it were a pageant or a procession. She dresses for it, and simpers and grins, and gesticulates for it. She pushes her neighbors, and struggles for a good place in the dismal march; she elbows, and writhes, and tramples, and prances to the one end of making the most of the misery. She gets up early and sits up late, and is loud, and restless, and noisy, and unpitying . . . They riot in battle, and murder, and clamor [in] desperation. If they can't agitate the universe and play at ball with hemispheres, they'll make mountains of warfare and vexation out of domestic molehills, and social storms in household teacups. Forbid them to hold forth upon the freedom of nations and the wrongs of mankind, and they'll quarrel with Mrs. Jones about the shape of a mantle or the character of a small maid-servant. To call them the weaker sex is to utter a hideous mockery. They are the stronger sex, the noisier, the more persevering, the most self-assertive sex. They want freedom of opinion, variety of occupation, do they?*

Let them have it. Let them be lawyers, doctors, preachers, teachers, soldiers, legislators—anything they like—but let them be quiet—if they can.

At this point in the novel's production, Mary Elizabeth Braddon must have felt conflicted in choosing how to proceed. She could kill off Lady Audley, debased and thus deserving of a Gothic death, but nonetheless an assertive female with whom she and many thousands of readers identified. She could let Lady Audley live on in freedom, and risk being condemned for inducing widespread admiration for a homicidal maniac. Or, she could do what she did: in a truly sparkling stroke of genius, she chalked it all up to latent, somewhat ill-defined "puerperal insanity" and sent Lady Audley to an institution to live out her days in peace. This last was a fantastic option, for it also allowed Mary to tease the reader with the biggest secret of all: that Lady Audley is actually sane. (In the novel, the family doctor will not support the insanity defense, finding no evidence of insanity in Helen's having run away from an unpleasant home, in using bigamy to obtain fortune, or in her having "employed intelligent means . . . [to] carr[y] out a conspiracy which required coolness and deliberation in its execution.")

LADY AUDLEY'S SECRET WASN'T THE FIRST SENSATION NOVEL—that honor is usually bestowed upon Wilkie Collins's *The Woman in White,* which Mary drew on heavily for her own work (even down to her heroine's physical attributes)*—but

* "I always say that I owe 'Lady Audley's Secret' to 'The Woman in White.' Wilkie Collins is assuredly my literary father. My admiration for 'The Woman in White' inspired me with the idea of 'Lady Audley's Secret' as a novel of constitution and character. Previously my efforts had been in the didactic direction of Bulwer, long

with its female villain, it is an early and groundbreaking example of female sensation fiction, where women were not victimized without consequence to others. As such, it was also the source of much consternation in the media. Critics at the *Christian Remembrancer* were aghast at "the utter unrestraint" with which Lady Audley and her growing cadre of unchaste female heroines were permitted "to expatiate and develop their stormy, impulsive, passionate characters." *Punch* referred to it as "Lady *Disorderly's* Secret." Others wrongly suspected that the sensationalist's worrisome ethics had been plagiarized from the pages of one of those dubious French novels that were "not in accordance with our rules of respectability." Yet for all their objections, the critics couldn't deny that the work was a titanic triumph, and that, despite its imperfections (its bumptious wit, its rushed dialogue), *Lady Audley* had met the public's demand with absolute precision.

JOHN MAXWELL, MARY ELIZABETH BRADDON, AND WILLIAM Tinsley all got rich off the proceeds of this novel—Tinsley even built a mansion and named it Audley Lodge. However, rather than removing herself from the stress of serialized production, perhaps by trying another form of literature at a more relaxed pace, Mary ramped up her efforts, bringing new meaning to the word *prolific*. While she was busily scratching away at *Lady Audley*, "from hand to mouth, as a serial, wherever I happened to be when the time of publication drew near," she'd written four

conversations, a great deal of sentiment." See Hatton, "Miss Braddon at Home," quoted in Carnell, *Literary Lives*, 154.

other novels concurrently—*The Black Band; or Mysteries of Midnight; The Octoroon; or Lily of Louisiana; Captain of the Vulture;* and *The Lady Lisle*—each of which was serialized in one of Maxwell's growing list of cheap publications during the whirlwind *Lady Audley* year. On top of all this writing—five novels in seven months!—Mary was also pregnant for the first time and moving house with her mother in tow.* Maxwell's five children were fortunately all away at school, thus sparing Mary many additional domestic duties. Still, the mind reels at her energy. It is perhaps more astonishing that this level of productivity was to continue for most of her life. Novel after novel flowed from Mary's pen, even as she kept delivering babies (six in total: Gerald, Fanny, Francis [who died in infancy], William Babington, Winifred Rosalie, and Edward Henry Harrington). She also acted as stepmother to Maxwell's children and would remain close to each of them until her death in 1915, with more than ninety titles to her name.

Less than a year after *Lady Audley's Secret,* just prior to baby Gerald's arrival on March 19, Mary hit a second knock-out with her next novel, *Aurora Floyd.* It was a perfect one-two punch; while *Aurora Floyd* was running its course in *Temple Bar* (yet another start-up periodical of Maxwell's), *Lady Audley* was appearing in book form in circulating libraries all over England. Therefore, both of Mary's most famous works—her scandalous "bigamy novels"—were on sale at the same time. This did not go unnoticed by the other publishers in London. By using her own

* Perhaps because of her own unpleasant marital experiences, Fanny Braddon was very much in support of Mary and John Maxwell's arrangement, and contentedly shared their home until her death in 1868.

name, Mary managed to avoid the frustrations of Jane Austen and the many other female writers who used "By a Lady" or went uncredited altogether, but achieving success under her real name inevitably led to accusations of purveying immodest "trumpery," or of having too much ambition. How could she commercialize herself so overtly? Was she not the most indecorous woman ever to draw breath? She and her publishers were heartily berated in the press for their eager pandering to public tastes, for their willful and vulgar disregard for "high" art in favor of an open quest for publicity and, in many cases, barely concealed notoriety—wasn't literature supposed to be above that kind of thing? The *Athenaeum* certainly thought so:

> *This sort of puffery is never used by the great houses; and we should think that few readers are likely to be taken in by it . . . we would prefer that the younger members of the publishing trade should exhibit that perfect decorum before the public which is the habit, as well as the interest, of their more eminent brethren in the craft.*

As for the rest of society, the real problem with Mary's work was its content. With every page of *Lady Audley* exceeding the boundaries of respectability, and nearly every scene of *Aurora Floyd* exuding immorality, many social commentators thought Mary was heralding an end to their way of life—she had sown the seeds of corruption and doubt into readers' hearts by satisfying an unspeakable craving within them, and now there was no going back. "[Sensationalist authors] want to persuade people that in almost every of the well-ordered houses of their neighbors there was a skeleton shut up in some cupboard; that their comfortable and easy-looking neighbor had in his breast a secret story," as the Archbishop of York preached in a sermon at the Huddersfield Church Institute in 1864. Mary was bringing crime into the home, lowering the bar, defying class biases by "making the literature of the Kitchen the favorite reading of the Drawing room."

Her work was also accused of being close to pornographic, due to her ample display of smutty alternatives to traditional marriage.* It should be known—there are fully zero scenes of actual sex in any of Mary's novels. Still, there was enough *hinting* at immoral varieties of it to rile Reverend Paget to snarling ire in his *Lucretia*:

> *The successful accomplishment of abductions, seductions, elopements, and illusive or clandestine marriages, are elaborately shown; and, to pass lightly over a subject on which these pages must not dwell, all breaches of the seventh commandment ["Thou shalt not commit adultery"] are provided with apologetic excuses: antenuptial connections are treated of as inevitable; adultery as a social necessity; and bigamy and polygamy are assumed to be the most natural of matrimonial arrangements, except the condition of divorce, which is better still!*
>
> *And the writers of these books, ay the very foulest*

* Mary took issue with this claim, and rightly so, for the takeaway from her work was more about an implied condemnation of a restrictive society than it was about sex. In point of fact, Mary's novels were permitted in Victorian school libraries when George Eliot's *The Mill on the Floss* was not. See Showalter, *A Literature of Their Own*, 161; and Amy Cruse, *The Victorians and Their Books* (London: G. Allen and Unwin, 1935), 326.

> *of them,—authors who have put forth confessions of the darkest profligacy that an utter reprobate could make, and who have degraded woman's love into an animal propensity so rabid and so exciting, as to profess an opinion that its gratification would be cheaply purchased* at the cost of an eternity in hell,—*these writers are, some by their own admission, some by internal evidence, (where the publication is anonymous,)* women; *and the worst of them, UNMARRIED WOMEN!*

Whether Paget was directing his anger and dismay at one novel in particular, we'll never know. Yet, considering the body of female sensation work on the market when he wrote *Lucretia*, and the astronomical popularity of Mary's material, it very well could have been one of hers—and the most likely candidate is *Aurora Floyd*. As far as sensation novels go, *Aurora Floyd* is fairly standard-issue (action, secrets, treachery, murder), but its few notable differences invited more hostility than usual into the critical response. Published by Tinsley a year after *Lady Audley*, in 1863—and in the United States by none other than the same publisher of *this* book, then called Harper and Brothers, in New York—*Aurora Floyd* is far riskier and a lot more daring, in particular with its eponymous protagonist. Aurora rides horses and can talk about dogs more readily than she can any "feminine" subject; she's bold and impetuous, and she doesn't think things through. (Where Lady Audley stops and ponders what to do next, Aurora powers right on past the problem with dizzying fearlessness.) She's also dark-haired, with "eyes that were like the stars of heaven" and "two rows of peerlessly white teeth," which are troublingly erotic attributes when superimposed over an indelicate personality such as hers. For all her flaws, however, Aurora is generous and kind, accustomed to truthfulness (as opposed to Victorian-style ambiguity), and sensitive to all forms of injustice: she's light and dark, like a real person (and like Sara Coleridge's Phantasmion). The difficulties that befall her happen as a result of her choice to realize her independent ideals, not, as would be the case in a Gothic novel, because she's inherently demonic.

Riding horses was especially improper for a female character, since it gave clear evidence that she'd been dabbling in the world of men. In Aurora's case it was an even greater infraction because of her love of dogs. What with these indecent proclivities, this heroine could potentially ride out on a hunt with her dogs, visit a young man unchaperoned, or get lost (whether on purpose or not) and have to spend the night at an inn many miles from home. Here was a girl with greater independence than should be afforded, who laughs in the face of convention, whose clothes are covered in straw and sawdust, who rustles up trouble wherever she goes. Worse yet is Aurora's blatant sensuality, which was what truly drove the Reverend Paget and the other critics mad with disgust (and, just as likely, mad with envy for the piles of money this kind of writing brought to Mary Braddon's doorstep). Again, there's no actual sex, but the heroine of *Aurora Floyd* is decidedly sultry—and it's not just those teeth and sparkling eyes. Her abundant "blue-black" hair is always delicious to behold, be it braided in thick plaits upon her forehead "crown[ing] her as an Eastern empress . . . who reigned by right divine of her eyes and hair," or "all tumbled and tossed about the pillows." Later she's seen lounging on a sofa, "wrapped in a loose white dressing-gown, her masses of ebony hair uncoiled and falling about her shoulder in serpentine tresses." . . . "[O]ne small hand lay under her head, twisted in the tangled mass of her glorious hair." Aurora also admits to having married her first husband partly because of his good looks, thereby acknowledging her sex drive and the uncouth truth that physical attraction plays a role in choosing a mate—a fact that is always hinted at but, according to Victorian society, should never be explicitly stated.

This could all be forgivable, however, considering that her worst sin is merely mistaking a bad man for a good one early in life, and seeing how she works so hard to prove herself worthy of the love of her second husband. She *could* redeem herself—that is, if it weren't for the whipping scene. For critics, these paragraphs simply went too far in their undisguised, unrepentant, sexy naughtiness:

> *Aurora sprang upon him like a beautiful tigress, and, catching the collar of his fustian [dark-colored twill] jacket in her slight hands, rooted him to the spot upon which he stood. The grasp of those slender hands, convulsed by passion, was not to be easily shaken off . . . she towered above him, her cheeks white with rage, her eyes flashing fury, her hat fallen off, and her black hair tumbling about her shoulders, sublime in her passion . . .*
>
> *"How dared you!" cried Aurora—"how dared you hurt him? My poor dog! My poor, lame, feeble dog! How dared you do it? You cowardly dastard! you—"*
>
> *She disengaged her right hand from his collar, and rained a shower of blows upon his clumsy shoulders with her slender whip; a mere toy, with emeralds set in its golden head, but stinging like a rod of flexible steel in that little hand.*

> *"How dared you!" she repeated again and again, her cheeks changing from white to scarlet in the effort to hold the man with one hand. Her tangled hair had fallen to her waist by this time, and the whip was broken in half a dozen places.*

This is no "Angel in the House"—Aurora expresses her emotions freely, even violently, and with no care for prudence or propriety (even if it requires falling into various stages of sexy undress). Thus, with defects aplenty, Aurora and her creator were quickly condemned by some reviewers for their brazen defiance of social law. Others, though, found themselves fascinated, and why shouldn't they have been? "Aurora is a woman," wrote Geraldine Jewsbury (who, it will be remembered, was a member of Catherine Crowe's ultraliberal fem-squad)—"not a fiend, nor a maniac, but a warm-hearted, generous, loving woman, with an earnest desire to do what is honorable . . . therefore, she is a far more pleasing heroine than her predecessor, Lady Audley; and we cannot help liking her and sympathizing with her, in spite of our better reason and judgment." Henry James agreed, writing for *The Nation* that "Lady Audley was diabolically wicked; Aurora Floyd, her successor, was simply foolish, or indiscreet, or indelicate—or anything you please to say of a young lady who runs off with a hostler." Even Dinah Mulock Craik's friend Margaret Oliphant, who in the same article criticized Mary's tendency to allow her heroines too much sexual license, had to concede that *Aurora Floyd* really was an excellent novel:

> *"Aurora Floyd," notwithstanding its unpleasant subject (though we don't doubt that its unpleasant subject has*

been in reality the cause of its great success), is a very clever story. It is well knit together, thoroughly interesting, and full of life. The life is certainly not of a high description, but it is genuine in its way; and few people with any appreciation of fiction could refuse to be attracted by a tale so well defined.

Indeed, few could. *Lady Audley's Secret* and *Aurora Floyd* together made Mary Elizabeth Braddon phenomenally successful. There were unprecedented print runs for the magazines that serialized them; multiple adaptations of them appearing on London stages; bitter competition between the two largest circulating libraries, Mudie's and the Library Company, over which could manage to purchase the greatest number of copies; and translations and pirated editions spreading overseas to continental Europe and the colonies. Mary became spectacularly wealthy after having all but taken over the London markets—in less than two years!—which enabled her to purchase and appoint a vast Georgian manse, Lichfield House in Surrey, for herself and Maxwell and their growing brood of children (their second baby, a son named Francis, had arrived in 1863). Yet with all this fame and fortune came an increased interest in her personal life, and by 1864, when she was still unwed and once again pregnant, the eccentricities of her faux-marital arrangement with Maxwell (along with his less-than-scrupulous approach to handling their troubles) could no longer be concealed from public view.

THAT THE MARRIAGE QUESTION WAS NOT HANDLED WELL seems to have been what led to rockier times for Mary. She was very famous; her writing rate had not slowed after *Aurora Floyd* (*Woman's Revenge; or, the Captain of the Guard; The White Phantom; John Marchmont's Legacy; The Factory Girl; or All Is Not Gold That Glitters; Eleanor's Victory*; and *The Outcasts* were the sum total of her stupefying productivity between 1862 and 1863), and stories of her increasing riches were told far and wide. Accordingly, then, the press was quick to jump on any shred of information that might serve to dethrone this Queen of the Lending Libraries. Insinuations flew back and forth in the periodicals—about her clear debasement, her acquaintance with "a very low type of female character," as one reviewer said—and these left her mostly unperturbed. Yet when *Athenaeum* suggested that, in her work, she'd shown ignorance of the protocol in the marriage vows, she balked; things had gotten personal. In their review of *John Marchmont's Legacy*—for which she was paid an astounding £4,000 (around £330,000 today)—its critics cast their aspersions bluntly: "When Miss Braddon knows more about the Marriage Service than she does at present, she will know that these words are uttered by the bridegroom—not the bride." (The troubling phrase referred to here is "with all my goods I thee endow," which Mary depicts a female character as remembering to have said in *John Marchmont*. In a traditional Victorian marriage ceremony, that sentence was actually spoken by the groom.)

Two months later, in an ill-conceived and high-handed attempt to quash the rumors of their situation, Maxwell placed an advertisement in two London papers announcing his recent marriage to Mary. Mary Ann Crowley's brother-in-law immediately refuted this, and the subsequent storm of suspicion that surrounded the couple grew more and more heated. Was Mary married? Were those children legitimate? Her public image, her sensational literature, her piles of money, her shadowy home life—was this the future of literature? By the spring of 1864, the critical response bordered on hysteria: Mary Elizabeth Braddon and her raunchy novels were "indications of a wide-spread corruption, of which they are in part both the effect and the cause; called into existence to supply the cravings of a diseased appetite, and contributing themselves to foster the disease, and to stimulate the want which they supply"; only "the unthinking crowd" could lend its support, ". . . [for] no discriminating reader ever laid down these volumes without regretting that he had taken them up."

Now that Mary's wobbly marital status was out in the open, Margaret Oliphant, who leaned toward conservativism in these matters, zoomed in for her own nasty sting:

> *There has been a good story now and then, a clever bit of construction, even an inkling of character. She is the inventor of the fair-haired demon of modern fiction. Wicked women used to be brunettes long ago, now they are the daintiest, softest, prettiest of blonde creatures; and this change has been wrought by Lady Audley, and her influence on contemporary novels. She has brought in the reign of bigamy as an interesting and fashionable crime, which no doubt shows a certain deference to the British relish for law and order. It goes against the seventh commandment, no doubt, but does it in a legitimate sort of way, and is an invention which could only have been possible to an Englishwoman knowing the attraction of impropriety, and yet loving the shelter of law.*

The rumors seethed for the next ten years, until, in 1874—after Mary had had four more children, weathered the death of her mother and sister, and become a colossal literary figure—Mary Ann Crowley died. At the time, more than thirty Braddon novels had been published; in addition, Mary was editing one of Maxwell's periodicals, *Belgravia,* while experimenting with playwriting. Yet when news of Mary Ann's passing arrived at Lichfield House, Mary and Maxwell were overwhelmed with a media frenzy the likes of which they'd never seen. Maxwell handled things very, very poorly, first by trying to persuade the Crowley family (in vain) to keep the news of Mary Ann's death out of the papers, and then by circulating a pamphlet among his neighbors and friends that read, "Mr and Mrs Maxwell present their Compliments to——— and beg to disclaim any knowledge of the maliciously-intentioned announcement of a death on the 5th." The Crowleys intercepted one of these, and responded with their own damning and widely read pamphlet describing Maxwell's marital history in full detail. The secret was out, Mary's own skeleton in the closet had been let out, and it was *big.*

Soon, the world was awash with the news of Queen Braddon's juicy disgrace. Friends were lost, confidantes were forfeited—even the staff at Lichfield House abandoned them, forcing Maxwell, Mary, and their eleven children and stepchildren to relocate to Chelsea for a year, to let the gossip die down. The rumors of 1864 had been true; Mary's children *were* illegitimate! "Having, like so many of her heroines, committed a species of bigamy, she has at last been found out," the *New York Times* reported on its front page—it was just too scrumptious. The troubles Mary Ann's death caused notwithstanding, there must have been a small part of Maxwell and Mary that quietly rejoiced in being released from the bondage his earlier marriage represented, because soon after, the two were legally wed at St. Bride's Church off Fleet Street. Mary went back to her writing, Maxwell to his publishing enterprises, and eventually both returned to their home at Lichfield with their problems safely and firmly behind them, the scandal forgotten.

At the time of her death, Mary Elizabeth Braddon had produced a phenomenal body of work that included poetry, plays, an opera, four songs, short stories both collected and not, and nearly one hundred novels spanning multiple styles. After the storm of controversy in the late 1860s, her sensational period evolved into a time of quieter, more delicate fiction (*Eleanor's Victory, The Doctor's Wife, The Lady's Mile*), which in turn developed into a skillful radicalism mingled with late-Victorian decorum—this allowed her to support middle-class values while subtly satirizing them at the same time. *Strangers and Pilgrims* and *Lost for Love*, for example, use this model in addressing hypocrisy in the Church; while *Vixen, Just as I Am, Gerard*, and *Rough Justice* use it to attack the idle, Old World aristocracy. Mary's older works were still in print during her later years, too—*Lady Audley's Secret* didn't leave the presses until after her death, in fact—and even as she slowly receded into ill health and infirmity, Mary Braddon still fanned the embers of her career. She kept up with the times and stayed in society, wrote more books (*A Lost Eden, Dead Love Has Chains*, and *The Green Curtain* are among her last), and when World War I broke out, she opened the doors of Lichfield House to Belgian refugees. By her death at age eighty, she had become a cultural mainstay, "a part of England," as the periodical *The Academy* wrote upon the release of her novel *The Infidel,* in 1900. "She has woven herself into it; without her it would be different . . . she is in the encyclopaedias; she ought to be in the dictionaries, a common noun, for she stands for something which only schoolboys need ask to be defined."

AFTERWORD

UNLIKE MANY OF THE MORE WELL-KNOWN WOMEN OF British literature—such as Fanny Burney, whose heroine Camilla was "always getting into some new scrape"—Mary Elizabeth Braddon never enjoyed wreaking undue havoc upon a passive, complicit character, for she found the social requirement of feminine frailty insupportable and, in truth, heartily annoying. Why, oh why must every woman be overwhelmed by outside forces? In a letter to her friend and fellow best-selling novelist Sir Edward Bulwer-Lytton, she tried to explain away her lack of attention to deep and tragic emotion in her characters, questioned the point of such emotion, and digressively wondered whether these doubts she nursed about the importance of interior goings-on hadn't "passed [her] beyond the power of feeling [them]." This, she wrote—this lack of emotional engagement—is what caused the "flippancy of tone" many critics had noticed in her work, a quality that could be perceived as, in her words, "jar[ring] upon [the] sense of the dignity of art." It was a characteristically unconventional position, yet, as becomes clear later in the letter, it was merely a tactful evasion of the real truth: in actuality, she simply struggled watching her heroes suffer "because I always have in mind the memory of wasted suffering of my own."

THE LIFE STORIES OF MARY ELIZABETH BRADDON, AND THE six other women featured in this book, exemplify the complicated, tumultuous, and often self-defeating world women were forced to inhabit during the eighteenth and nineteenth centuries—and they transferred these experiences onto the page without holding back.

For Charlotte Turner Smith—and indeed, for many of these women—marriage was an entrapment from which there was very little means of escape (though it wasn't impossible, as we've seen), and the realistic portrayals of it in her works show this frustration. Helen Maria Williams is an archetype of those brazen women who sought to engage with politics as an equal—but such women were often not forgiven for their boldness, and completely written out of history to ensure their silence. Left with no other option, Mary Robinson used her body as leverage in a rigid and patriarchal social system, and thereafter she was forever engaged in an uphill battle against those who would besmirch her intellectual and moral reputation to control, and ultimately contort, her legacy (a battle she lost). Poor Catherine Crowe witnessed the unraveling of her literary career at the hands of rumormongers, who seized on a moment of weakness to portray her as mentally unstable. Drug addiction haunted sweet Sara Coleridge—to a lesser extent, Mary Robinson, too—and though invalidism gave her a breath of air in an otherwise choking existence, the resulting waste of talent in her situation is unmistakable. Dear, dear Dinah Craik, for whom spinsterhood was a confirmed reality until middle age—she couldn't *not* write in support of women finding their strength because, for her, spinsterhood was a daily reminder of her shortcomings as a female, of the emptiness of a life with no story. Then, finally, there was Mary Elizabeth Braddon, a woman who made a fortune off morally ambiguous novels and paid a price for it (though not a financial one).

However limited their careers, however much they were impeded, these seven women embraced the reality of their time, and in doing so they transformed Britain's literary tradition. They all broke major barriers through their work, from shaping new genres, as in the case of Sara and Catherine; to recognizing opportunities in a burgeoning periodical market that changed the way people read; to weaving plotlines and narrative structures that ploughed through class divides, revealed the true nature of women's plight, or highlighted the unfairness of the status quo. Whether by flagrant and unmissable self-portraiture (think *Vancenza,* and dejected Mrs. Stafford in *Emmeline*), by subversive implantation of controversial values (Craik's *Olive,* Coleridge's *Phantasmion,* the whole of Williams's body of work), or by condemnation—subtle and not—of the world in which they were written (*The Night-Side of Nature, Lady Audley's Secret, Aurora Floyd*), the authors of these works did what Anne Brontë also tried to do in her work: paint a true portrait of England, with all its flaws and incongruencies.

I came to realize the beauty of this not just in my reading of these seven women's work, but also in the midst of my research into their lives: First, when I was in Edinburgh, standing outside Catherine Crowe's elegant four-story sash-windowed town house at 2 Darnaway Street—the house she paid for with her own money, the house where she started her life anew, where the shapes and specters of the "other" world crept slowly down the walls and onto the pages of *The Night-Side of Nature*. A week later, in the Lake District, it happened again as I hiked out of Keswick and up to the windswept summit of Skiddaw Mountain, just as thirteen-year-old Sara Coleridge did with Robert Southey, William Wordsworth, and their respective families (along with a host of servants and a cartful of beef and plum pudding to cook over the fire)—and just as Phantasmion does, when he travels over the mountains of Palmland to find his place in the world. Then, again, in Brighton, after I'd spent days digging through Geoffrey Larken's invaluable Catherine Crowe material at the University of Kent: staring out at the English Channel on a blustery Sunday morning, I wondered how Charlotte Turner Smith and Helen Maria Williams must have felt when they themselves stood there, waiting for the passage to France—one tortured (like many of her characters), one hopeful (as her political beliefs would show), and both poised on the edge of seminal change.

I saw it as I wandered around Mecklenburgh Square, where Mary Elizabeth Braddon first settled with John Maxwell and where, it can be assumed, the premise for *Lady Audley's Secret* first popped into her mind; as I gawked at Drury Lane's cavernous interior, where Mary Robinson honed her talents, became famous, fell in love, and gathered material for her smash success, *Vancenza;* as I strolled down Shortlands Road, where Dinah Mulock Craik built her home with such pride, having at last found, to everyone's surprise (probably not least her own), the kind of love her eponymous heroine in *Olive* finds: warm, safe, smiling attachment. And as a result of my time among these seven special women, absorbing from their perspectives the realities of life during this turbulent one-hundred-fifty-year period, my understanding and perception of British social and literary history has greatly evolved; the past is colored in, rendered in three dimensions, filled with the sounds of long-forgotten voices.

AS WE'VE SEEN WITH THE GLORIOUS POSTHUMOUS RISE OF Jane, and with the ennobling of Charlotte—Elizabeth Gaskell's famous biography, *The Life of Charlotte Brontë*, turned this strange, isolated authoress into a Victorian icon of "duty" and "solitude" and "sensitiveness of soul"—and, more recently, with the groundswell of attention and appreciation directed toward Anne, it takes only a handful of adoring fans to revive an authoress and her work, to invite her to be read once again; to light the torch that will move from generation to generation; and to ensure that today, tomorrow, and beyond, we will continue to read and reread works, study times, and wonder about the nature of England. What will it take to resurrect the literary gifts and inspirational lives of Charlotte and Helen Maria, Mary and Catherine, Sara and Dinah, and Mary Elizabeth, so that they, too, can be enjoyed today, tomorrow, and beyond?

You, dear reader, it really takes only *you*. You and your unending capacity for love—of stories, of books, and, maybe most important, of women who defy the conventions of their times in order to make their voices heard. This is what history depends on; this is what the future of literature depends on, because the words of the present are made possible by those of the past (and because the present *mirrors* the past—methods of creation and distribution are changing now, in the digital age, just as they did then). Of all the wonderful things I experienced during this journey, the best occurred at the end, as I stood in front of a bookshelf full of new titles, each of which introduced me to new women, new worlds, new windows into British history. It is to these treasures that I wish to turn your attention in this final moment. Find their works, whether in used-book stores or by way of the many websites that generously provide them (Archive.org, Project Gutenberg, and Google Books are especially helpful), and then, *read*. Open your arms to these women, just as you have (and should continue to do) with Jane and Charlotte and Emily and Mary Ann (George) and Virginia. Fall in love with these women, just as I did. Embrace the fullest spectrum of female literary accomplishment you can. Allow these women to tuck in close and take your imagination to a whole new place. The only thing better than British literature is *more* British literature, so go, reader, rediscover it all over again.

ACKNOWLEDGMENTS

For their generous support and assistance—without which this project would never have been possible—I am deeply indebted to the following people.

First, to my editor at Harper, Hannah Wood, whose patience and kindness during the creation of this book were matched only by incredible proficiency and skill: thank you for all you've done, and for being *exactly* the kind of editor writers want. Noah Ballard, too, my agent at Curtis Brown—he deserves equal praise for his generous attention to the project, and for the unflagging enthusiasm and encouragement he exhibited from the very, very beginning.

In England, for their direction and assistance, much appreciation goes out to Jeronime Palmer—who, on a beautiful summer day, gave me a tour of Sara Coleridge's home in Keswick (while simultaneously cooking falafel) and was a great help in unraveling several mysteries surrounding the place—and Gerry Masters, Ilchester's local history buff, for his careful analyses and delightful emails. The good people in Special Collections at the University of Kent's Templeman Library are also in my thoughts (thank you for staying late!), along with the unsung heroes in the reading rooms at the British Library, to whom I became attached during many long days in their midst. Special acknowledgment goes out to Dr. Deborah Kennedy at Saint Mary's University in Halifax, Dr. Joanne Wilkes at the University of Auckland, Gillian Anderton, Alli Kildahl, Jennifer Thorp, Simon Elliott, Emily Walhout, Darren Bevin at Chawton House Library, Donna Ainsworth, and Brianna Cregle for their assistance with my research.

To Laurel Ann Nattress of Austenprose.com: thank you for welcoming me so readily into the Janeite community all those years ago and for your continued support of my work. I'm lucky to know you!

To my family—especially my twin sister, Colleen—and my parents: thank you for weathering so many storms with me, and for listening oh-so-patiently as I blathered on about my obsession with these seven women. Thank you for helping me keep Montana in my heart.

And finally, we turn to the person who deserves the biggest thanks of them all, the one to whom I am forever beholden for his limitless patience and love: my husband, AJ. He's the real champion of this project, because he experienced it right alongside me, in the trenches, even as the romance of it waxed and waned across three years, two countries, and four apartments. As I write this, our nine-day-old son is sleeping peacefully on my chest, and I can't help but be overwhelmed. Thank you for everything you are.

NOTES ON SOURCES

FOR THOSE WHO WISH TO PURSUE THE TOPIC FURTHER, there are limited yet excellent resources on the explosive relationship between female authorship and British society. Sandra M. Gilbert and Susan Gubar's groundbreaking study *The Madwoman in the Attic: The Woman Writer and the Nineteenth-Century Imagination,* Elaine Showalter's *A Literature of Their Own: British Women Novelists from Brontë to Lessing,* and Eva Figes's *Sex and Subterfuge: Women Writers to 1850* are all excellent places to start, as is the deservingly oft-quoted manifesto *A Room of One's Own,* by Virginia Woolf. *The Fallen Angel: Chastity, Class and Women's Reading, 1835–1880* by Sally Mitchell and *The Proper Lady and the Woman Writer: Ideology as Style in the Works of Mary Wollstonecraft, Mary Shelley, and Jane Austen* by Mary Poovey are also useful. In addition, Judith Flanders's *Inside the Victorian Home: A Portrait of Domestic Life in Victorian England* and Roy and Leslie Adkins's *Jane Austen's England: Daily Life in the Georgian and Regency Periods* both serve very well as introductory historical studies.

Of the scant published primary resources available for our seven women, three are readily accessible: *The Collected Letters of*

Charlotte Smith, edited by Judith Phillips Stanton, *Memoirs of the Late Mrs. Robinson*, and *Memoir and Letters of Sara Coleridge* (the latter two of which are online at Archives.org). Others in manuscript form can be found on Sara Coleridge and Mary Elizabeth Braddon at the Harry Ransom Center, University of Texas, and on Dinah Mulock Craik at UCLA's Charles E. Young Research Library. And there are the incredible Geoffrey Larken papers on Catherine Crowe—the most complete cache of documents extant on this authoress (and decidedly crucial to this book)—in Special Collections at the University of Kent, Canterbury.

There are also reliable biographies on some (though not all—not yet!) of the women mentioned here, for those who'd like to read more into a specific figure. Works from the academic presses include *Charlotte Smith: A Critical Biography* by Loraine Fletcher, *Helen Maria Williams and the Age of Revolution* by Deborah Kennedy, Bradford Keyes Mudge's *Sara Coleridge, A Victorian Daughter*, which also includes her epistolary autobiography and a selection of her hard-to-find essays, and *The Literary Lives of Mary Elizabeth Braddon* by Jennifer Carnell. Available on the wider market is Paula Byrne's 2004 study, *Perdita: The Literary, Theatrical, Scandalous Life of Mary Robinson.*

BIBLIOGRAPHIES

CHARLOTTE TURNER SMITH

Elegiac Sonnets, and Other Essays. London: Dodsley, 1784.

Emmeline, The Orphan of the Castle. London: Cadell, 1788.

Ethelinde; or The Recluse of the Lake. London: Cadell, 1789.

Celestina. London: Cadell, 1791.

Desmond. London: G. G. and J. Robinson, 1792.

The Old Manor House. London: J. Bell, 1793.

Rural Walks: in dialogues intended for the use of young persons. London: Cadell, 1795.

Rambles Farther: a Continuation of Rural Walks, in dialogues intended for the use of young persons. London: Cadell, 1796.

The Letters of a Solitary Wanderer. London: Sampson Low, 1801.

A History of England, from the earliest records, to the peace of Amiens in a series of letters to a young lady at school. London: Phillips, 1806.

A Natural History of Birds, intended chiefly for young persons. London: J. Johnson, 1807.

Beachy Head, Fables, and Other Poems. London: J. Johnson, 1807.

HELEN MARIA WILLIAMS

Edwin and Eltruda, A Legendary Tale. London: Cadell, 1782.

An Ode on the Peace. London: Cadell, 1783.

Peru, A Poem. London: Cadell, 1784.

A Poem on the Bill Lately Passed for Regulating the Slave Trade. London: Cadell, 1788.

Poems in Two Volumes. Includes "An American Tale" and "Part of an Irregular Fragment, Found in a Dark Passage of the Tower." London: Cadell, 1786.

Letters Written in France in the Summer 1790, to a friend in England: containing various anecdotes relative to the French Revolution; and Memoirs of Mons. and Madame du Fossé. London: Cadell, 1790.

Julia, A Novel. London: Cadell, 1790.

A Farewell, for Two Years, To England. London: Cadell, 1791.
A Tour in Switzerland; or, A View of the Present State of the Governments and Manners of those Cantons: with Comparative Sketches of the Present State of Paris. London: G.G. and J. Robinson, 1798.
Personal Narrative of Travels to Equinoctial Regions of the New Continent. Trans. *Researches Concerning the Institutions and Monuments of the Ancient Inhabitants of America, with Descriptions and Views of Some of the Most Striking Scenes in the Cordilleras!*, by Alexander von Humboldt. London: Longman: 1814.
A Narrative of the Events Which Have Taken Place in France from the Landing of Napoleon Bonaparte to the Restoration of Louis XVIII. London: Murray, 1815.
Letters on the Events Which Have Passed in France Since the Restoration in 1815. London: Baldwin, 1819.
Souvenirs de la Révolution française. Paris: Dondey-Dupré, 1827.

MARY ROBINSON

Poems by Mrs. Robinson. London: C. Parker, 1775.
Captivity, A Poem; And Celedon and Lydia, a Tale. London: T. Becket, 1777.
Ainsi va le Monde. London: John Bell, 1790.
Impartial Reflections on the Present Situation of the Queen of France. London: John Bell, 1791.
Poems by Mrs. Robinson. Includes "The Maniac." Vol. 1, London: J. Bell, 1791. Vol. 2, London: T. Spilsbury, 1793.
Vancenza; or the Dangers of Credulity. London: J. Bell, 1792.
The Widow, or a Picture of Modern Times: A Novel in a Series of Letters. London: Hookham and Carpenter, 1794.
Angelina, A Novel. London: Hookham and Carpenter, 1796.
Hubert de Sevrac: A Romance of the Eighteenth Century. London: Hookham and Carpenter, 1796.
Walsingham; or, the Pupil of Nature. London: Longman, 1797.
The False Friend. London: Longman, 1799.
The Natural Daughter. London: Longman, 1799.
A Letter to the Women of England, on the Injustice of Mental Subordination. London: Longman, 1799.
Memoirs of the Late Mrs. Robinson. London: R. Phillips, 1801.

CATHERINE CROWE

Aristodemus: A Tragedy. Edinburgh: Tait, 1838.
The Adventures of Susan Hopley; or, Circumstantial Evidence. Edinburgh: Tait, 1842.
Men and Women; or, Manorial Rights. London: Saunders and Otley, 1844.
The Story of Lilly Dawson. London: Colburn, 1847.
Pippie's Warning; or, Mind Your Temper. London: Arthur Hall & Co., 1848.
The Night-Side of Nature: Or, Ghosts and Ghost Seers. London: Newby, 1848.

The Juvenile Uncle Tom's Cabin, arranged for young readers. London: Routledge & Co., 1853.
Linny Lockwood, A Novel. London: Routledge & Co., 1854.
The Story of Arthur Hunter and His First Shilling. London: James Hogg and Sons, 1861.
The Adventures of a Monkey. London: Dean and Son, 1862.

SARA COLERIDGE

An Account of the Abiphones, an Equestrian People of Paraguay. London: Murray, 1822.
The Right Joyous and Pleasant History of the Facts, Tests, and Prowesses of the Chevalier Bayard, the Good Knight Without Fear and Without Reproach. London: Murray, 1825.
Pretty Lessons in Verse for Good Children; With Some Lessons in Latin in Easy Rhyme. London: Parker and Son, 1834.
Specimens of the Table Talk to the Late Samuel Taylor Coleridge. (unattributed) London: Murray, 1835.
Phantasmion. London: William Pickering, 1837.
The Literary Remains of Samuel Taylor Coleridge. (unattributed) London: William Pickering, 1836–1839.
Aids to Reflection in the Formation of a Manly Character. Ed. Sara Coleridge. Includes her long essay "On Rationalism." London: William Pickering, 1843.
Biographia Literaria. Ed. Sara Coleridge. London: William Pickering, 1847.
Notes and Lectures Upon Shakespeare. Ed. Sara Coleridge. London: William Pickering, 1849.
Essays on His Own Times, forming a Second Series of The Friend. Ed. Sara Coleridge. London: William Pickering, 1850.
The Poems of Samuel Taylor Coleridge. Ed. Sara Coleridge. London: Edward Moxon, 1852.

DINAH MULOCK CRAIK

SHORT STORIES:

"Good Seed," *Chambers's Edinburgh Journal,* 1845.
"The Motherless Children," *Chambers's Edinburgh Journal,* 1845.
"Minor Trials," *Chambers's Edinburgh Journal,* 1846.
"All For the Best," *Chambers's Edinburgh Journal,* 1847.
"The Half-Caste: An Old Governess's Tale," *Chambers's Papers for the People,* 1851.

BOOKS AND COLLECTED TALES:

Michael the Miner. London: Religious Tract Society, 1846.
How to Win Love, or Rhoda's Lesson. London: 1848.
Cola Monti. London: 1849.
The Ogilvies. London: Chapman and Hall, 1849.

Olive, A Novel. London: Chapman and Hall, 1850.
Head of the Family. London: Chapman and Hall, 1852.
Agatha's Husband. London: Chapman and Hall, 1853.
Avillion and Other Tales. Includes "The Self-Seer," "The Wife of King Tolv," "Hyas the Athenian," and "Miss Letty's Experiences," originally published in *Bentley's Miscellany* and *Fraser's*. London: Smith, Elder, & Co., 1853.
John Halifax, Gentleman. London: Hurst and Blackett, 1856.
A Woman's Thoughts About Women. Originally published in *Chambers's Edinburgh Journal*, 1857. London: Hurst and Blackett, 1858.
A Life for a Life. London: Hurst and Blackett, 1859.
Mistress and Maid. Originally published in *Good Words*, 1862. London: Hurst and Blackett, 1863.
Christian's Mistake. London: Hurst and Blackett, 1865.
A Noble Life. London: Hurst and Blackett, 1866.
Two Marriages. London: Hurst and Blackett, 1867.
The Woman's Kingdom. Originally published in *Good Words*, 1868. London: Hurst and Blackett, 1869.
A Brave Lady. Originally published in *Macmillan's Magazine*, 1870. London: Hurst and Blackett, 1870.
Fair France: Impressions of a Traveller. London: Hurst and Blackett, 1871.
Hannah. Originally published in *Saint Pauls*, 1871. London: Hurst and Blackett, 1872.
The Little Lame Prince and His Traveling Cloak. London: Daldy, Isbister, & Co., 1875.
Young Mrs. Jardine. Originally published in *Good Words*, 1879. London: Hurst and Blackett, 1879.
An Unsentimental Journey Through Cornwall. Originally published in *English Illustrated Magazine*, 1884. London: Macmillan, 1884.
King Arthur: Not a Love Story. New York: Harper, 1886.

MARY ELIZABETH BRADDON

Essays and Uncollected Serialized Stories:

"London on Four Feet," *Welcome Guest*, 1860.
"How the Romans Supped," *Welcome Guest*, 1860.
The Octoroon; or, The Lily of Louisiana, *The Halfpenny Journal*, 1861–1862.
The Woman's Revenge; or, The Captain of the Guard, *The Halfpenny Journal*, 1862.
The White Phantom, *The Halfpenny Journal*, 1862–1863.
The Factory Girl; or, All is Not Gold That Glitters, *The Halfpenny Journal*, 1863.

Books and Collected Tales:

Three Times Dead. Beverley: Empson, 1860. Republished as *The Trail of the Serpent* by W.&M. Clark, 1861.

Ralph the Bailiff and Other Stories. Includes "Captain Thomas," "The Cold Embrace," "My Daughters," "My First Happy Christmas," "Samuel Lowgood's Revenge," and "The Lawyer's Secret," all originally published in *The Welcome Guest*, 1860–1861. London: Ward, Lock, & Tyler, 1862.

Garibaldi and Other Poems. London: Bosworth & Harrison, 1861.

Captain of the Vulture. Originally published in *The Sixpenny Journal*, 1861. London: Ward, Lock, & Tyler, 1863.

John Marchmont's Legacy. Originally published in *Temple Bar*, 1861. London: Tinsley, 1863.

Lady Audley's Secret. Originally published in *Robin Goodfellow*, 1861, before moving to *Sixpenny Magazine*. London: Tinsley, 1862.

The Black Band; or, The Mysteries of Midnight. Originally published in *The Halfpenny Journal*, 1861–1862. London: Vickers, 1877.

The Lady Lisle. London: Ward, Lock, Tyler, 1862.

Aurora Floyd. Originally published in *Temple Bar*, 1862. London: Tinsley, 1863.

Eleanor's Victory. Originally published in *Once a Week*, 1863. London: Tinsley, 1863.

The Outcasts. Originally published in *London Journal*, 1863–1864. Republished as *Henry Dunbar* by John Maxwell, 1864.

The Doctor's Wife. Originally published in *Temple Bar*, 1864. London: Maxwell, 1864.

The Lady's Mile. Originally published in *St. James's Magazine*, 1865–1866. London: Ward, Lock, & Tyler, 1866.

Strangers and Pilgrims. Originally published in *Belgravia*, 1872–1873. London: Maxwell, 1873.

Lost for Love. Originally published in *Belgravia*, 1873–1874. London: Chatto & Windus, 1874.

Vixen. Originally published in *All the Year Round*, 1878–1879. London: Maxwell, 1879.

Just as I Am. Originally published in *Bolton Weekly Journal*, 1880. London: Maxwell, 1880.

The World, the Flesh, and the Devil. Originally published in *Sheffield Weekly Telegraph*. Republished as *Gerard* by Simpkin & Marshall, 1891.

A Shadowed Life. Originally published in *Sheffield Weekly Telegraph*, 1897. Republished as *Rough Justice* by Simpkin & Marshall, 1898.

The Infidel. London: Simpkin & Marshall, 1900.

A Lost Eden. London: Hutchinson, 1904.

Alias Jane Brown. Originally published in *Northern Newspaper Syndicate*, 1906. Republished as *Dead Love Has Chains* by Hurst and Blackett, 1907.

The Green Curtain. London: Hutchinson, 1911.

END NOTES

INTRODUCTION

3. "carefully-fenced, highly cultivated garden": Charlotte Brontë, *Letters of Charlotte Brontë*, ed. Margaret Smith (New York: Oxford University Press, 1995), 2:10.

8. "gentle and kind obedience": Francis Lye, *The Single Married and the Married Happy, Being a Series of Wholesome Advice Designed to Promote the Discreet Union of the Sexes, and Their Mutual Happiness When United* (Cheltenham: E. Matthews, 1828), 22, quoted in Hazel Jones, *Jane Austen and Marriage* (London: Continuum, 2009), 121.

8. "exercise of the most splendid talents": Elizabeth Gaskell, *The Life of Charlotte Brontë* (New York: Harper, 1900), 357.

8. "what but domestic misery can be expected?": Thomas Gisborne, *An Enquiry into the Duties of the Female Sex* (London: Cadell, 1796), 256. Gisborne recommends that women use friendships only "as instruments of comfort, of virtue, and of usefulness," which leaves no room for connections with any of those husband-hunting females who obsess over "tinsel and glitter."

9. "children of a larger growth": Philip Stanhope, Earl of Chesterfield, *Letters to His Son and Others* (London: Dent, 1984), 66, quoted in Robert W. Uphaus, "Jane Austen and Female Reading," *Studies in the Novel* 19, no. 3 (1987): 340.

10. "My mind is worked up": Diary entry, Jan. 27, 1793, in *English Diaries: A Review of English Diaries from the Sixteenth to the Twentieth Century* (London: Methuen, 1923), 247. In 1797 Elizabeth's husband divorced her on the grounds of adultery. Two days later, after the papers were finalized, she married her longtime lover, Lord Holland, and lived with him until his death in 1840. They had seven children together.

10. "a life without external events": Hans Eichner, "The Eternal Feminine: An Aspect of Goethe's Ethics," in Johann Wolfgang von Goethe, *Faust*, trans.

Walter Arndt, ed. Cyrus Hamlin (New York: W. W. Norton, 1976), 620, quoted in Sandra M. Gilbert and Susan Gubar, *The Madwoman in the Attic: The Woman Writer and the Nineteenth-Century Literary Imagination* (New Haven, CT: Yale University Press, 1979), 22. Italics mine.

10. strict cosmetic and dietary practices: Gilbert and Gubar, *Madwoman in the Attic*, 25.

10. for anyone of intelligence it was intolerable: Eva Figes, *Sex and Subterfuge: Women Writers to 1850* (New York: Persea, 1982), 9.

11. "the method's origins are also tied to France": Thomas Hodgson, *An Essay on the Origin and Progress of Stereotype Printing; Including a Description of the Various Processes* (Newcastle: Hodgson, 1820), 77. Stereotyping was used during the French Revolution to issue a form of paper money, the assignat, but due to the shortcomings of the print method, most especially its ability to create like and imitative images rather than identical ones, the assignat was very readily counterfeited. Stereotype printing made great progress, then, in the hands of the French, as they worked to correct this problem by creating cleaner, better-cut plate molds and more efficient machinery.

12. more than twenty thousand titles: Edward Jacobs, "Circulating Libraries," in David Scott Kastan, ed., *Oxford Encyclopedia of British Literature* (Oxford: Oxford University Press, 2006), 2:5.

13. "They tell us, we mistake our sex": Anne Finch, *The Poems of Anne Countess of Winchilsea*, ed. Myra Reynolds (Chicago: University of Chicago Press, 1903), 5. The original edition of Finch's poetry was published in 1713.

21. *Susan Hopley* was the antecedent: Lucy Sussex, "The Detective Maidservant: Catherine Crowe's *Susan Hopley*," in *Silent Voices: Forgotten Novels by Victorian Women Writers*, ed. Brenda Ayres (Westport, CT: Praeger, 2003).

21. singular attention to worldbuilding: Matthew David Surridge, "Worlds Within Worlds: The First Heroic Fantasy, Part IV," *Black Gate: Adventures in Fantasy Literature*, 2010. http://www.blackgate.com/2010/09/19/worlds-within-worlds-the-first-heroic-fantasy-part-iv/.

22. "more widely read": "Mrs. Craik," *Academy*, Oct. 1887.

22. novel's placement just behind *Uncle Tom's Cabin*: Sally Mitchell, *Dinah Mulock Craik* (Boston: Twayne, 1983), 51.

24. "a critic's novelist": B. C. Southam, introduction, in B. C. Southam, ed., *Jane Austen: The Critical Heritage* (Routledge: London, 1979), 1:2.

25. paved the way for her enduring posthumous celebrity: Claire Harman, *Jane's Fame: How Jane Austen Conquered the World* (New York: Picador, 2009), 155–59.

26. Whereas they embraced: Beulah Maud Devaney, "Anne Brontë: the unsung sister, who turned the gaze on men," Guardian.com, January 17, 2014, (http://www.theguardian.com/books/booksblog/2014/jan/17/anne-bronte-sister-men-charlotte-emily).

27. "Jane Eyre is, in comparison": Sally Shuttleworth, "Jane Eyre and the 19th-century Woman," The British Library, http://www.bl.uk/romantics-and-victorians/articles/jane-eyre-and-the-19th-century-woman.
27. Thanks to the Irish critic: Arthur Boyars, "Ebury Street and Cinderella," *The Spectator*, July 16, 1959, p. 30.
27. But she is still "the forgotten Brontë sister": Devaney, "Anne Brontë."
28. the unshakable "moral taxonomy" of her characters: Paula Marantz Cohen, "Why Read George Eliot?" *The American Scholar*, March 1, 2006 https://theamericanscholar.org/why-read-george-eliot
29. "most popular novel to that point written by a woman": *British Women Writers: A Critical Reference Guide*, ed. Janet Todd (New York: Continuum, 1989), 576.

CHAPTER ONE

32. "We awake in the morning": "On the Cause of the Popularity of Novels," *The Universal Magazine of Knowledge and Pleasure*, 1798.
32. "people that marry can never part": Jane Austen, *Northanger Abbey* (London: Murray, 1818).
33. "the most eminent men": Thomas Gisborne, *An Enquiry into the Duties of the Female Sex* (London: Cadell, 1796), 32.
36. a form of legal prostitution: Charlotte Turner Smith to Sarah Rose, June 15, 1804.
36. "disadvantages belonging to your sex": George Savile, Marquis of Halifax, *The Ladys New-years Gift: or, Advice to a Daughter* (London, 1688), 25.
37. "If marriage be such a blessed state": Mary Astell, *Some Reflections upon Marriage* (London: John Nutt, 1700), 12.
37. "daily preparations for my journey to Hell": Lady Mary Wortley Montagu, *Complete Letters*, ed. Robert Halsband (New York: Oxford University Press, 1965), 1:122. Wortley Montagu was related, by marriage, to the leader of the Bluestockings, Elizabeth Montagu.
37. She really was quite happy: Loraine Fletcher, *Charlotte Smith: A Critical Biography* (Basingstoke, UK: Palgrave, 2001), 27–28.
38. "I pass almost every day": Charlotte Smith to "an early friend," c. 1765–66, *Collected Letters*, ed. Judith Phillips Stanton (Bloomington, IN: Indiana University Press, 2003), 2.
39. "No disadvantage could equal": Smith to an unnamed recipient, c. 1768–70, Stanton, ed., *Collected Letters*.
39. "would empower her to act": Fletcher, *Charlotte Smith*, 36.
39. "in for it": Jane Austen to her sister, Cassandra Austen, Jan. 5, 1801, *Jane Austen's Letters*, ed. Deirdre Le Faye (Oxford: Oxford University Press, 2011), 71.
39. "simple regimen of separate rooms": Austen to Fanny Knight, Feb. 21, 1817, *Jane Austen's Letters*, 344.

40. "unending cycle of gestation": S. Ryan Johansson, "Medics, Monarchs and Mortality, 1600–1800: Origins of the Knowledge-Driven Health Transition in Europe," *University of Oxford Discussion Papers in Economic and Social History*, No. 85 (2010): 1, http://www.nuff.ox.ac.uk/economics/history/Paper85/johansson85.pdf. Average life expectancy during the last half of the eighteenth century hovered around age forty.
40. "more avidity than judgment": Mary Hays, *British Public Characters of 1800–1801* (Dublin, 1801), 3:37.
40. "without provocation at all": Charlotte Turner Smith to the Earl of Egremont, quoted in Fletcher, *Charlotte Smith*, 59.
41. a mixture of pity and concern: Fletcher, *Charlotte Smith*, 63.
41. "fierce and stern faces of the keepers": Charlotte Smith, *Ethelinde; or the Recluse of the Lake* (London: Cadell, 1789), 5:31, quoted in Fletcher, *Charlotte Smith*, 63–64. This scene represents a reality Charlotte came to know all too well that winter in King's Bench, where the "wrangling from other figures, who were by the gloomy light discovered among them, all gave a new shock . . . as the men who surrounded her looked with inquisitive and attentive eyes into her face, she was terrified."
41. she would do it now: Fletcher, *Charlotte Smith*, 64. Fletcher has theorized that given Charlotte's penchant for writing and the pressing need for money, her first thoughts upon entering King's Bench would likely have been about capitalizing on her talents by publishing *Sonnets*.
42. "Queen of the silver bow!": Charlotte Turner Smith, *The Poems of Charlotte Smith*, ed. Stuart Curran (Oxford: Oxford University Press, 1993), 15.
43. "My native hills": Smith to an unnamed recipient, c. July 1784, Stanton, ed., *Collected Letters*, 5–6.
44. through gambling buddies: Fletcher, *Charlotte Smith*, 6.
45. she knew then and there: Ibid., 77.
45. only three hundred people attempted it: Roy and Lesley Adkins, *Jane Austen's England* (New York: Viking, 2013), 16.
47. "Amid the interruptions": Smith to Thomas Cadell, Jan. 3, 1787, Gillian M. Anderton, *An Analysis of the Preston Manor Letters: An Unpublished Collection of Letters by Charlotte Turner Smith to Her Publishers Cadell and Davies, 1786 to 1794* (2008), 7, http://www.charlottesmithpmletters.co.uk/pdf-docs/an_analysis_of_the_preston_manor_letters.pdf.
48. "highest branch of fictitious narrative": Sir Walter Scott, in a note to Catherine Ann Dorset's "Charlotte Smith," in *Miscellaneous Prose Works of Sir Walter Scott* (London: Longman, 1827), 4:33.
48. in an action that appears to reflect Charlotte's dissenting opinion: Loraine Fletcher, introduction to *Emmeline* (Peterborough, ON: Broadview, 2003), 17.
48. "accustomed from his infancy": Charlotte Smith, *Emmeline, The Orphan of the Castle* (London: Cadell, 1788), 1:68–69.

49. "I have a mind": Ibid., 1: 61.
49. "ever in pursuit of some wild scheme": Ibid., 2:180.
49. "Mr. Stafford was one of those unfortunate characters": Ibid., 2:147.
50. "vices yet more fatal": Ibid.
50. "'till the tears streamed down her cheeks": Ibid., 1:107.
50. "I, when not older than you now are": Ibid., 1:109.
52. the most significant wages: Jacqueline Labbe, *Charlotte Smith: Romanticism, Poetry, and the Culture of Gender* (Manchester: Manchester University Press, 2003), 9.
52. "lively company": Fletcher, *Charlotte Smith*, 123.
52. "[dragged] its dreary length": Charles Dickens, *Bleak House* (London: Bradbury and Evans, 1853), 3. It is not known if Charles Dickens based the central plot of his novel on any real-life happenings, but it has been proposed that the inheritance proceedings of Charlotte's father-in-law, Richard Smith, were a likely incitement, along with the 117-year-long *Jennens v. Jennens* case. See William Dunstan, "The Real Jarndyce and Jarndyce," *The Dickensian* 93 (1997).
53. "caught the contagion": Dorset, "Charlotte Smith," *Miscellaneous Prose Works*, 4:23.
53. "good for nothing but to make a show": Charlotte Smith, *Desmond*, ed. Antje Blank and Janet Todd (Peterborough, ON: Broadview Press, 2001), 171.
54. "As to the political passages": Ibid., 45.
54. refused to ever be in the same room: Smith to Lucy Hill Lowe, Nov. 27, 1791, *Letters*, 39. The end of this letter features some brusk commentary apparently written by Mrs. Lowe's husband, Thomas Lowe, that demonstrates his hatred of Charlotte's political position after the Revolution had turned into a bloodbath. "After this," he writes, "I never w[oul]d see Charlotte."
54. "armed with all the malignity": Dorset, "Charlotte Smith," 4:39.
55. "[to] the Women of Great Britain": David V. Erdman, *Commerce des Lumières: John Oswald and the British in Paris, 1790–1793* (Columbia: University of Missouri Press, 1986), 230.
55. had met and befriended each other: Deborah Kennedy, *Helen Maria Williams and the Age of Revolution* (Lewisburg, PA: Bucknell University Press, 2002), 27.
55. "great novel-readers": Austen to Cassandra, Dec. 18, 1798, *Jane Austen's Letters*, 26.
56. "I was near a month at Mr. Hayley's": Evenlyn Morchard Bishop, *Blake's Hayley: The Life, Works, and Friendships of William Hayley* (London: Gollancz, 1951), 165.
57. "But she said to me": Charlotte Smith, *The Old Manor House*, ed. Jacqueline Labbe (Peterborough, ON: Broadview Press, 2002), 263.
58. "knowing they are to expect no mercy": Ibid., 155.

58. "where the elderly police the young": Loraine Fletcher, "Emblematic Castles," *Critical Survey* 4, no. 1 (1992): 7, http://www.jstor.org/stable/41555617.
59. she began to have doubts about her spirited nose-thumbing: Fletcher, *Charlotte Smith*, 167.
59. "troops had to be called out": Florence May Anna Hilbish, "Charlotte Smith, Poet and Novelist, 1749–1806," PhD diss., University of Pennsylvania, 1941, 227.
60. choosing not to write of the present day: Fletcher, *Charlotte Smith*, 174.
60. "half shaded with brush-wood": Smith, *Old Manor House*, 463.
61. "While he pursued these contemplations": Ibid., 462–63.
61. "being rather solicitous": Ibid., 520.
62. a broad decline in readership: Sarah M. Zimmerman, "Charlotte Smith," in *Oxford Dictionary of National Biography*, ed. H. C. G. Matthew and Brian Harrison (Oxford: Oxford University Press, 2004); online edition, ed. Lawrence Goldman, Oct. 2007, http://www.oxforddnb.com/view/article/25790.
62. "I wrote mournfully": Smith, *Poems*, 5–6.
63. "Charlotte, my dear!": Ticklepitcher, "Ode to Charlotte Smith," *Morning Post* and *Daily Advertiser* (London), Dec. 14, 1789, quoted in David Hall Radcliffe, "Charlotte Smith," *Spenser and the Tradition: English Poetry 1579–1830*, http://spenserians.cath.vt.edu/CommentRecord.php?action=GET&cmmtid=6783.
63. "too frequently whining or frisking": Thomas James Mathias, *The Pursuits of Literature: A Satirical Poem in Four Dialogues* (London: Becket, 1798), 58.
63. "You say Mrs. Smith's sonnets are pretty": Anna Seward to Miss Weston, July 20, 1786, *Letters of Anna Seward: Written Between the Years 1784 and 1807* (Edinburgh: Archibald Constable and Co., 1811), 1:163.
64. "deserving of admiration": Dorset, "Charlotte Smith," 4:25.
64. of what was probably uterine cancer: Stuart Curran, "Charlotte Smith and British Romanticism," *South Central Review* 11, no. 2 (1994): 67, http://www.jstor.org/stable/3189989.
65. "husband of the justly celebrated Mrs Charlotte Smith": *Gentlemen's Magazine*, March 1806.
65. poor access to her novels and poetry: Curran, "Charlotte Smith and British Romanticism," 71.
66. "Though she has done more": Robert Southey, *Selections from the Letters of Robert Southey*, ed. John Wood Warter (London: Longman, 1856), 1:184.
66. "Literature cannot be the business of a woman's life": Charlotte Brontë, *Letters of Charlotte Brontë*, ed. Margaret Smith (New York: Oxford University Press, 1995), 1:166–67.
66. "preserves in her landscapes the truth and precision": Sir Walter Scott, in a note to Dorset's "Charlotte Smith," 4:37.
66. "with true feeling for rural nature": William Wordsworth, in a note to his

"Stanzas Suggested in a Steamboat off Saint Bees' Heads," *Poetical Works* (London: Macmillan, 1898), 843.

67. "so much better than any of the others": Jane Austen, *Jane Austen's Manuscript Works,* ed. Linda Bree, Peter Sabor, and Janet Todd (Peterborough, ON: Broadview Press, 2013), 170.

CHAPTER TWO

68. "She wept": *European Magazine,* March 1787.
70. he departed for France: William Wordsworth, *The Letters of William and Dorothy Wordsworth,* ed. Ernest de Selincourt (New York: Oxford University Press, 2004), 1:66.
70. "a considerable disappointment": Ibid.
71. "notable for many things": Richard Gravil, *Wordsworth and Helen Maria Williams; or, the Perils of Sensibility* (Penrith, UK: Humanities-Ebooks LLP, 2010), 15.
71. "early sorrows": Helen Maria Williams, *Poems on Various Subjects: With Introductory Remarks on the Present State of Science and Literature in France* (London: Whittaker, 1823), poem ix. Deborah Kennedy also denotes this passage as having revealed Williams's generally gloomy disposition. See *Helen Maria Williams,* 22n11.
71. strict reverence for Protestant values: Kennedy, *Helen Maria Williams,* 23.
72. "confined," she later called it: Helen Maria Williams, *Poems in Two Volumes* (London: Cadell, 1786), preface.
72. "the graces of her mind": Percival Stockdale, *The Memoirs of the Life, and Writings of Percival Stockdale; Containing Many Interesting Anecdotes of the Illustrious Men with Whom he Was Connected* (London: Longman, Hurst, Rees, and Orne, 1809), 2:218. Original emphasis.
73. "The young Lady who is the writer of the following": Helen Maria Williams, *Edwin and Eltruda* (London: Cadell, 1782), i–iii.
73. "To feel the fulness of despair": Ibid., 2–3.
74. "EDWIN, of every grace possest": Ibid., 6.
74. "He feels within his shivering veins": Ibid., 31.
75. "the very drollest of the droll": Charlotte Burney, *The Early Diary of Frances Burney 1768–1778 with a Selection from Her Correspondence, and from the Journals of Her Sisters Susan and Charlotte Burney,* ed. Annie Raine Ellis (London: George Bell and Sons, 1889), 2:301–5.
76. "I am engaged to drink tea": William Hayley, *Memoirs of the Life and Writings of William Hayley, Esq,* ed. John Johnson (London: Colburn, 1823), 1:294.
76. "behaved with the most friendly politeness": Ibid., 289–93.
77. "I proceeded to the great Mrs. Montagu": Ibid.
77. "Far other homage claims than flatt'ry brings": Helen Maria Williams, *Peru,* ed. Paula R. Feldman (Peterborough, ON: Broadview Press, 2015), 25.
78. "has not had the presumption": Ibid., 49.

78. "partial, prejudiced, and ignorant": Jane Austen, *The History of England* (Chapel Hill, NC: Algonquin, 1994), iv.
79. "an innocent and amiable people": Ibid., 229.
79. "arbiter of moral standards": Angela Keane, *Revolutionary Women Writers* (Horndon, Devon: Northcote, 2013), 71.
80. "tender, pathetic, and pleasing": *The Critical Review*, 1790.
80. "no small degree of sublimity": Andrew Kippis, *The New Annual Register . . . for the Year 1783* (London: Robinson, 1784), 275.
80. "seized the epic lyre": Anna Seward, "Sonnet to Miss Williams, on her epic poem PERU," *London Magazine*, Feb. 1785.
80. "We feel their sorrows": Elizabeth Ogilvy Benger, *The Female Geniad: A Poem* (London: Hookham and Carpenter, 1791), 20.
81. "harmonious virgins": Horace Walpole, *Horace Walpole's Correspondence with the Countess of Ossory*, ed. W. S. Lewis and A. Doyle Wallace (New Haven, CT: Yale University Press, 1965), 33:533.
81. "literary star of the first magnitude": Mark Ledden, "Perishable Goods: Feminine Virtue, Selfhood and History in the Early Writings of Helen Maria Williams," *Michigan Feminist Studies* 9 (1994–1995): 37.
81. "the most distinguished man of letters": Pat Rogers, "Samuel Johnson," in *Oxford Dictionary of National Biography*, Oxford University Press, 2004; online ed., May 2009, http://www.oxforddnb.com/view/article/14918.
81. "He had dined that day at Mr. Hoole's": James Boswell, *The Life of Samuel Johnson* (Dublin: R. Cross, et al., 1792), 3:428–29.
82. "simplicity, tenderness, and harmony": *Monthly Review*, 1786.
83. "As, starting at each step, I fly": Helen Maria Williams, *Poems in Two Volumes* (London: Cadell, 1786).
84. "What, indeed, but friendship": Helen Maria Williams, *Letters Written in France in the Summer 1790, to a Friend in England: Containing Various Anecdotes Relative to the French Revolution; and Memoirs of Mons. and Madame du Fossé* (London: Cadell, 1790), 195. This work would later become the first volume of the first series of *Letters from France* (1790–93).
84. "Rather to be dreaded than beloved": Ibid., 123.
84. "[He] considered the lower order of people": Ibid., 124.
84. "in the bosom of conjugal felicity": Ibid., 129.
85. "Oh, my dear, my ever beloved friends!": Ibid., 135.
86. "A friend's having been persecuted": Ibid., 195.
86. "imbibe, from their earliest age": Ibid., 9.
87. "transported with joy": Ibid.
87. "Nous sommes mouillés à la nation": Ibid., 14–15.
88. showed unmistakably that a full-on revolution was at hand: Introduction, in Helen Maria Williams, *Letters Written in France*, ed. Neil Fraistat and Susan S. Lanser (Peterborough, ON: Broadview Press, 2002), 11.

88. United Nations' 1948 Universal Declaration of Human Rights: Ibid., 12.
89. France was progressing faster than any other country: Ibid.
89. "a triumph in the warm hope": Hannah More, *Remarks on the Speech of M. Dupont* (London: Cadell, 1793), 7.
89. "I think myself happy": Samuel Romilly, *Memoirs of The Life of Sir Samuel Romilly* (London: Murray, 1840), 1:356. This astute claim is made by Deborah Kennedy in *Helen Maria Williams*, 53.
89. "the triumph of human kind": Williams, *Letters . . . Summer of 1790*, 14.
90. "every sword was drawn": Ibid., 13–14.
90. "which so many wretches have entered": Ibid., 23.
91. distancing herself and her heroine from the politics: Deborah Kennedy, "Responding to the French Revolution: Williams's *Julia* and Burney's *The Wanderer*," in *Jane Austen and Mary Shelley, and Their Sisters*, ed. Laura Dabundo (UPA, 2000), 6, quoted in Stephanie Mathilde Hilger, *Women Write Back: Strategies of Response and the Dynamics of European Literary Culture, 1790–1805* (Amsterdam: Rodopi, 2009), 51.
91. "if any thing were wanting": *Monthly Review*, Dec. 1790.
92. "part history, part journalism": Deborah Kennedy, "Spectacle of the Guillotine: Helen Maria Williams and the Reign of Terror," *Philological Quarterly* 73, no. 1 (1994), 96.
92. "talent of chatting on paper": *The Analytical Review*, Dec. 1790.
92. "so much the air of romance": *The English Review; or, an Abstract of English and Foreign Literature*, Jan. 1791.
93. "conformity to nature": Edmund Burke, *Reflections of the Revolution in France, and on the Proceedings in Certain Societies in London Relative to That Event, in a Letter Intended to Have Been Sent to a Gentleman in Paris* (London: J. Dodsley, 1790), 49.
93. "if you pleased, have profited": Ibid., 50.
93. "Laws overturned; tribunals subverted": Ibid., 56–57.
94. "[The Queen] bears the imprisonment": Ibid., 112.
95. "events the most astonishing": Helen Maria Williams, *Letters from France: Containing Many New Anecdotes Relative to the French Revolution, and the Present State of French Manners* (1792), 4. This work would become the second volume of the first series of *Letters from France* (1790–93).
95. "pure and sensitive heart": Williams, *Letters from France*, ed. Fraistat and Lanser, 225. Translation of this letter and of Helen Maria's response are based on text quoted in Lionel D. Woodward, *Une Anglaise, amie de la révolution française, Helene-Maria Williams, et ses amis* (Paris: Honoré Champion, 1930), 43–46.
96. "Revolution is an event": Ibid.
96. "the most famous English woman": Kennedy, *Helen Maria Williams*, 81.
97. "join the universal voice": Williams, *Letters . . . Summer of 1790*, 21.

98. intimately connected to France: Mark Ledden, "Perishable Goods," 41.
98. "All the stupendous events": Helen Maria Williams, *Letters on the Events in France Since the Restoration in 1815* (London: Baldwin, Cradock and Joy, 1819), 3–4.
99. "As our English women excel": *Spectator*, June 1711.
100. "monstrous political and sexual desires": Steven Blakemore, "Revolution and the French Disease: Laetitia Matilda Hawkins's Letter to Helen Maria Williams," *Studies in English Literature, 1500–1900* 36, no. 3 (1996): 676.
100. "debased her sex": *The Gentleman's Magazine*, 1795.
100. "[She] received a severe lesson": Lewis Goldsmith, *Female Revolutionary Plutarch, Containing Biographical, Historical, and Revolutionary Sketches, Characters, and Anecdotes* (London: John Murray, 1806), 3:404. Deborah Kennedy made this astute connection in "Spectacle of the Guillotine," 101.
100. "reasoning backwards": Laetitia Matilda Hawkins, *Letters on the Female Mind, Its Powers and Pursuits. Addressed to Miss H. M. Williams, with Particular Reference to Her "Letters" from France* (London: Hookham and Carpenter, 1793), 185.
100. "We are not formed for these deep investigations": Ibid., 6–8.
101. "Those whom nature, not withstanding all modern levelling": Ibid., 33–34.
101. "the incense of flattery": Stockdale, *Memoirs*, 2:220.
102. "in a state of cold alienation": Anna Seward, *Letters of Anna Seward: Written Between the Year 1784 and 1807* (Edinburgh: George Ramsay and Co., 1811), 3:209.
102. "the electrical fire": Helen Maria Williams, *A Tour in Switzerland; or, a View of the Present State of the Governments and Manners of those Cantons: with Comparative Sketches of the Present State of Paris* (London: G. G. and J. Robinson, 1798), 1:ii.
103. "particularly corresponding to her style of society": Catherine Wilmot, *An Irish Peer on the Continent (1801–1803): Being a Narrative of the Tour of Stephen, 2nd Earl Mount Cashell, Through France, Italy, etc., as Related by Catherine Wilmot*, ed. Thomas U. Sadleir (London: Williams and Norgate, 1920), 38–39.
103. "Must I be told that my mind is perverted?": Williams, *Letters . . . Summer of 1790*, 218.
104. "forgot the lessons of her youth": William Beloe, *The Sexagenarian; or The Recollections of a Literary Life* (London: Rivington, 1818), 1:356–58.

CHAPTER THREE

105. In the late 1790s: Great approbation is due to William Stafford, whose work *English Feminists and Their Opponents in the 1790s* was of immeasurable assistance in the research for this chapter.
105. "lime twigs of Lust": Mary Tattlewell and Joanne Hit-him-Home, *The Wom-*

en's *Sharp Revenge* (London: Beckett, 1640). This and the following three rare texts have been reprinted in *Half Humankind: Contexts and Texts of the Controversy About Women in England, 1540–1640*, ed. Katherine Usher Herderson and Barbara F. McManus (Chicago: University of Illinois Press, 1985).

106. "sober shows without": Anonymous, *Hic Mulier; or, The Man-Woman* (London, 1620).

106. "foul water will quench fire": John Taylor, *A Juniper Lecture, with the Description of All Sorts of Women, Good and Bad* (London: William Ley, 1639).

106. "like rich Jewels hang[ing] at your ears": Anonymous, *Haec Vir; or, The Womanish Man* (London, 1620).

106. "be so ridiculous": Quoted in Virginia Woolf, *A Room of One's Own* (New York: Fountain, 1929), 63. Osborne was herself a gifted letter writer, and enjoyed a years-long epistolary romance with her future husband, William Temple, but she was vehemently against women publishing books—this remark, in fact, was in response to the recent publication of Margaret Cavendish's 1653 *Poems and Fancies*. For purposes of comprehension, spelling and punctuation of this passage have been modernized.

106. "what ne'er our fathers saw": Richard Polwhele, *The Unsex'd Females, A Poem* (London: Cadell, 1798).

107. "[A] mix with sparkling humour": Ibid.

107. "sp[u]n webs of feeble reasoning": *The British Critic*, Aug. 1793.

108. "[Wollstonecraft] spoke": Polwhele, *Unsex'd Females*.

108. "she may still produce entertainment": *Anti-Jacobin Review*, Aug. 1798; and *British Critic*, Nov. 1795.

109. "vigorous and impatient": *Monthly Review*, Aug. 1799; and *Anti-Jacobin Review*, Feb. 1800.

109. "confine[d] herself to the fashions": *Anti-Jacobin Review*, May 1799 and Aug. 1798.

109. "Is not a woman a human being": Mary Robinson, *Thoughts on the Condition of Women, and on the Injustice of Mental Subordination* (London: Longman and Rees, 1799), 8–9.

110. memorized moving poetry: Mary Robinson, *Memoirs of the Late Mrs. Robinson, Written by Herself, from the Edition Edited by Her Daughter* (London: Hunt and Clarke, 1827), 12.

110. "too unlimited indulgence": Ibid., 14.

111. "She was the most extensively accomplished female": Ibid., 19–20.

113. "Take care": Ibid., 26.

113. "He was 'the kindest, the best of mortals!'": Ibid., 30–31. Original emphasis.

113. "contemplating a thousand triumphs": Ibid., 27.

113. "the source of all my succeeding sorrows": Ibid., 31.

114. "My heart, even when I knelt": Ibid., 34–35.

114. "the most wretched of mortals": Ibid.
115. "broad hemisphere of fashionable folly": Ibid., 45.
115. "sure to attract attention": Ibid.
115. "known by name": Ibid., 58.
115. "Had Mr. Harris generously assisted": Ibid., 59. Original emphasis.
116. "fidelity and affection": Ibid., 61.
116. "My little collection of poems": Ibid., 71.
116. "Mrs. Robinson is by no means an Aiken": *The Monthly Review,* Sept. 1775.
116. "distinguished by an elegant simplicity": *The Critical Review,* July 1775.
117. "Ye nymphs, ah!": Mary Robinson, *Selected Poems,* ed. Judith Pascoe (Peterborough, ON: Broadview Press, 2000), 67.
117. "Gladly I leave the town": Ibid., 72.
118. "mildness and sensibility": Robinson, *Memoirs,* 76.
119. "Patroness of the Unhappy": Mary Robinson, *Captivity, A Poem and Celadon and Lydia, a Tale. Dedicated, by Permission, to Her Grace the Duchess of Devonshire* (London: Beckett, 1777), 3.
119. "Bear me, sweet Freedom": Ibid., 9–10.
120. "Even though I was the partner of his captivity": Robinson, *Memoirs,* 77.
120. "with zeal bordering on delight": Ibid., 83–84.
121. "with uncommon and universal applause": Reviews from the Dec. 11, 1779, edition of each respective publication.
121. turned and curtsied: Robert D. Bass, *The Green Dragoon: The Lives of Banastre Tarleton and Mary Robinson* (Orangeburg, SC: Sandlapper, 1973), 65.
121. "That curtsy": Robinson, *Memoirs,* 85.
122. "The piece was well got up": *Morning Post,* May 1, 1778, quoted in Bass, *Green Dragoon,* 66.
122. "ill-bestowed upon a man": Robinson, *Memoirs,* 95–96.
123. "strange degree of alarm": Ibid., 98.
123. milkmaid's outfit with red ribbons: Paula Byrne, *Perdita: The Literary, Theatrical, Scandalous Life of Mary Robinson* (New York: Random House, 2004), 99.
123. "Just as the curtain was falling": Robinson, *Memoirs,* 99. Original emphasis.
123. "greatest and most perfect beauty": Anson Papers, folder 2, Prince of Wales to Mary Hamilton, letter 74, quoted in Byrne, *Perdita,* 101.
124. "the most admired": Robinson, *Memoirs,* 102.
124. "inviolable affection": Ibid., 105.
124. "A promise of the sum of twenty thousand": Ibid., 112.
124. A few clandestine meetings: Byrne, *Perdita,* 113. Their wild, love-struck consummation may have occurred instead at the inn on Eel Pie Island, a romantic spot where they first met in person and later visited often, but Mary claims they were always accompanied by friends at this location and could therefore not have sneaked away. See Byrne, *Perdita,* 113–14.
124. "How would my soul have idolized such a *husband!*": Ibid., 110.

124. "a certain *young actress*": *Morning Post,* 20 and 22 July 1780.
125. "Whenever I appeared in public": Robinson, *Memoirs,* 112.
126. "hourly augmenting torrent": Ibid., 111.
126. "The audacity of Mrs. R": *Morning Post,* Sept. 27, 1780.
126. feeling the creeping hand of envy: Byrne, *Perdita,* 124.
127. "in blows and reproaches": *Morning Post,* Oct. 7, 1780.
127. Mary was becoming a liability: Byrne, *Perdita,* 124.
127. "*we must meet no more!*": Robinson, *Memoirs,* 113.
127. scores, from an almost daily correspondence: Byrne, *Perdita,* 128.
128. outgoing payments: Byrne, *Perdita,* 217. Account books on file at the Royal Archives, Windsor.
128. "most superb and elegant piece": *Rambler's Magazine,* 18 March 1783, quoted in Byrne, *Perdita,* 208.
128. "standard of taste": *Morning Herald,* Jan. 9, 1782.
128. Such a "naked" dress led to a national scandal: Byrne, *Perdita,* 190. Accusations of indecency were accompanied by assertions of anti-France sentiment: by wearing imported muslin, Marie Antoinette was showing disregard for the French silk industry.
129. new trends in fashion: Ibid.
129. "The *wit* of the *eye*": *Morning Herald,* Jan. 18, 1781. Original emphasis.
130. "an imprudent exposure": Robinson, *Memoirs,* 123.
130. It is suspected: Byrne, *Perdita,* 213. Martin J. Levy, "Mary Robinson," in *Oxford Dictionary of National Biography,* Oxford University Press, 2004; online ed., Jan. 2008, http://www.oxforddnb.com/view/article/23857. Paula Byrne surmises that a miscarriage was the most likely cause of Mary's paralysis, but she doesn't rule out hypothermia despite the warm summer weather. Martin Levy describes the sickness as "a paralytic stroke, possibly brought on by a miscarriage."
130. never became pregnant again: Byrne, *Perdita,* 214.
130. "receptacles of loathsome mud": Robinson, *Memoirs,* 129.
130. "the more assiduous cultivation": Ibid., 123.
131. "*vastly pretty*": Ibid., 136. Original emphasis.
132. "This poetic address": *The Monthly Review,* April 1791.
132. "very refined sensibility": *General Magazine,* Dec. 1790.
132. "WHAT is the charm": Mary Robinson, *Ainsi va le monde: A Poem* (London: Bell, 1790), 13–16.
133. "beyond her most sanguine hopes": Robinson, *Memoirs,* 137.
133. single most popular novel: *British Women Writers: A Critical Reference Guide,* ed. Janet Todd (New York: Continuum, 1989), 576. Dawn M. Vernooy-Epp, introduction to *The Works of Mary Robinson,* ed. Daniel Robinson and Dawn M. Vernooy-Epp (London: Pickering, 2011), 2:225.
133. "animated portrait of her mind": Robinson, *Works,* 2:256.

134. "I considered the Prince as my friend": Ibid., 331.
135. a decidedly melodramatic work: Stephanie Russo, "'Where Virtue Struggles Midst a Maze of Snares': Mary Robinson's *Vancenza* (1792) and the Gothic Novel," *Women's Writing* 20, no. 4 (2014): 586.
135. "nothing short of revolutionary": Ibid., 591.
135. "Little and contracted minds": Robinson, *Works,* 2:305. Original emphasis.
136. "[A] record of domestic woe": *European Magazine,* May 1792; *The Monthly Review,* March 1792; and *The English Review,* 1792.
136. "The sentiments in these volumes": *Analytical Review,* Feb. 1796.
137. all manner of favored themes: Byrne, *Perdita,* 357.
138. "a woman of undoubted genius": Samuel Taylor Coleridge, *Collected Letters of Samuel Taylor Coleridge,* ed. Earl Leslie Griggs (Oxford: Clarendon, 2000), 1:562–63. Original emphasis.
138. "Ay! that Woman has an Ear": Ibid., 576.
138. "AH! WHAT ART THOU": Robinson, *Selected Poems,* 122.
139. "Have you seen Mrs. Robinson lately?": Coleridge, *Letters,* 589.
139. "an *injunction*": Robinson, *Memoirs,* 150. Original emphasis.
139. "pressing to her heart": Ibid., 151.
139. "most refined and elegant conversation": Pierce Egan, *The Mistress of Royalty; or, the Loves of Florizel and Perdita* (London, 1814), 124–42, quoted in Byrne, *Perdita,* 393.
140. outrageous sums on harebrained fun: Saul David, *Prince of Pleasure: The Prince of Wales and the Making of the Regency* (New York: Grove, 1998), 364. Carolly Erickson, *Our Tempestuous Day: A History of Regency England* (New York: Harper, 2011), 235.
140. "being patronized by nincompoops": Claire Harman, *Jane's Fame: How Jane Austen Conquered the World* (New York: Picador, 2009), 52.
140. the true love of his life: Byrne, *Perdita,* 396. To support her claim, Byrne references a little-known letter from Charles James Fox to Mary Benwell describing "a curious document attesting his [George's] *penchant* for Mrs. Robinson, via Walter Sichel, *Sheridan* (New York: Houghton Mifflin, 1909), 2:52.
140. "appear in the white muslin frocks": *Ladies Magazine,* July 1787.
140. She also popularized: *Ladies Magazine,* April–Dec. 1783. Credit is due to Paula Byrne for having discovered these "Robinsonian" influences on fashion.
141. "with flattering avidity": Robinson, *Memoirs,* 97.
141. no woman was more notorious: Levy, *Oxford Dictionary of National Biography,* "Mary Robinson."

CHAPTER FOUR

142. "the smallest creature": Harriet Martineau, *Autobiography,* ed. Maria Weston Chapman (Boston: Houghton, Mifflin and Co., 1877, 1900), 23.

143. handpicked the guest list: Anne Thackeray Ritchie, *Chapters from Some Memoirs* (London: Macmillan, 1894), 62.
143. Thackeray paced fussily: Ibid., 60.
143. "tiny, delicate, serious": Ibid.
143. "she believed there were books being published": Charles and Frances Brookfield, *Mrs. Brookfield and Her Circle* (New York: Scribner, 1905), 2:305. My emphasis.
143. "Do you like London, Miss Brontë?": Thackeray Ritchie, *Memoirs*, 63.
144. "the great *Jane Eyre*": Ibid., 61.
144. an extra dish of cookies: Ibid., 64.
144. "female horrors": G. H. Lewes (aka "Vivian"), "Flight of the Authoresses," *Leader*, June 15, 1850.
145. "some few others have claims": Ibid. My emphasis.
145. "if her story had not been so good": Ibid.
145. "How many of us can write novels": G. H. Lewes (aka "Vivian), "A Gentle Hint to Writing-Women," *Leader*, May 18, 1850. Despite his complimentary words here, Lewes was never in favor of authoresses: "They are ruining our profession. Wherever we carry our skilful pens, we find the place preoccupied by women . . . What am I to do—what are my brother-pens to do, when such rivalry is permitted?" His objections must've been purely professional, though, because he would later enjoy a twenty-four-year romance with George Eliot.
145. Catherine Crowe was a dynamic personality: Generous credit is due to the University of Kent for granting me access to the Geoffrey Larken Catherine Crowe Collection (hereafter "Larken Papers"). Gathered between 1970 and 1990 in the course of Larken's research for a biography, the materials were instrumental in helping the fragments of Mrs. Crowe's life come together for this chapter.
146. "thirty or forty saddle-horses": Rees Howell Gronow, *Reminiscences of Captain Gronow, Formerly of the Grenadier Guards, and M.P. for Stafford: Being Anecdotes of the Camp, the Court, and the Clubs, at the Close of the War with France* (London: Smith, Elder and Co., 1862), 75.
148. To his deep regret: Larken Papers. Larken has surmised that, considering the length and breadth of John Crowe's military service, his unexpected discharge in 1825 would likely have been a source of great consternation for this upstanding, dedicated soldier.
148. "a colony of half-pay notables": A. B. Granville, *The Spas of England and Principle Sea-Bathing Places* (London: Colburn, 1841), 359.
149. "the Smith of Smiths": Lord Macaulay to his father, Zachary Macaulay, July 21, 1826, in *The Life and Letters of Lord Macaulay*, ed. George Otto Trevelyan (London: Longmans, Green, and Co., 1881), 103.
149. lots of jocose commentary: Larken Papers.

150. of whom she considered herself a disciple: Ibid.
151. "forgotten and forgettable": Lucy Sussex, "The Detective Maidservant: Catherine Crowe's *Susan Hopley*," in *Silent Voices: Forgotten Novels by Victorian Women Writers*, ed. Brenda Ayres (Westport, CT: Praeger, 2003), 60.
151. "Old men live long": Catherine Crowe, *Aristodemus: A Tragedy* (Edinburgh: Tait, 1838), 25–26.
152. title character of Voltaire's novel *Zadig*: Kenneth Silverman, *Edgar A. Poe: A Mournful and Never-Ending Remembrance* (New York: Harper, 1992), 171.
152. Lucy Sussex points to: Sussex, "Detective Maidservant," 57.
153. "It is powerful, beyond all question": *Examiner*, Feb. 28, 1841.
153. "Worthy, excellent Susan!": Catherine Crowe, *Susan Hopley; or, the Adventures of a Maid-Servant* (Edinburgh: Tait, 1842), 1. This edition of the novel and those printed afterward featured a modified title, whereas the title for the original 1841 version, published in London by Saunders and Otley, was *Susan Hopley; or, Circumstantial Evidence.*
154. "sweetened exactly to my liking": Ibid.
154. "go over to the house": Ibid., 22.
154. "a pair of little studs": Ibid., 24.
155. "unhappy story": Ibid., 30.
155. "Mr. Gaveston, when he left the court": Ibid., 279.
156. among all classes of society: Sussex, "Detective Maidservant," 62.
156. "We hardly know what to say": *Examiner*, Feb. 28, 1841.
156. "through all the intricacies": *Athenaeum*, Jan. 1841.
156. "in certain states of mind": Elizabeth Gaskell to Catherine Winkworth, Nov. 2, 1848. *Letters of Mrs. Gaskell*, ed. J. A. V. Chapple and Arthur Pollard (Manchester: Mandolin, 1997), 60; and *Letters and Memorials of Catherine Winkworth* (Clifton, UK: E. Austin and Son, 1883), 1:160. Original emphasis.
156. "A boy goes on board a frigate": Sydney Smith to Mrs. Crowe, Jan., 31, 1841, in Saba Smith Holland, *A Memoir of the Reverend Sydney Smith, by His Daughter Lady Holland, with a Selection from His Letters* (London: Longman, et al., 1855), 1:442.
156. after a run of three hundred nights: *Cumberland's Minor Theatre*, 8, quoted in Sussex, "Detective Maidservant," 63.
157. initiating regular mail runs: Kevin Hillstrom and Laurie Collier Hillstrom, *The Industrial Revolution in America: Steam Shipping* (Santa Barbara, CA: ABC-CLIO, 2005), 7.
157. "admirable psychological ingenuity": P. Quin Keegan, "Mrs. Crowe's and Mrs. Gaskell's Novels," *Victoria Magazine* 33, 1879.
159. "very clever, eccentric person": Alexander Ireland, introduction to Robert Chambers, *Vestiges of the Natural History of Creation* (London: W and R Chambers, 1884), xx.

159. "The situation was delicious": Ibid., xx–xxi. Ireland does not name Mrs. Crowe, but she was later identified by James Secord in the course of his research for *Victorian Sensation: The Extraordinary Publication, Reception, and Secret Authorship of Vestiges of the Natural History of Creation* (Chicago: University of Chicago Press, 2000). See Sussex, "Detective Maidservant."
160. "instantly answered": Arthur Conan Doyle, *The History of Spiritualism* (London: Cassell and Co., 1926), 1:59.
161. "the spiritual telegraph was at last working": Ibid.
161. "Extend the bounds of nature": Catherine Crowe, *The Night-Side of Nature: Or, Ghosts and Ghost Seers* (London: Newby, 1848). All citations for our purposes refer to the 1901 edition, printed in Philadelphia by Coates and Co.
162. "laughed with open, dead eyes": Aug. 17, 1847, in Elias Bredsdorff, *Hans Christian Andersen: The Story of His Life and Work, 1805–75* (New York: Scribner, 1975), 194.
162. Could people accommodate a reality: Robert F. Geary, "The Corpse in the Dung Cart: *The Night-Side of Nature* and the Victorian Supernatural Tale," in *Functions of the Fantastic: Selected Essays from the Thirteenth International Conference on the Fantastic in the Arts*, ed. Joe Sanders (Westport, CT: Greenwood, 1995), 50.
162. "Somewhat of the mystery of our own being": Crowe, *Night-Side of Nature*, 9.
163. "nobody thought of seeking the explanation": Ibid., 46.
163. "From believing in everything": Ibid., 47.
163. "the wise men of the world": Ibid. That "much quoted axiom" of Shakespeare's is from *Hamlet*.
163. "shadowy borderland": *New Monthly Magazine*, Dec. 1852.
164. a literary chorus: Geary, "Corpse in the Dung Cart," 51.
164. "enlightened age": Bram Stoker, *Dracula* (New York: Bantam, 1981), 339.
164. "horribly dismal": Charles Dickens to W. H. Wills, Feb. 28, 1850, *Letters of Charles Dickens*, ed. M. House, G. Storey, and K. Tillotson (Oxford: Clarendon, 1988), 6:50. Credit is due to Deborah Wynne of Keele University for her astute observations of the Dickens-Crowe relationship in "Dickens's Changing Responses to Hereditary Insanity in *Household Words* and *All the Year Round*," *Notes and Queries* 46, no. 1 (March 1999).
165. she pored over texts: Larken Papers.
165. "much that is most perplexing": Catherine Crowe to James Thomas Fields, Jan. 30, 1854, on file with Special Collections at the University of Kent, Canterbury.
166. "terrible condition of mad exposure": Robert Chambers to Alexander Ireland, March 4, 1854, on file with the National Library of Scotland.
166. "She received the assurance": Francis Ann Kemble, *Records of Later Life* (New York: Holt, 1883), 233.
166. "One of the curious manifestations": Charles Dickens to Rev. James White, March 7, 1854, Dickens, *Letters*, 7:285–86.

167. suffering from stress: Larken Papers.
167. wandering about the body of its own volition: "Hysteria," *Encyclopedia of Gender and Society*, ed. Jodi O'Brien (Thousand Oaks, CA: SAGE, 2009), 2:448.
167. use her story to protest: Sussex, "Detective Maidservant," 64.
168. "she is now under restraint": Charles Dickens to Emile de la Rue, March 9, 1854, Dickens, *Letters*, 7:288.
168. "The authoress of 'Susan Hopley'": *Examiner*, Feb. 1848.
169. "a medium, and an Ass": Charles Dickens to Emile de la Rue, March 9, 1854, Dickens, *Letters*, 7:288.
169. "obviously troubled": Diana Basham, *The Trial of Woman: Feminism and the Occult Sciences in Victorian Literature and Society* (London: Macmillan, 1992), 154.
170. "good-natured Mrs. Crowe": W. M. Thackeray to John Brown, Dec. 31, 1854, *Letters of Dr. John Brown*, ed. D. W. Forrest (London: Black, 1907), 323.
170. dined several times: Gaskell, *Letters*, 778–79.
170. "The writer, in a word": *Examiner*, Feb. 28, 1841. Original emphasis.
170. women and their predicament: Joanne Wilkes, "Catherine Crowe," in *Oxford Dictionary of National Biography*, Oxford University Press, 2004; online ed., May 2008, http://www.oxforddnb.com/view/article/6822.
171. "The circumstances of her heroines": Adeline Sergeant et al., *Women Novelists of Queen Victoria's Reign: A Book of Appreciations* (London: Hurst and Blackett, 1897), 156–60.

CHAPTER FIVE

172. "most delightfully situated": Mrs. Coleridge to her sister-in law Mrs. George Coleridge, July 1800, on file with the Harry Ransom Humanities Research Center at the University of Texas, Austin (hereafter "Harry Ransom Center").
173. "Some Mountain or Peak": *Collected Letters of Samuel Taylor Coleridge*, ed. E. L. Griggs (Oxford: Clarendon, 1971), quoted in Kathleen Jones, *A Passionate Sisterhood: Women of the Wordsworth Circle* (New York: St. Martin's, 2000), 103. Coleridge's letters are also available online at http://inamidst.com/coleridge/letters/.
175. "Angel in the House": Bradford Keyes Mudge, *Sara Coleridge, A Victorian Daughter: Her Life and Essays* (New Haven, CT: Yale University Press, 1989), 14.
175. "a remarkably interesting Baby": Sara Coleridge, *Memoir and Letters of Sara Coleridge*, ed. Edith Coleridge (New York: Harper, 1874), 35. There are several versions of this work, including one each for the years 1873 and 1874 (published by King in London and Harper in New York, respectively), and a third, abridged edition that appeared in 1875. Because this third *Memoir and*

Letters is the most readily available (via the generous people at Archives.org), most of the citations for our purposes, unless otherwise noted, are from it. Here, Sara is quoting an Oct. 1803 letter from her father to Thomas Poole, a lifelong family friend. See Griggs, *Collected Letters*, 2:1014.

176. played on the floor: Dennis Low, *Literary Protégées of the Lake Poets* (Burlington, VT: Ashgate, 2006), 103.
177. "[a] GIRL!": Samuel Taylor Coleridge, *Collected Letters*, 3:902, quoted in Mudge, *Sara Coleridge*, 19.
176. "an omen of our lifelong separation": Sara Coleridge, *Memoir and Letters*, 2.
176. enthusiastic about all things literary and linguistic: Ibid., 25.
176. "[She] has received an education": Robert Southey to John Prior Estlin, March 17, 1815, *New Letters of Robert Southey*, ed. Kenneth Curran (New York: Columbia University Press, 1965), 2:119. Robert Southey's letters are also online, at http://www.rc.umd.edu/editions/southey_letters.
177. caught anemones: Sara Coleridge, *Memoir and Letters*, 18. Sara also mentions her childhood fearlessness here—that she was "ever ready to take the difficult mountain-path and outgo my companions' daring in tree-climbing."
177. pulled from the comfort of his second-floor study: Jones, *Passionate Sisterhood*, 171.
177. there were kittens: Ibid.
178. Murray's desk was piled up: Claire Harman, *Jane's Fame: How Jane Austen Conquered the World* (New York: Picador, 2009), 50–51.
178. "How she Dobrizhoffered it all out": Charles Lamb to Robert Southey, Aug. 10, 1825, *The Works of Charles and Mary Lamb*, ed. Edward Verrall Lucas (London, Methuen and Co., 1905), 7:692.
178. "Yes, I have seen Miss Coleridge": Charles Lamb to Bernard Barton, Feb. 17, 1823, *The Works of Charles and Mary Lamb*, 599.
179. "My dear daughter's translation": "Dobrizhoffer," *Specimens of the Table Talk of the Late Samuel Taylor Coleridge*, ed. Henry Nelson Coleridge (London: John Murray, 1835), 2:81. This was written Aug. 4, 1832, ten years and seven months after *An Account of the Abiphones* was published.
180. "Tell her nothing": Sally Mitchell, *The Fallen Angel: Chastity, Class and Women's Reading, 1835–1880* (Bowling Green, OH: Bowling Green University Press, 1981), xii. Mitchell is quoting Cecil Willett Cunnington, *Feminine Attitudes in the Nineteenth Century* (New York: Haskell, 1973), 214.
180. "She is never weary": Mrs. Coleridge to Thomas Poole, in Stephen Potter, ed., *Minnow Among Tritons: Mrs. S. T. Coleridge's Letters to Thomas Poole* (Bloomsbury: Nonesuch Press, 1934), 111, quoted in Mudge, *Sara Coleridge*, 34.
181. "those duties": Robert Southey, *New Letters*, 2:280, quoted in Mudge, *Sara Coleridge*, 38.
181. "You once mentioned": Sara Coleridge to Elizabeth Crumpe, Feb. 2, 1828, on file with the Wordsworth Trust at Dove Cottage. Mrs. Rundell's *A New*

System of Domestic Cookery was a smash success in the first half of the nineteenth century and, it will be remembered, enabled John Murray to purchase his London Mayfair home. As Dennis Low notes, it was Murray's second best seller behind Byron's *Childe Harolde's Pilgrimage*. See *Literary Protégées of the Lake Poets,* 118.

181. "I should have been much happier": Sara Coleridge to Derwent Coleridge, June 6, 1825, Harry Ransom Center.

182. "I regret that I cannot make more use": Sara Coleridge to Elizabeth Crumpe, Feb. 2, 1828, Wordsworth Trust, Dove Cottage, Ambleside, Cumbria, UK.

182. "infinitely for the better": Sara Coleridge, *Memoir and Letters* (1874), 58, quoted in Mudge, *Sara Coleridge*, 53.

182. "half reduced to idiotcy": Robert Southey to John Rickman, April 24, 1807, *New Letters,* 1:451.

183. "It has done me much good": Sara Coleridge to Derwent Coleridge, Nov. 5, 1825, Harry Ransom Center. Henrietta Boyle O'Neil's poem was first published in Charlotte Turner Smith's *Desmond,* under the title "Ode to the Poppy." Smith and O'Neil were close friends, and Smith grieved deeply at the death of O'Neil a year later, in 1793. She memorialized the loss in her second volume of *Elegiac Sonnets,* with a recounting of an earlier note: "Sent to the Honorable Mrs O'Neil, with painted flowers."

183. O'Neil's "lovely blossom" had a history: Mudge, *Sara Coleridge,* 37.

183. to hush fussy babies: Alethea Hayter, *Opium and the Romantic Imagination* (Berkeley: University of California Press, 1968), 31.

183. before the advent of psychology, it was impossible: Mudge, *Sara Coleridge,* 57–58.

184. "despair[ing] of being entirely healthful": Sara Coleridge to Emily Trevenen, Dec. 1830, quoted in Mudge, *Sara Coleridge,* 55.

184. her menstrual cycle stopped entirely: Ibid., 58.

184. "My childish and girlish castles": Sara Coleridge to Henry Nelson Coleridge, Feb. 9, 1827, Harry Ransom Center.

184. "mark the Talent and Industry": Quoted in Earl Leslie Griggs, *Coleridge Fille* (Oxford: Oxford University Press, 1940), 66.

185. "from a *too* bustling family": Mrs. Coleridge to Thomas Poole, July 1829, in Potter, ed., *Minnow Among Tritons,* 147, quoted in Mudge, *Sara Coleridge,* 54.

185. "sit in a Carriage": Potter, ed., *Minnow Among Tritons,* 170, quoted in Mudge, *Sara Coleridge,* 56.

185. "the delicate mirth": Sara Coleridge to Emily Trevenen, Aug. 3, 1834, Harry Ransom Center.

186. "Children mark what you *do* much more": Sara Coleridge to Henry Coleridge, Oct. 1833, Sara Coleridge, *Memoir and Letters,* 74.

186. "'O, sister!'": Sara Coleridge, *Pretty Lessons in Verse for Good Children; with Some Lessons in Latin in Easy Rhyme* (London: Parker and Son, 1834), 43.

186. "The Tiger, confined in a cage": Ibid., 42.
187. "When Herbert can say all his nouns": Ibid., 99.
187. "I envy the beasts": Sara Coleridge, "The Melancholy Prince," *Sara Coleridge: Collected Poems*, ed. Peter Swaab (Manchester: Carcanet, 2007), 183.
188. "There was everything in the circumstances": Sara Coleridge to Thomas Poole, Sept. 5, 1834, Mrs. Henry Sanford, *Thomas Poole and His Friends* (London: Macmillan, 1888), 297.
189. "STC's works must be reissued": Sara Coleridge to Henry Nelson Coleridge, Sept. 30, 1834, Harry Ransom Center.
189. "[Wilson] is a fool": Quoted in Griggs, *Coleridge Fille*, 107.
190. "No work is so inadequately rewarded": Sara Coleridge, diary entry, Oct. 28, 1848, Harry Ransom Center.
191. children hustled out of the room: Mudge, *Sara Coleridge*, 88.
191. "Your feelings will be sad": Sara Coleridge to Henry Nelson Coleridge, Oct. 16, 1836, Harry Ransom Center.
192. dependent on Henry: Mudge, *Sara Coleridge*, 90.
192. Each morning, she would write: Sara Coleridge to Henry Nelson Coleridge, Oct. 17, Nov. 10, and Nov. 6, respectively, 1836, Harry Ransom Center.
193. "burlesque child's tale": Sara Coleridge, diary entry, 1836, Harry Ransom Center. The term *wondertale* is from Vladimir Propp's *Theory and History of Folklore* (Minneapolis: University of Minnesota Press, 1984), quoted in Mudge, *Sara Coleridge*, 95.
193. print run of just two hundred fifty copies: Lord John Coleridge, preface to Sara Coleridge, *Phantasmion* (Boston: Roberts Brothers, 1874), iii.
193. "It is . . . a Fairy Tale": *Quarterly Review*, Sept. 1840.
194. "To print a Fairy Tale": Sara Coleridge, *Memoir and Letters*, 82.
194. what disqualified Lewis Carroll's *Alice's Adventures:* D. L. Ashliman, *Greenwood Encyclopedia*, 331–32. Ashliman is referencing Tolkien's essay "On Fairy Stories," whereby an attempt is made to differentiate the newly emerged fantasy genre from others.
195. "Phantasmion looked round in momentary dread": Sara Coleridge, *Phantasmion*, 347–48.
195. "crushed and mangled": Ibid., 295.
195. "dazzling in whiteness": Ibid., 37.
196. uncanny, and unprecedented, attention: Matthew David Surridge, "Worlds Within Worlds: The First Heroic Fantasy, Part IV," *Black Gate: Adventures in Fantasy Literature*, 2010, http://www.blackgate.com/2010/09/19/worlds-within-worlds-the-first-heroic-fantasy-part-iv/.
196. "given to agriculture": Sara Coleridge, *Phantasmion*, 25.
196. "tissues of unrealities": Sara Coleridge to Derwent Coleridge, Aug. 16, 1837, quoted in Mudge, *Sara Coleridge*, 96.
196. "Go, little book": Sara Coleridge, *Memoir and Letters*, 82.

197. "a bellyful of macaroons": Henry Crabb Robinson, *Henry Crabb Robinson on Books and Their Writers* (London: J. M. Dent, 1938), 2:538.
197. in the hands of the transcendentalist movement: Jeffrey W. Barbeau, *Sara Coleridge: Her Life and Thought* (New York: Palgrave, 2014), 67–68.
197. "Rev. Mr. N [reading]": *Boston Quarterly Review*, Jan. 1840.
199. confidence to reevaluate: Mudge, *Sara Coleridge*, 93.
199. systematic reread: Bradford K. Mudge, "Sara Coleridge," in *Oxford Dictionary of National Biography*, Oxford University Press, 2004; online ed., Oct. 2007, http://www.oxforddnb.com/view/article/5889.
199. "Our loss, indeed": Sara Coleridge to Mrs. Joshua Stanger, Aug. 10, 1840, Sara Coleridge, *Memoir and Letters*, 117.
200. forced to confront a new domestic arrangement: Mudge, *Sara Coleridge*, 107.
200. "No two beings could be more intimately united": Sara Coleridge to Mrs. Gillman, Feb. 1843, Sara Coleridge, *Memoir and Letters*, 131.
200. "*I have cultivated cheerfulness*": Sara Coleridge to Mrs. Henry Jones, Oct. 13, 1843, Coleridge, *Memoir and Letters*, 146.
201. many of London's most famous: Mudge, "Sara Coleridge," in *Oxford Dictionary of National Biography*.
202. "chequered dappled figure": Virginia Woolf, "Sara Coleridge," in *The Death of the Moth* (London: Hogarth, 1942), 98–103.

CHAPTER SIX

204. "we are always *to be* married": Mary Heber, *Dear Miss Heber: An Eighteenth Century Correspondence*, ed. Francis Bamford (London: Constable, 1936), 120.
204. 5 percent of upper-class girls: Lawrence Stone, *The Family, Sex, and Marriage in England 1500–1800* (London: Harper and Row, 1977), 380; Hazel Jones, *Jane Austen and Marriage* (New York: Continuum, 2009), 179.
204. Just thirty-four years after Austen's death: Mary Poovey, *Uneven Developments: The Ideological Work of Gender in Mid-Victorian England* (Chicago: University of Chicago Press, 1988), 4; and Elizabeth K. Helsigner, Robin Lauterbach Sheets, and William Veeder, *The Woman Question: Society and Literature in Britain and America, 1837–1883* (New York: Garland, 1983), 2:135.
204. "in place of completing, sweetening": William Rathbone Greg, *Why Are Women Redundant?* (London: N. Trübner and Co., 1869), 5.
205. 365,000 more women than men: Stone, *Family, Sex, and Marriage*, 381. For more on British emigration and the many reasons a person might have attempted it, see C. E. Snow, "Emigration from Great Britain," in *International Migrations: Interpretations*, ed. Walter F. Wilcox (Washington, DC: National Bureau of Economic Research, 1931), 237–60, http://www.nber.org/chapters/c5111.pdf.

205. as middle- and upper-class Victorian wives did often: Judith Flanders, *Inside the Victorian Home: A Portrait of Domestic Life in Victorian England* (New York: W. W. Norton, 2004), 285.
205. an insulated, protected space in the new Victorian fashion: Ibid., 5–6.
206. "so much liberty of action": Robert Kemp Philp, *The Practical Housewife, Forming a Complete Encyclopaedia of Domestic Economy* (London: Ward and Lock, 1855), 2, quoted in Flanders, *Victorian Home*, 18.
206. unrelenting single-mindedness: Elaine Showalter, "Dinah Mulock Craik and the Tactics of Sentiment: A Case Study in Victorian Female Authorship," *Feminist Studies* 2, no. 2/3 (1975): 12.
206. "a kind of excrescence": John Stuart Mill, "Early Essays on Marriage and Divorce," in *Essays on Sex Equality*, ed. Alice Rossi (Chicago: Chicago University Press, 1970), 72. Original emphasis. Mill was a loud voice in the early fight for gender equality. His piece *The Subjection of Women* laid claim to women's individual rights and called for a change in public opinion on the role of marriage in a lady's life. (In his opinion, husbands were essentially slave owners.)
207. "My papa and mamma": *The Lady's Monthly Museum*, 1798, quoted in Stone, *Family, Sex, and Marriage*, 381.
207. "What else could she do?": Samuel Butler, *The Way of All Flesh* (New York: E. P. Dutton and Co., 1917), 49.
207. "a star of promise": *Good Words*, 1861.
208. "At your age": Anne Judith Penny, *The Afternoon of Unmarried Life* (New York: Rudd and Carleton, 1859), 340–41. Original emphasis.
208. well-publicized rhetoric: Janet C. Myers, "Performing the Voyage Out: Victorian Female Emigration and the Class Dynamics of Displacement," *Victorian Literature and Culture* 29, no. 1 (2001): 129–46.
209. "every article of dress": Miss Weeton, *Journal of a Governess 1811–1825*, ed. Edward Hall (1939), 1:178, quoted in Stone, *Family, Sex, and Marriage*, 386.
209. "felt all the good luck of it": Jane Austen, *Pride and Prejudice* (London: T. Egerton, 1813).
210. "wasting life and soul": Greg, *Why Are Women Redundant?*, 6.
210. "We *must* help ourselves": Dinah Mulock Craik, *A Woman's Thoughts About Women* (London: Hurst and Blackett), 34.
210. "This lot is probably the hardest": Ibid., 267.
211. "evening-parties, dresses, and gloves": Ibid., 236.
211. "Every girl ought to be taught": Ibid., 344–45.
211. "withdraw[ing] from public inspection": Penny, *Afternoon of Unmarried Life*, xii.
212. "groups of dirty, happy little rogues": Dinah Mulock Craik, "Going Out to Play," *Chambers Edinburgh Journal*, March 6, 1858.
213. "good general knowledge": Dinah Mulock Craik, "Want Something to Read," *Chambers Edinburgh Journal*, May 8, 1858.

213. his modest lending library: Sally Mitchell, *Dinah Mulock Craik* (Boston: Twayne, 1983), 4.
214. "the present race of juveniles": Dinah Mulock Craik to Rebecca Hallam, 1843, in Aleyn Lyell Reade, *The Mellards and Their Descendants, Including the Bibbys of Liverpool, with Memoirs of Dinah Maria Mulock and Thomas Mellard Reade* (London: Reade, 1915), 66.
214. "After all childhood is a very pleasant thing": Dinah Mulock Craik to Rebecca Hellam, 1841, in Reade, *The Mellards and Their Descendants*, 61.
214. "entirely destitute": Ibid., 70.
215. "on level ground": Craik, *A Woman's Thoughts*, 50.
215. works by "D.M.M." were a regular sight: Mitchell, *Dinah Mulock Craik*, 8. Her initials "D.M.M." includes that for her middle name, Maria
215. energetically walking: Ibid., 9.
215. writing to these audiences: Credit for the astute conclusions surrounding Craik's purposeful and premeditated placement of her stories is due to Sally Mitchell and her 1983 biography, *Dinah Mulock Craik*.
216. edited with a very heavy hand: Mitchell, *Dinah Mulock Craik*, 21.
216. the evolution of her style: Ibid., 21–23.
217. "I am quite a *giantess*": Reade, *Mellards*, 59.
217. "She was a tall young woman": Margaret Oliphant, *Autobiography and Letters of Mrs. M. O. W. Oliphant*, ed. Mrs. Harry Coghill (New York: Dodd, Meade, and Co., 1899), 38.
218. "in the most independent manner": *Memorials of Two Sisters: Susanna and Catherine Winkworth*, ed. Margaret J. Shaen (London: Longmans, Green, and Co., 1908), 64. Elizabeth Gaskell had been socializing with Dinah and Francis in London and is quoted in a note by Catherine Winkworth. The Working Women's College, founded in 1864, functioned as a sister institution of the Working Men's College until the two merged in 1966.
218. "wonderful vitality": Mrs. E. M. Ward, *Memories of Ninety Years* (New York: H. Holt and Company, 1925), 107. Dinah loved reaching out to other professional women. Her sixty-pound-per-year Civil List pension was always given away to a struggling female, and later in life, she used her travelogue writing as an excuse to take along with her those in need of a vacation. Significantly, however, she was against many of the organized feminist movements, including universal suffrage, preferring instead to bolster women's capacity for individual, interior strength. See Mitchell, *Dinah Mulock Craik*, and Showalter, "Dinah Mulock Craik and the Tactics of Sentiment."
218. unconvinced by mysticism: Mitchell, *Dinah Mulock Craik*, 22.
218. the only novels she was familiar with: Ibid., 28.
219. "Hump-backed": Dinah Mulock Craik, *Olive* (Leipzig: Bernhard Tauchnitz, 1866), 11. The first edition of *Olive* was published by Edward Chapman in 1850.

219. "She had no maiden doubts": Ibid., 118.
220. Linton Heathcliff: See Emily Brontë, *Wuthering Heights* (London: Newby, 1847); George Eliot, *The Mill on the Floss* (London: Blackwood, 1860); and Charlotte Brontë, *Jane Eyre* (London: Smith, Elder, and Co., 1847).
220. "smiling, nestled": Craik, *Olive*, 303.
220. rejection, loneliness, discomfort: Mitchell, *Dinah Mulock Craik*, 30–31.
221. "heroic beneath the broadcloth": *Colburn's New Monthly Magazine*, 1852.
221. she was paid one hundred fifty: Dinah Mulock Craik to Frederic Chapman, Jan. 23, no year, on file with the Morgan Library, New York, quoted in Bourrier, "Rereading Dinah Mulock Craik," 289.
221. better than the going rate: Bourrier, "Rereading Dinah Mulock Craik," 289.
222. "Do you think that out of the profits of all": Dinah Mulock Craik to Frederic Chapman, n.d., on file with the Morris L. Parrish collection at Princeton University, quoted in Elaine Showalter, *A Literature of Their Own: British Women Novelists from Brontë to Lessing* (Princeton, NJ: Princeton University Press, 1977), 50.
222. "mechanical literary work": Dinah Mulock Craik to Alexander Macmillan, June 26, 1856, on file with the Berg Collection at the New York Public Library.
223. demonstrating a latent uncertainty: Mitchell, *Dinah Mulock Craik*, 8.
223. the venue itself: Bill Bryson, *At Home: A Short History of Private Life* (New York: Anchor, 2010), 9.
224. the most revolutionary aspect: Jeffrey A. Auerbach, *The Great Exhibition of 1851: A Nation on Display* (New Haven, CT: Yale University Press, 1999), 2.
225. "Thus he stood, principal figure": Dinah Mulock Craik, *John Halifax, Gentleman* (Leipzig: Bernhard Tauchnitz, 1857), 3. The first edition was published by Hurst and Blackett in 1856.
225. "Shall I give thee [money] now?": Ibid., 5.
225. "I don't care what it is": Ibid., 26.
227. other printings: Mitchell, *Dinah Mulock Craik*, 51.
227. just behind *Uncle Tom's Cabin*: Ibid.
227. "more widely read": "Mrs. Craik," *Academy*, Oct. 1887.
227. "he could not, attain the bearing and manners of a fine gentleman": *Athenaeum*, April 26, 1856.
227. "Neither before nor after": Henry James, *Notes and Reviews* (Cambridge, UK: Dunster, 1921), 167–68.
228. "with affright, very grave": Margaret Oliphant, *Autobiography*, 85.
229. "giving anxieties much grudged": Margaret Oliphant, *Macmillan's Magazine*, Dec. 1887.
229. "given her affection for affection": Reade, *Mellards*, 84.
229. "All the funeral arrangements": Ibid., 84–85.
230. centered on the loss: Mitchell, *Dinah Mulock Craik*, 9.
230. "extraordinary case of life imitating art": Ibid., 14.

232. "I do believe": Dinah Mulock Craik to Ben Mulock, Sept. 20 (no year), Mulock Family Papers, UCLA.
232. "a tale on a new plan": Reade, *Mellards*, 87.
233. "perfect nonsense": Ibid., 88.
233. "When people are happily married": Dinah Mulock Craik to Miss Rawkin, n.d., on file with the Morris L. Parrish collection at Princeton University, quoted in Showalter, "Dinah Mulock Craik and the Tactics of Sentiment," 19. Original emphasis.
233. "the exquisite absorption": Craik, *Woman's Thoughts*, 63.
234. helped George read manuscripts: Mitchell, *Dinah Mulock Craik*, 16.
234. "We shall be Gothic": Dinah Mulock Craik to her cousin Thomas Mellard Reade, Dec. 29, 1868, quoted in Reade, *Mellards*, 92.
234. "books bedded in the recesses": *Life and Letters of J. H. Shorthouse*, ed. Mrs. Shorthouse (London: Macmillan, 1905), 118–19.
234. "the delicious retirement": Craik, *Woman's Thoughts*, 63.
234. "dainty little soul": Dinah Mulock Craik to Mrs. Jolly, Jan. 24, 1869, quoted in Reade, *Mellards*, 93.
235. "twenty thousand times": Ibid.
235. "Drunkenness, dissoluteness": Dinah Mulock Craik, "Young Mrs. Jardine," *Good Words*, 1879.
236. "as perfect as the novel can well be": Dinah Mulock Craik, "To Novelists—and a Novelist," *Macmillan's Magazine*, 1861.

CHAPTER SEVEN

239. "feminine genius of this generation": *British Quarterly Review*, 1869, quoted in Elaine Showalter, *A Literature of Their Own: British Women Novelists from Brontë to Lessing* (Princeton, NJ: Princeton University Press, 1977), 153.
239. "We women can't go in search": George Eliot, *Daniel Deronda* (Boston: Little, Brown, and Co., 1900), 1:134.
240. "well-disciplined mind": Unnamed fashion magazine cited in Cecil Willett Cunnington, *A Perfect Lady* (London: Parrish, 1948), 42, quoted in Judith Flanders, *Inside the Victorian Home* (New York: W. W. Norton, 2003), 309.
240. "Woman, whose whole life": Sarah Stickney Ellis, *The Daughters of England: Their Position in Society, Character, and Responsibilities* (London: Fisher, Son, and Co., 1845), 133.
241. "in fits of sensual passion": Margaret Oliphant, "Novels," *Blackwoods*, 1867.
241. "beautiful women of elegant figure": "Recent Novels: Their Moral and Religious Teaching," *London Quarterly*, 1866.
242. One such magazine: Alvar Ellegård, "The Readership of the Periodical Press in Mid-Victorian Britain," *Victorian Periodicals Newsletter* 13 (1971): 18.
242. "clever, pushing, semi-educated": Arthur Austin, "Art and Democracy," *Cornhill*, 1879.

243. "no divine influence": Henry Mansel, "Sensation Novels," *The Quarterly Review*, 1863. Mansel's comments were suited to *The Quarterly Review*, for this was one of the old establishment periodicals: it was relatively expensive (six shillings) and had an average circulation of about eight thousand copies per year, which, compared with the new penny and half-penny papers, didn't stand for much. See Ellegård, "Readership of the Periodical Press," 13.
243. fairer sex represented a formidable competitor: Showalter, *A Literature of Their Own*, 155.
243. everything not expressly forbidden was compulsory: Ibid., 158.
244. "sits at home and works sham roses": Mary Elizabeth Braddon, *The Doctor's Wife* (London: Maxwell, 1864), 3:49.
244. "the mixture of crime and crinoline": "Homicidal Heroines," *Saturday Review*, April 7, 1866.
244. "machinations of ruthless schemers": "Recent Novels," *London Quarterly*, 1866.
244. "accelerate the occurrence of menstruation": George Black, *The Young Wife's Advice Book: A Guide for Mothers on Health and Self-Management* (London: Ward, Lock and Co., 1888), 5, quoted in Showalter, *A Literature of Their Own*, 160.
244. "a series of little orthographic explosions": Showalter, *A Literature of Their Own*, 160.
245. "No man *would have dared*": Francis Paget, *Lucretia; or, the Heroine of the Nineteenth Century* (London: Masters, 1868), 304–5. Original emphasis.
246. Sarah Hobbs, who sang bawdy songs: Jennifer Carnell, *The Literary Lives of Mary Elizabeth Braddon: A Study of Her Life and Work* (Hastings: Sensation Press, 2000), 7.
247. "not a dry page": Mary Elizabeth Braddon, "Before the Knowledge of Evil" (c. 1914), 171, unpublished autobiographical manuscript included in the Robert Lee Wolff Collection, Harry Ransom Center, quoted in Carnell, *Literary Lives*, 88.
247. "the interval between the ages": Mary Elizabeth Braddon, "My First Novel," *Idler*, 1893.
247. "a historical novel on the Siege of Calais": Ibid.
247. "Her work was fleeting": Fanny Braddon contributed to *Bentley's Miscellany* in the 1840s and ghosted her husband's column in *Sporting Magazine* prior to their separation. See Carnell, *Literary Lives*, 89–90.
247. "Mary traveled all over rural England": Valerie Pedlar, "Behind the Scenes, Before the Gaze: Mary Braddon's Theatrical World," in *Popular Victorian Women Writers*, ed. Kay Boardman and Shirley Jones (Manchester: Manchester University Press, 2004), 189. For an extensive chronology of Braddon's billed roles as an actress, see Carnell, *Literary Lives*.
247. "ha[d] been applauded": *Cumberland's Minor Theatre*, 7, quoted in Lucy

Sussex, "The Detective Maidservant: Catherine Crowe's *Susan Hopley,*" in *Silent Voices: Forgotten Novels by Victorian Women Writers,* ed. Brenda Ayres (Westport, CT: Praeger, 2003), 63.

248. "I am glad you are [now] in Buckinghamshire": Mary Elizabeth Braddon to George Augustus Sala, 1861, quoted in Robert Lee Wolff, *Sensational Victorian: The Life and Fiction of Mary Elizabeth Braddon* (New York: Garland, 1979) and in Sussex, "Detective Maidservant," 63.
248. "everything from Carlyle to Ruskin": Richard Foulkes, *The Calverts: Actors of Some Importance* (London: Society for Theatrical Research, 1992), 8, quoted in Pedlar, "Behind the Scenes, Before the Gaze."
248. "She always managed to alight": Carnell, *Literary Lives,* 71.
249. her writing style was so perfectly in tune: Ibid., 143.
250. "wild eyes": Emily Brontë, *Wuthering Heights* (London: Newby, 1847).
251. the chased chaste: Sally Mitchell, *The Fallen Angel: Chastity, Class and Women's Reading, 1835–1880* (Bowling Green, OH: Bowling Green University Press, 1981), 92.
251. "I—*I* had furnished this house!": Mary Elizabeth Braddon, "Captain Thomas," in *Ralph the Bailiff and Other Tales* (London: Ward, Lock and Tyler, 1862), 63. First published in *Welcome Guest,* Sept. 1, 1860. Original emphasis.
251. "O how I hate": Ibid., 56.
251. "taken off her chenille": Mary Elizabeth Braddon, "My Daughters," in *Ralph the Bailiff,* 83. Originally published in *Welcome Guest,* Oct. 20, 1860.
253. the same condition: Saverio Tomaiuolo, *In Lady Audley's Shadow: Mary Elizabeth Braddon and Victorian Literary Genres* (Edinburgh: Edinburgh University Press, 2010), 11.
253. it almost didn't happen at all: Carnell, *Literary Lives,* 143–44.
254. "Another new journal?": *Athenaeum,* July 13, 1861.
254. "The day before a decision was necessary": Joseph Hatton, "Miss Braddon at Home: A Sketch and an Interview," *London Society Magazine,* Jan. 1888, quoted in Carnell, *Literary Lives,* 143–44.
255. in the interval between being reduced to trembling: Mitchell, *Fallen Angel,* 82.
255. nickname his blue-eyed daughter: J. B. Buckstone to Mary Elizabeth Braddon, March 12, 1866, quoted in Carnell, *Literary Lives,* 144.
255. "very exciting tale": *Court Journal,* July 5, 1862, quoted in Carnell, *Literary Lives,* 146.
256. "amiable and gentle": Mary Elizabeth Braddon, *Lady Audley's Secret* (Oxford: Oxford University Press, 2009), 5.
256. requires secrecy and underhand action: Showalter, *A Literature of Their Own,* 165.
256. "Every one loved, admired, and praised": Braddon, *Lady Audley,* 6.

257. "soft and melting blue eyes": Ibid.
257. "I cannot be blind": Ibid., 11.
258. "a practiced and consummate flirt": Ibid., 102.
258. "Who ever heard of a woman": Ibid., 206–7.
259. Lady Audley is actually sane: Showalter, *A Literature of Their Own*, 167. Showalter surmises that by showing Lady Audley's mental condition to be vague and ambiguous, Braddon has tempted her readers to consider whether this "madness" is real, thereby subversively luring them into admiring a cold-blooded yet strongly feminist killer.
259. "employed intelligent means": Braddon, *Lady Audley*, 377.
260. "the utter unrestraint": *Christian Remembrancer*, n.d., quoted in Showalter, *A Literature of Their Own*, and in Walter C. Phillips, *Dickens, Reade, and Collins: Sensation Novelists* (New York: Columbia University Press, 1919), 26.
260. "not in accordance with our rules": *The Reader*, Jan. 3, 1863.
260. "from hand to mouth": Clive Holland, "Fifty Years of Novel Writing: Miss Braddon at Home." *Pall Mall*, Nov. 1911, quoted in Carnell, *Literary Lives*, 144. Carnell has also determined that an additional work, *The White Phantom*, was in its beginning stages. It was published in Maxwell's *Halfpenny Journal* the following year.
262. "This sort of puffery": *Athenaeum*, May 28, 1864. This criticism was aimed particularly at Maxwell, who over the course of the first print runs of his publications would frequently report false sales figures in order to create the appearance of success. His actions seemed unprofessional from the standpoint of the *Athenaeum* critics, but as always, the paper still needed to cleave to public opinion if it hoped to stay in business: In 1866, *Athenaeum* ran an advertisement for Braddon novels that occupied an entire page. As Jennifer Carnell points out, she was the only author to be promoted in such a fashion. See Carnell, *Literary Lives*, 149.
262. "[Sensationalist authors]": W. Fraser Rae, "Sensation Novelists: Miss Braddon," *North British Review*, 1865.
263. "making the literature of the Kitchen": Ibid.
263. "The successful accomplishment of abductions": Paget, *Lucretia*, 304–5. Original emphasis.
264. "eyes that were like the stars": Mary Elizabeth Braddon, *Aurora Floyd* (New York: Harper, 1863), 10.
265. What with these indecent proclivities: Mitchell, *Fallen Angel*, 74–75. "Aside from the new plots she creates," Mitchell further explains, "the figure of a woman riding gives clear evidence of conservative reaction to a new social phenomenon. When a woman is introduced in a riding habit—or even more dangerously, on the hunting field—we can be virtually certain that trouble and impropriety will follow."
265. "crown[ing] her as an Eastern empress": Braddon, *Aurora Floyd*, 18.

265. "all tumbled and tossed": Ibid., 41.
265. "wrapped in a loose white dressing-gown": Ibid., 100.
266. "Aurora sprang upon him": Ibid., 52.
267. "Aurora is a woman": *Athenaeum*, Jan. 31, 1863.
267. "Lady Audley was diabolically wicked": *Nation*, Nov. 9, 1865. See also Henry James, *Notes and Reviews* (Cambridge, UK: Dunster, 1921), 108–16.
267. "notwithstanding its unpleasant subject": Oliphant, "Novels," *Blackwoods*, 1867.
269. "a very low type of female character": W. Fraser Rae, "Miss Braddon," *North British Review*, September 1865.
269. "When Miss Braddon knows more": *Athenaeum*, Dec. 12, 1863.
269. placed an advertisement: Wolff, *Sensational Victorian*, 104.
270. "indications of a wide-spread corruption": H. L. Manse, "Sensation Novels," *Quarterly Review*, April 1863.
270. "the unthinking crowd": Fraser Rae, "Miss Braddon."
270. "There has been a good story": Oliphant, "Novels," *Blackwoods*, 1867.
271. "Mr and Mrs Maxwell present": Carnell, *Literary Lives*, 182. Great approbation is due to Jennifer Carnell in uncovering the rare documents surrounding this history, most especially the Crowleys' private circular written on Sept. 28, 1874, by Richard Brinsley Knowles.
271. "Having, like so many of her heroines": "Miss Braddon as a Bigamist," *New York Times*, Nov. 22, 1874.
272. St. Bride's Church off Fleet Street: Carnell, *Literary Lives*, 183.
272. "a part of England": *Academy*, Aug. 25, 1900.
275. "always getting into some new scrape": Robert Lee Wolff, "Devoted Disciple: The Letters of Mary Elizabeth Braddon to Sir Edward Bulwer-Lytton 1862–1873," *Harvard Library Bulletin* 12 (1974), 150, quoted in Elaine Showalter, *A Literature of Their Own*, 164.
275. found the social requirement of feminine frailty insupportable: Showalter, *A Literature of Their Own*, 164.
275. "passed [her] beyond the power of feeling [them]": Wolff, "Devoted Disciple," 15–16, quoted in ibid.
275. tactful evasion of the real truth: Showalter, *A Literature of Their Own*, 164.
276. "I always have in mind the memory of wasted suffering": Wolff, "Devoted Disciple," 15–16, quoted in ibid.
279. "duty" and "solitude": Catherine Malone, "'We Have Learnt to Love Her More Than Her Books': The Critical Reception of Brontë's *Professor*," *The Review of English Studies* 47, no. 186 (1996): 175–87.

ABOUT THE AUTHOR

SHELLEY DEWEES has a graduate degree in ethnomusicology, several tattoos, and a documented obsession with British literature. Her writing has appeared on *Austenprose, Jane Austen's World,* and *Jane Austen Today,* and after time spent teaching in Korea she recently moved back to Minneapolis with her husband.